JO JACKS

The Station
at Austin Downs

ABC
Books

Permissions

Thank you to the following copyright holders for permission to quote from their works:

Hodder Headline for *The Joy of Snow* by Elizabeth Goudge

Neil Murray and Island Music for 'My Island Home'

Life Rhythm Books and Bodo Baginski & Shalila Sharamon for *Reiki: Universal Life Energy*. Life Rhythm Books, PO Box 806, Mendochino, CA 95460, USA. www.liferhythm.com

HarperCollins for JRR Tolkien's *The Fellowship of the Ring* and *The Hobbit*

Published by ABC Books for the
AUSTRALIAN BROADCASTING CORPORATION
GPO Box 9994 Sydney NSW 2001

ISBN 0 7333 1378 7.

Cover design by Lore Foye
Front cover photograph by David Bent
Back cover photographs by Amanda Jackson, except peaches by photolibrary.com
Text design by Lore Foye
Typeset in 11/15pt Berkeley Book by Kirby Jones
Colour reproduction by Colorwize, Adelaide
Printed and bound by Griffin Press, Adelaide

5 4 3 2 1

For my family

Acknowledgments

I have discovered that a book is never just the work of one person. *The Station at Austin Downs* began life as a radio series on the ABC. I'd like to thank all those people who listened to me on the radio — without you there would never have been a book.

I would like to thank Barry O'Sullivan who introduced me to Deborah Leavitt from the ABC (my good fairy). I would also like to thank Kathy Gollan, Grant Woodhams, Ted Bull, Sarah Knight, Jim Shaw, Jean Brown, Steve Altham, Bernadette Neubecker and Jane Finemore who are all from the ABC as well.

My editor Jo Mackay has proved to be an 'ideal reader' — like my sister Megan she always knows what I'm trying to say on those occasions I've failed to say it.

I'd like to thank all of the people in the book who have kindly allowed me to write a little about their lives — and particularly those people who have read through my work and approved it. My most sincere thanks to Cathi Montague, Minnie King, Gladys King, Paul King, Susan Hamilton, Joyce Tunzie (and Margaret McConnell), Kaye Bodie, Adrian Cutler, Des Thompson, Helen Webb, Allan Savory, Mike and Annette Prendergast, Bill and Kaye Degens, Lynette Gillam, Sandy and Michael Clinch, Janine and Chris Varley, Jane Morling, Sylvia Byers, Melissa O'Connor, Debbie and Ashley Dowden, Anne and Geoff Pilkington, Deborah Pitter and Tony Gaspar.

Thanks to David Bent and Amanda Jackson for the cover photography, and thanks to Lore Foye — for not just the cover design but the look of the book altogether.

Before the book went to Jo Mackay for editing it was 'pre-edited' by my family. I'd especially like to thank my sisters Megan and Stephanie, my sister-in-law Amanda, my brother-in-law Bradley, my dad, my mum, my gran Elizabeth Jackson, my sister-in-law Minnie and my husband Martin King — all of whom spent a lot of time ensuring what I had written was correct and comprehensible. As soon as I began to write, I understood why so many 'Acknowledgments' contain lines like, 'Thank you to my family for supporting me and most of all for simply putting up with me while I wrote this book.'

Thanks to Barbara Prentice (Revise Teacher), the Meekatharra School of the Air, Amanda, the Flylady team and particularly Martin and Mum for helping me cope with the remainder of my responsibilities as I wrote. (This book would just not have been possible without Martin and Mum!) My sons Tim and Sam have also been very tolerant of my writing, and are just wonderful little boys.

Jo Jackson King

1	THE SOUND OF GRASS GROWING	1
2	A FAMILY OF MAVERICKS	6
3	TEAMWORK	18
4	BACK TO SCHOOL	28
5	TRAVELLING HOPEFULLY	38
6	GOING HOME	49
7	THE ROAD LESS TRAVELLED BY	66
8	PIECES OF GOLD	82
9	FROM FARM TO STATION	97
10	SAYING GOODBYE	117
11	THE FIRST MUSTER	123
12	PLANTING AN ORCHARD	138
13	OF SHEEP AND SOIL AND GHOSTS	150
14	DROUGHT	163
15	FESTIVAL TIME	177
16	RAIN	189
17	EVERYDAY PLEASURES	203
18	TRIAL AND ERROR	217
19	PEACH-PICKING TIME	233

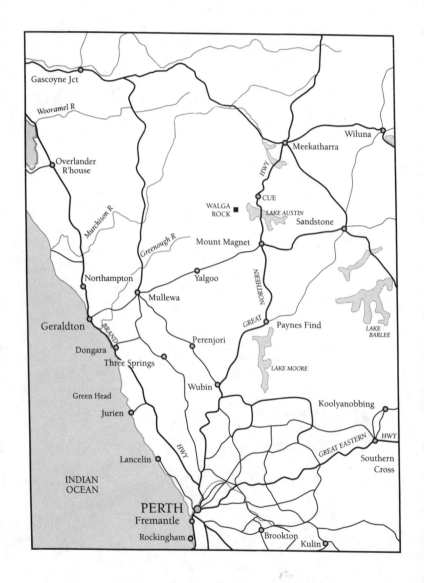

THE SOUND OF GRASS GROWING

'You cannot judge the value of what happens to you until many years afterwards. Then you see how one thing led to another and how it was all … somehow necessary …'
ELIZABETH GOUDGE, *THE JOY OF SNOW*

When I was a little girl my dad would say to me: the sound of rain is the sound of grass growing, the sound of grass growing is the sound of coins clinking in the bank. So from very early, I loved the green months for the soft air and wet ground, the calling lambs in the paddocks, the wild ducklings and the tadpoles in the creeks, but I also loved them for bringing us money.

Even now that I'm grown-up, a mother, a partner in the family business, I cannot tell whether my longing for rain is more to do with wanting to see the land green and glorious with new life, or more because we need those coins clinking in the bank. They are caught together in my imagination and my heart.

I grew up on a farm, but now we live on a station. This is the story of my family's big adventure, which has taken us from farm to station, immediately into the worst drought in a hundred years and perhaps, by this story's end, out the other side.

I remember when Dad first suggested the idea of moving to a station. He was sitting on the verandah of my house at our farm at Wannamal; it was an afternoon at the end of winter; I was nursing a four-month-old Sam; and Dad had that intense, invigorated expression that meant an alarming idea was on its way. My husband Martin and I were watching him with some trepidation.

'Of course,' Dad said, 'the really sensible thing to do would be to sell this expensive land, find some land with good water that we can lease from the government, and then use the remaining money for capital development. But I know none of you wants to move.'

When I think of it now, I realise that this last statement was delivered in the way that a three-year-old Sam trying to disguise forbidden behaviour would tell me loudly that he was never allowed to do anything. For example, he would say, 'You never let me take knives,' all the time glaring at me accusingly, while removing one of these forbidden implements from a drawer. And in spite of his air of having just come up with the idea, Dad had already been talking to a real estate agent about pastoral properties with irrigation potential. The agent had quickly directed him to a property called Austin Downs, 650 kilometres north of Perth.

In recent years it had become harder and harder to keep the farm going and survive financially. Dad was simply putting in action what all of us had been thinking.

'Austin Downs,' said Dad, 'sounds really positive. There is a special irrigation lease on the property, so we could start development right away. I think we could do vines, but first we'd need to test the water, and the soil … What do you think?'

He was looking at me, but it was Martin who spoke first, which was not usually the way it happened. 'I wouldn't mind,' he said, 'I've no family left in Perth.'

Our farm was just two hours drive from Perth, which had seemed a long way when we first moved out there. Austin Downs was an eight-hour drive.

'What do you think, Jo?' asked Dad.

I did not know what to think, and eventually settled on a vague (and probably lengthy) expression of my willingness to look at all options — if the others thought so, too — it would be an adventure, anyway — and would Dad like another cup of tea?

That night Martin and I talked some more about Dad's idea. We agreed that a move to a station was not likely to happen, because we had discussed many such ideas recently and none had actually come to pass. In fact, a new plan was arising for remaking the family business and ourselves every week. Over the past year we had slowly come to realise, financial problems aside, that we were no longer a happy family.

I think it was Mandy, my sister-in-law who first noticed that the family was not happy. From deep inside the situation, which had changed slowly over the years, we didn't see the extent of our unhappiness. We didn't even notice that we had stopped laughing — and we had been a great family for laughter.

For years we had been a family who worked hard and had fun. When Mandy began, gently at first, to tell me that we had simply become a family who worked too hard, I did not believe her. She had been doing her best to turn us back into the family she had married into — with full support from Martin, who also felt that the happy family he had joined had long vanished. She had been organising monthly family outings and it was after one of these trips — a night-time visit to the zoo — that I realised something was wrong. We had fun, falling back into our old ways, telling stories about each other, and laughing all night.

Perhaps the contrast between this night and everyday life finally alerted me, for it was after the night at the zoo that I began to understand what Mandy had been saying for so long. We were on a walk together, Mandy bumping Lachlan along in the pram, me heavily pregnant with Sam, walking a firebreak that bordered a cropped paddock, when she finally got the message through.

'Come on Jo,' she had said, 'when was the last time you saw your parents tease each other?'

Mandy has a beautiful and rich voice, and I can still hear the gentleness, empathy and touch of exasperated humour with which she infused her words.

'At the zoo,' I said obliviously. 'That was nice!'

At this point Mandy must have tried not to sigh.

'But apart from that? And when did you and Martin last walk along hand in hand?'

'We did at the zoo …'

Mandy raised her eyebrows.

'Well, it's been busy,' I said slowly, but suddenly I could feel the scales rattling from my eyes and dropping to the hot, dry ground as we walked along.

'Are you saying that we aren't a happy family?' I asked. 'That's how it looks to you?'

'You haven't been a happy family for a long time, Jo,' said Mandy, very gently. 'And none of you is much fun to be around! But I'm sure that there's a way that we can change that.'

Even writing this, three years later, I can still feel the hollow sickness of this moment, when I gave up denying that there was a problem. I gave up my illusions, and there was suddenly nothing — no certainty, no security. But it was not a feeling that lasted long. Once I had given up the illusion, I saw that we needed to change a great many things. We had tried being nicer to each other. We had tried making small changes to the farm operation. But we had found those things did not solve our unhappiness. It was time for major change.

On the face of it, we had no reason to be unhappy. We were all healthy. The farm was a good one: the best bit of dirt in the district, according to many friends and neighbours.

But we were all worried all the time now. We had experienced two poor seasons in succession, the big dams were not filling, and the timelines for success were pushing out. And none of us were happy in this world, where success appeared just ahead, only to vanish as we came closer. Over shared informal meals, within formal meetings moderated by the Better Business process, over one-on-one cups of tea, on our long walks over the property, we discussed what further changes we could make. Should we give up farming and move into tourism? Should we sell all stock and all equipment and rest the farm and start afresh? Should we sell the farm?

Selling the farm did not seem possible. For when you know every corner of every paddock, where trees have watched you grow, where you know the different rocks in each pile of rocks, land is not just land but home and self. Somehow we could no longer make the farm work for us, yet we loved it still.

A FAMILY OF MAVERICKS

*'Experience shows us that love does not consist in gazing at
each other, but in looking together in the same direction.'*
ANTOINE DE SAINT-EXUPÉRY, *WIND, SUN AND STARS* (1939)

A s I said, the farm was probably the best bit of dirt in the
area. It was certainly the best cared-for bit of dirt, as my
grandfather, then my father and mother, had always been
aware of the need to manage water and feed so that we didn't lose
topsoil.

Of course, the farm had been my grandparents' adventure
once. In 1960 my grandparents had sold their tobacco and cattle
farm in Rhodesia to move to Western Australia. Their decision to
move made headlines in the tiny country of Rhodesia because,
although they kept their reasons private, people could easily
guess that it was a vote of 'no confidence' in the country. It was a
deeply unpopular decision. But what other people thought never
ranked very highly with Grandad. That's not quite right — the
truth was that opposition merely strengthened an already iron
intention to go his way.

On buying the farm at Wannamal, his first action was to map
the way the water moved and on that basis add contour drains to
prevent erosion. These were ridged banks that guided water into
dams, stopping the topsoil from disappearing into creeks. Forty
years ago the erosion gullies that now hollow the neighbouring
properties didn't exist, so no one understood why Grandad had

done it. As far as the neighbours was concerned, he was simply making the paddocks difficult to drive over. And they were quite right. Contour drains did make it hard to move around the paddocks. Standing with my siblings on the back of the ute, my sister Steph and I would take the sight of a contour fast approaching as a cue to stand with our arms around Megan and Kynan, the two little ones, and take a firm hold of the bars of the ute. Dad would not slow down at all. Instead, he would climb the ute up sideways onto the bank. Then he would ride along it, the ute angled sharply toward the ground, until he saw a place to cross, then the ute would angle just as sharply the other way, and we would be over, the back of the ute horizontal once more. On the back we would ungrit our teeth, unglue our hands from the bars and grin at each other. We had survived another crossing!

So I grew up with the contour drains — and I grew up gradually realising that I was part of a family of mavericks. We didn't eat the same kind of food as the other people, my mum and dad didn't behave the same way as other parents, and the paddocks on our farm didn't look anything like other people's paddocks and, in case I was imagining those things, we weren't related to anyone else in the district.

But I didn't think I was imagining that my parents were unusual. When I was seven, the whole family drove across to Queensland to look at bulls. Mum and Dad had modified the car so that all the children had room to sleep as they drove. The seats were altered so that Steph and I could extend our legs into the boot, Kynan slept between Mum and Dad in the front, and Megan slept on the back window ledge. In case the suspense is too much, I'll tell you now that there were no accidents at all.

The trip took just a few days, and we children were all very well behaved; remarkably well behaved, considering that there was nothing but days of driving. This is because we knew that if we were very, very good, we would see the Kari cows.

Mum and Dad told us that the Kari cows were a kind of cow that only live in Queensland. They were nocturnal, small and black-skinned, with green glowing eyes and curly tails, a bit like pig tails. Our eager questions brought forward extraordinary details of breeding, habits and preferred food. Even today I can still remember a lot of these details, but even more vividly can I remember the disbelief when, as we crossed the Queensland border, Mum and Dad admitted that they had invented Kari cows to keep us entertained! It should not have been such a surprise, for Mum and Dad had always told us stories. They read us stories too, but the best stories were the ones they made up. The problem with the story of the Kari cows is that it had been too fascinating, too appealing.

Later on that holiday, we stayed at a house where there was a little bush with fascinating, appealing red shapes hanging from it. Mum said to us: 'That is a chilli, and those little fruits are called chillies. Don't touch them, and if you do touch them, don't touch your mouth until you have washed your fingers first, or they will burn your mouth.'

After the Kari cows, Steph and I decided that we needed to test the veracity of everything either of them said. We waited carefully until the last morning of the holiday. Just before we got in the car, Steph and I each touched a little red fruit and then touched our lips. Nothing happened: what terrible liars our parents were!

Twenty minutes later the burning began. We asked for the vaseline, complaining of dry lips. When Mum turned around to discover us smearing the vaseline inside our mouths, she must have guessed, for she began to laugh uncontrollably, at the same time expressing heartfelt sympathy as well as she could.

Someone once asked me at about this time why I thought Mum and Dad had decided to have so many children. 'So there were more to laugh at,' I said. And I still feel this response is as good as any other.

While I remember chiefly the laughing and the work, other children (for there were often other children who stayed with us, sometimes for weeks at a time) remember the discipline. My friend Cathi was enjoyably terrified of Dad all through her childhood. During her stays she would describe him to me as a 'barbarian'. Mum and Dad strictly enforced table manners, consideration for others and pulling your own weight. 'Chew with your mouth shut, or go and eat with the dogs' was one of Dad's chief exhortations at mealtimes. While we were used to this statement (and it wasn't an empty threat, almost all of us were sent out to eat with dogs at least once), it always shocked any visitors.

Many things did. Dad chose to support my interest in natural history by bringing me lamb foetuses if he accidentally slaughtered a ewe in lamb for family eating. I was very proud of the continuum of pickling jars in my room, which showed lambs at different stages of development. But, strangely, very few of the visitors were interested in looking at them with me. I had a good understanding of life and death — I was even terrified at the thought of dying — but somehow these sad little relics never brought death to mind. It is a curious part of childhood, what you can know and not know. I knew we ate our own sheep. Dad would allow me to come and watch while he gutted the sheep. He would show me the lungs and, as a special treat, breathe into them so I could watch them inflate. Years later I discovered that this made him feel very sick (as well it might!), and yet he would always do it if I asked. But while I knew that we killed our own sheep for food, I was ten before I worked out what the 'killers' really were.

Mum and Dad called a little gang of unshorn micky rams the 'killers'. Micky rams are rams who are not meant to be rams: one or both testicles had resisted the castration procedure. The killers had woollen dreadlocks and untidy daggy backsides. They loitered where the lines of creek and fence intersected. This meant they always had a way to escape us, for between the creek bed and the bottom wire of the fence there was always a gap. When we approached them, we were usually moving another mob of sheep. We kids would be on the back of the ute, listening for the command to 'hop off and push 'em up'. The killers would watch us and wait, wait till the last moment, then suddenly belt for the nearest creek, dreads flying. They would reappear with a complacent air of having gone one better than the humans yet again. Coupled with the name, it was this air of delinquency that had persuaded me that these sheep were called the killers because they were sheep of murderous intent.

Over the year their numbers would steadily decline, likewise their casual demeanour: no longer did they wait until the last minute to run for the creek. As their numbers decreased, it was apparent to me that they lived a dangerous life, and this just added to their mythic appeal. Mum and Dad never corrected our interesting idea about the killers. I can see now they got a great deal of enjoyment from our nervous fascination whenever the killers appeared.

When I was ten, Dad's osteoarthritis became very severe: old sporting injuries and new farming injuries had combined to make walking difficult. Dad's ineradicable habit of throwing himself at the ball, at the opposition, at the stock or at the problem was apparently to blame. 'Wear and tear,' said the doctor. 'He's a young man with old joints.' Dad was told that he would be in a wheelchair by the age of forty. There was nothing that could be done.

I remember this particularly, not because this was what happened, but because it was the first time I remember noticing my mother's ability to face and solve seemingly insurmountable problems.

When the verdict and matching second opinion were delivered, Mum began to talk to people about arthritis. Stories of farms being sold surfaced, as did stories of people functioning despite the pain. But eventually came the stories Mum was looking for: the stories of people who had overcome arthritis. All of them had changed the way they ate.

So that was what Dad had to do. I can remember Mum, at the end of a day's shopping in town, still in her boots and skirt, emptying the long white pantry cupboards of packet mixes for jellies, custards and soups. Then the potatoes and tomatoes Dad loved so much. And the empty places being filled with rice, and with new and strange foods: dried seaweed, dried mushrooms and nuts. I remember Dad protesting, Mum laughing, remorseful but unyielding. And Dad's joints slowly getting better.

And this is when I learnt that there is nearly always something you can do that will help; you just have to look and experiment until you find it. And then keep looking and keep experimenting, because you can always learn more. This was the beginning of my admiration of Mum as a person; and also the beginning of what has become a whole family fascination with food: not just for flavour, but for how it affects health. A visitor may find that complaining about a persistent facial tic will mean that he is given a banana to eat. People with high blood pressure are told to stay away from sugar but eat pineapple, and people with depression will have butter secretly added to the meals we give them. Although seeing food through the lens of health is not yet mainstream, it's not so very unusual now. But in the 1970s removing perfectly normal foods from the diet was not at all understood: Mum's views were considered very weird indeed.

Not just her views on food, either. I often think that if Mum had looked in some way offbeat, or if her manner had been eccentric, then people might have had some warning. Mum looked serene and conventional and she was able to do all the things that women on farms can: ear-tagging, monitoring the play of children out-of-sight, calling the sheep dog to push 'em up, all while breastfeeding the baby.

But Mum was interested in educational techniques to the extent that she used a different one to teach each of us to read. I, the eldest, was taught using the Doman method: 'sight word' reading then 'number picture' maths. I became a confident reader very early, but it was the baby on the floor (Steph) who really benefited from the maths. The big number pictures were appealing to a baby, and this early exposure gave Steph an understanding of number patterns, the basis of mathematics. Steph was taught to read phonetically, and Megs (the third baby) was taught everything using the Montessori method (the tools are provided and the child teaches themself). Kynan was taught with an idiosyncratic blend of techniques, with a particular focus on problem-solving. Now I wonder: did this early teaching give us our vocations? For words are still my thing, and Steph can explain any maths concept to any listener. Meg has become the kind of all-rounder Montessori dreamed of producing, and Kynan is a gun problem-solver. Mum was experimenting, deciding in advance what teaching style she would try and seeing what the results were. She is still surprised by the influence her choice of teaching techniques has had on our lives.

Somehow Mum fitted all this playful teaching into the hours between housework and farmwork. She has a need to push the envelope, and back then this was her way of doing it. And there was another reason for teaching us in addition to the envelope pushing: at age six, Mum could not read. Every morning the nun at the convent school would stand in front of her desk and say, 'Barbara, open your reading book, and read page 10 to the class.' Mum could open her book, but do no more. She could not understand how there were such exciting, vivid pictures and just a few words. How could a picture of a dog galloping through green grass toward a little girl with plaits like her own, the little girl smiling and calling to the dog, with a blue bird overhead, possibly be paired with words like 'Run, Rover, run'? There had to have been something she was missing.

So one morning, when the nun stood and said, 'Barbara, open your reading book,' the little girl thumbed vainly at the pages and said with satisfaction, 'I can't.'

'What do you mean?'

'I can't open my reading book.'

The nun picked up the reading book and it was true; the book would not open. Someone had glued it shut.

I think the sight of the nun attempting to prise open the reading book that she had glued shut must have appealed to Mum's anarchic sense of humour, and made up a little for not being able to work out how to read. I hope so. But it was this experience that made Mum determine that if she ever had children, they were going to be able to read before they got to school.

So we all went to school reading well. This was unusual, but it wasn't the quality that made us *most* unusual: that was something else altogether.

When Mum met Dad and his sisters, she immediately noticed their closeness. Perhaps they were closer because they were all new Australians, strangers together? But it wasn't just that. Soon she realised that these siblings had been brought up to be each other's support group. They rejoiced in each other's successes. Had this happened by accident, Mum wondered?

She soon found that this special sibling relationship was carried through from my gran's family. Gran's friendship with her brothers is something I saw for myself. Great-uncle Phil and Great Uncle Bob were part of my childhood. In Uncle Bob's case, this is something of an achievement, for the Second World War had left my Uncle Bob without a leg, and blind, and he still lived in Rhodesia. He would visit us and astound us by telling us apart by the weight of our footfalls on Gran's soft lino floor.

'Is it Joanna?' he would say (but it was never a question) as, on Gran's suggestion, we came toward him one by one. All of us slight, thin-faced and freckled, gazed at him in admiration as he sat in the sun, warmed by it, but made no wiser by its light — for he had lost the sight in his other eye to an infection. He would take out his glass eye and take off his wooden leg. He would laugh robustly as Grandad told the story of how Bob fought to keep the rest of his leg when the doctor wanted to amputate the remainder to save him from gangrene.

'The doctor warned him, "If it goes past your leg, you'll die." And your Uncle Bob said to him, "Don't cut off another inch, I'll be buggered if I die!" He was in hospital a long time, and the doctor always called him "my little bugger", but he didn't die and he didn't lose another inch off his leg.'

It was an inspirational story with a forbidden word in it too! We loved to hear it. But of course for Gran, it was also a sad story, and once I saw a tear sliding down her cheek and then her finger, as Grandad told it. Now I know she was remembering her mother's distress when the letter came from Bob telling them that he had lost his leg and his eye and had gangrene. He was miles away in a military hospital in South Africa, miles away from his mother and sister. They had heard he was hurt, but that his injuries were minor. The letter had been a terrible shock. Those weeks of thinking that he might die alone were what she remembered; that and the grief of him losing an eye and a leg.

When Uncle Bob was not there, tapes were exchanged. We kids would help with these, saying poems, singing songs, awkwardly telling stories. 'This morning we looked at tracks with Grandad. We could see bird prints and lizard prints and there were fox prints going near the chooks! Grandad is going to try and shoot it tomorrow.' Gran found taped books to send him too, as they were not readily available in Rhodesia.

This closeness with siblings often counts in childhood then is lost to adult life, but in old age siblings often support each other again. But in the case of Gran and Dad, their sibling friendships were maintained all the way from childhood to old age. Mum decided that this lifelong support group was a wonderful gift, and one that she would give her children. What were the barriers to it happening? What were the circumstances that would bring it about? She studied Gran's mothering style; she listened carefully to the stories Gran told of her own mother. Then Mum read books on sibling rivalry. She decided that getting those early years right was critical, and she spent hours thinking about it while pregnant with my sister Steph. When she came home with her new baby, she also came home with a plan.

At first, she simply aimed to make Steph and me friends, to prevent me from resenting the new baby as much as possible, and to teach us to play together. Breastfeeding was not a special time for Steph alone, it was also a special time for me because it was then that Mum read me stories.

Mum praised all my attempts to help care for and amuse Stephanie. She would describe to Dad (with me in eager earshot) the games I had invented to play with Steph. 'Hidey' was a favourite game — Mum would help Steph find me. Helping dress the baby in 'dress-ups' was another shared game. As Steph grew old enough to participate in the making of fun, Mum would reward us for inventing a new game by coming and joining in.

As we grew up Mum's aims expanded. From teaching us to play cooperatively, she began to teach us to work cooperatively. The rule at our house was that when there were jobs to do whoever finished their task first had to help the other children finish theirs. No one got to finish early and have playtime which belonged to them alone. When the work was done, we could all play together. So we understood from early in our lives that the nature of work was a shared effort and shared reward. She was teaching us to be a team.

I remember discovering from friends that parents had favourites. 'Favourite' was a word I often heard at school, used with resentment and envy by one sister, complacency by the other. Eventually, with a pang of uneasy horror, I worked out what it meant. It meant that parents liked one of their children better than the others! Soon I realised you could actually tell when you met another child if they were the favourite or not: 'favourites' seemed more contented, non-favourites had an air of striving against something invisible.

It was a revolutionary idea for me, for Mum and Dad just didn't seem to have one. No, insisted my friends, there is always a favourite. I concluded that my parents must have a favourite, as everyone else's Mum and Dad did, but that they were just good at keeping it secret. And this idea is so prevalent in our culture that it was not until I had two children of my own that I realised that Mum and Dad had been telling the truth.

And what trouble being or not being the favourite seemed to make between siblings! I remember friends encouraging us to try and work out who was the favourite: something Mum and Dad found hilarious. Eventually the friends would realise that this was a language we couldn't talk with them; and sadly, I found this was an important language. My inability to speak it sometimes became a barrier to close friendship with other children. I did not have either of those wounds: 'being favourite' meant a loss of friendship with your siblings and high parental expectations, or 'not being favourite' meant feeling belittled by your parents.

There is a cost to every parenting decision! School showed me I had another kind of wound: I was different. The contour banks on our farm, the early education, the lack of favourites in our family, no television — only books — all of these things would have made me different on their own, and to this concoction I added my own ingredient: an inability to keep my mouth shut. At twenty-six I wrote on my hand, as a visual prompt, the initials SU, which stood for 'Shut Up'. I kept them there for a year and sometimes I still glance at my left hand to remind myself to wait and listen a little longer. But for most of my childhood and my youth, every impulsive word branded me as different.

Now I know that this is the fate most people fear at school. Everyone is different, but they hide it and know that it must always be kept secret, and worry that some stray action will reveal them and that they will be branded and cast out! It is nearly twenty years since I left school, and a surprising number of people — even the most admired, the very coolest people — have said to me: 'I was like you, you know. I just kept it quiet.' I never could.

But being different also has its advantages.

One of the main questions I get asked about my life right now, about my life in a family business, is how do we all get on? How can I work with my husband, brother and sister-in-law and my parents? How does the family relationship affect the business? Don't we get sick of each other? It is not always easy, of course; there are dark times as well as the bright. But it was those hours of thought that Mum put in, so long ago, on how to teach her children to support each other, that have proved one of the main building blocks of our business.

3

TEAMWORK

'Grown-ups never understand anything for themselves, and it is tiresome for children to be always and forever explaining things to them.'

ANTOINE DE SAINT-EXUPÉRY, *LE PETIT PRINCE* (1943)

Mum and Dad taught us that we were a team: part of the family business. Mum taught us to work and play as a team so that we would be better friends. For her, teamwork was about sharing and mutual respect. She wanted big children and little children to respect each other, something teamwork both requires and builds. Respect of peers also builds confidence, and she wanted each of us to be confident enough to think for ourselves. And there were more prosaic reasons too. Children on farms are safer if they stay together for, if the need arises there is always someone to stay beside the injured child, and someone to go for help. And children who work well as a team are an asset to a family business.

Like all farm kids, we had plenty of jobs to do. When I was a little girl, we lived near the sheds. Before breakfast we would all walk down the laneway that ran the length of the cattleyards. They had a pungent, dungy smell, which changed 'flavour' depending on whether it was summer or winter and how recently the cattle had been in. I especially loved their smell in late summer; it seemed an intensification of the baked grass smell that was everywhere around me, and it's still one of the smells that reminds me of the reassuring, terrifying heat of the sun. One of us would run forward to try and open the gate, which had a pincher-like metal clasp that fitted around a pole. Sometimes I could open it, but on frosty or dewy mornings it would defeat my spidery cold fingers. Mum would have to do it, hitching the baby high on her hip, handing the milk pail to a child to hold.

And then she would go down to let out the calf and milk the cow, with a couple of us to help. One person would be nominated to let off the dog and speed toward the shed, spurred by Mum's parting words: 'Quick, or Dad will have done it.' But he never had, he would be bent over an engine, looking up to give an approving smile to the child, and a pat to the dog.

Then it was down to see how the milking was going. The cow-milking arrangement made me feel guilty. At night the calf and cow were separated into neighbouring byres. Just so we could have milk, the calf didn't get to have a drink all night! Even worse, it couldn't cuddle up next to its mum, as the other calves did. But in the morning I would usually be too fascinated by the sight of the milk going into the pail to remember my guilt, although the calf would be hollering outside in the paddock.

The sound of the milk going into the bucket! At first it sounded a little like heavy rain beating on the roof, liquid against iron. And then the sound would soften, lose its pattern, sometimes banging the iron at the side of the bucket, other times fizzing into the rising milk level. This middle sound was not so satisfying. But at the end of the milking came the sound I liked the most: the thick, creamy hind-milk squirting through the fluff gathering on the top made a noise that reminded me of the regular crash of heavy waves on the sand.

The milking cow was always nice to look at too. We had bought some Jerseys as milkers. Mum and Dad quickly named them 'the Apricosas', after a coconut and apricot sweet we occasionally purchased. The match between the name and the cows was perfect. They were apricot-coloured, freckled like apricots, their eyes apricot-shaped; and the cows themselves were demure and elegant, cosy and sweet, all at once. Only one cow would be milked at a time; the other three would be scattered among the herds of Angus and Brahman cows on the rest of the property. Spotting an Apricosa, like a golden sweet amongst the rangy cool-coloured Brahmans or the bead-round black Anguses was easy, but thrilling. 'Look, there's an Apricosa,' we would scream from the back of the ute.

While Mum milked, we children would perch behind her, sometimes half up the wall, wedging ourselves into gaps between railings, uncomfortable but not caring. Sometimes there were kittens and Mum would lose her helpers to the task of 'training' them to be friendly.

We would let the cow out and push her into the paddock; we would lay the hay out for the night to come. And then we would go back down the laneway to the house and breakfast, with warm milk to go on our porridge. If there was porridge left over, Mum would make biscuits from it. When we kids noticed this, we decided that one of us would ask for a smaller serving each morning so the biscuits would get made: just the kind of collaborative behaviour Mum and Dad were hoping to develop in us.

After breakfast the day's jobs would be divided between my parents and my grandparents. In the mornings Mum would make dinner and lunch, while we were sent to make our beds or to collect kindling, then we would go and do an outside job.

Mum would earmark small tasks that we kids could do within a bigger job. In stock-work we would be shown a place that we needed to be, told to run there, get in position and block the sheep or cattle going in that direction. Standing up to sheep took little resolve; cattle were a different matter. To reassure me, Dad had explained to me that cattle have four legs so that they think you have too. Behind what they can see of you they imagine you have the rest of your body and your other set of legs. Actually, reading what I've written here makes me suspect that this may be another lie! Anyway, that was what he said. As the cattle approached, I would remind myself that the cattle thought I was much bigger than I actually was. I would also take care not stand side-on, so that the cattle never became disillusioned.

We all knew the rules about waiting for stock. You had to be quiet and keep alert: who knew how long it would take for the mob to arrive? They could come easily, and there would be a yell of, 'Jo, where are you?', which was the cue to stand up. Or from behind the hill would come Mum's scream, 'Tom, they're breaking', followed by the howl of a motorbike engine revved past its capacity and orders to the dog, 'Right, right, right, back.' If the sounds then dwindled away, I knew they had needed to start again. I would settle contentedly back to whatever game I was playing: throwing one rock and trying to hit it with a second before it hit the ground, making daisy chains, scratching the hard ground with a stick, examining leaves or just dreaming.

But sometimes the stock would be fetched back on the verge of breaking and be steered rapidly and unsteadily toward me. It was too noisy to hear a command to stand. My heart would beat rapidly for if I stood up too soon, I would precipitate another break. Too late, and they would be going the wrong way. Making this judgement was a big responsibility. I don't ever remember getting it wrong, though I must have. I just remember the quick praise on getting it right: 'Thanks kids, we couldn't have done it without you.' I loved hearing those words.

'You kids worked well together on that,' was another phrase we often heard, and it was usually followed by, 'You saved me a lot of time this morning.' Mum would smile proudly at us as Dad said this, usually while boosting us onto the back of the ute. And we would go home in good spirits, ready for lunch.

On the days where it didn't go well, we shared that too. 'I'll fix the fence where the cattle knocked it down,' Dad would say, trying for equilibrium, 'and we'll have another go tomorrow. I know you kids did your best.' Dad does not easily accept reversals of fortune and he could never really disguise his annoyance and frustration. We would go home knowing we had tried, but that was no consolation, the job hadn't got done. Time Had Been Wasted!

We would eat lunch in the correct frame of mind — serious and thoughtful — but were never able to prevent ourselves from becoming cheerful before Dad did. Eventually, as we finished lunch, he would give one last sad backward-looking smile to us and the failed morning, set his mind to the afternoon's work and stride out the door.

After we had rested, we would be allowed to run up the hill to Gran. This was a kilometre's run, up and down hills, stopping to rest just once at the Halfway Rock, from which a wattle grew. Every day this was presented to us as a wonderful treat. And it was! For Gran would always lay on a special afternoon tea; she would make pikelets. She would walk around the garden with us, she would read us stories and play games. Very often she would try clothes on us, for Gran had been a dressmaker before she married, and she still loved to sew.

There was a real delight in try-on sessions. We all thought we were beautiful, of course, as children should think, so we were happy to stand before the glass and give our opinion. And our taste seems to have altered little since then. My favourite dress was rose-red, and covered in lacy flowers of cornflower blue and pink and stems of living green. Even after it was long outgrown, I kept a scrap of the material that I'd rescued from the shed where all clothes eventually went as rags. I still love those colours and flowers that delicately interlace. Steph wanted pink as a little girl — she wears it still! Megan still chooses the long flowing lines she wore as a child.

The feeling of the new material on our skin was a good one. Gran looking, tugging, pinning or unpinning, discussing with Mum what should be done: how satisfying! For Gran, making clothes was one of her ways of helping Mum. Gran always feels it's a very good way of saving money, so she made clothes for all her grandchildren as a gift to their parents. But trying-on sessions never had that feel: to me it seemed as if it was another way of acknowledging that I was important, that time had to be taken to get something right for me. Shopping for clothes is a very unsatisfactory experience compared with having the two women I loved best fussing over the length of my play-shorts!

So Gran made all of our clothes; even our knickers! Sometimes she would give us clothing to deliver to Mum and invite us to come back up the hill to see her after the job was done. I now see this arrangement doubled as an ingenious way to tire out children!

When we returned home, it would be time to shut up the cow and calf for tomorrow's milking (and I would feel very sad for cow and calf), to collect the kindling and wood for the next day's fire, to feed and tie up the dog. Dad would read a story to us as we ate; in this way we encountered some wonderful books. Susan Cooper's *The Dark Is Rising* series is one I particularly remember, and I cannot re-read it without hearing Dad's voice. I remember *The Hobbit* well, too.

When writers wish to add suspense and a feeling of dread, they add detail. The adventurers are in a cave. Tolkien describes the cave, and then in great detail outlines the relaxed behaviour of the dwarves. They fall asleep, but Bilbo has nasty dreams. If you have read the book, you will know the sense of doom that comes as Bilbo dreams of the crack in the wall and the sliding down to nowhere. Just a sentence before the words, 'At that he woke up with a horrible start …' came a scream. It was Steph. 'Shut the book, shut the book, stop reading, something awful's going to happen'. *The Hobbit* could never be opened at the table again.

Even though Steph and I were the big kids and carried more of the responsibility for jobs getting done, we were never given any power over Megs and Kyn. Naturally, we would have liked it! But Mum believed that no child should become a second parent: responsibility for your own actions is enough for any child, more robs children of some of their childhood. 'Teams are built among equals,' is one of Mum's favourite sayings, and she had made us as equal as she could.

What do you get if you have a group of children, equals, each taking responsibility for their own actions but not having responsibility for the actions of the others, encouraged to be loyal to each other, undivided by sibling rivalry, trained to work as a team to reach a shared goal? I'm not sure Mum foresaw this particular consequence (though she probably did), but what you get is a gang. And we were. We loved our parents, we liked to help them, we liked to do things with them, but they were also the only Enemy that our gang had in the early years. We needed to flout, to elude, to trick and to disobey!

But Mum and Dad were not very satisfying enemies. When I look back, I think that early wickedness consisted of giggling at the table, going to the mud patch when it wasn't allowed, riding on the back of sheep in the yards; and I suspect Mum and Dad of letting us think that minor misdemeanours were the height of naughtiness. They were always very cunning! It was when we went to school that we discovered the very best enemy of all: The Headmaster.

The local school was a one-teacher school and a source of pride to the district. Where all the neighbouring districts had lost their little school, Wannamal had kept theirs. I can remember the Schadenfreude-like shudder that went through Wannamal society when the news that the Mogumber school would be closed. Keeping a school open was achieved by birth-rate and the loyalty of parents: sending your child to one of the larger schools nearby would be an act of disloyalty to the district.

At the school all grades were taught in a single-room transportable by a young man in one of his first positions. As the only teacher, he was also the headmaster. I feel sorry now for any teacher in such a situation. How is it possible to teach twenty-three children in seven grades simultaneously and well? It would require a person of extraordinary talent and experience. But what we got were anxious, moustachioed young men, quick to avenge any hint of disrespect, jealous of their status and clinging to The Rules. They were a natural enemy. But not just that: they were natural victims as well.

In my first years I spent most of my time outside class, often talking to the lovely woman who did the gardening at the school. It was she who finally alerted Mum and Dad to the fact that if the teacher sent me outside, I did not sit by the door crying, as was correct. Instead I disappeared into the surrounding bush for long periods of time and could be heard giggling when the headmaster called me back.

In Year Three, because Steph was now at school too and part of the Gang were together again, I became braver. One day I hid the school bell and encouraged the other students to stay outside 'because the bell hasn't rung'. I remember the teacher saying, 'Come on Joanna, don't be silly.' But I didn't think I was silly, I thought I was clever. Steph thought I was clever, and it was the teacher who was silly. He had spent the whole year saying 'The bell has rung, so it's time to come in.' Now the bell was missing, he was saying, 'It doesn't matter if the bell hasn't rung.' So convinced were Steph and I, that the other students were too.

Mum and Dad intervened on behalf of the various headmasters many times. They became friendly with one teacher so that I saw him on weekends: they gave him permission to smack me if he felt it was required (he did). Mum and Dad would carefully explain that teachers had feelings too, and I would feel sad and guilty for a little while and be good. But soon the headmaster himself would undo my good intentions. He used 'favourites' as a management tool and also, 'You'll obey me because I am the headmaster.' I despised these methods, and my determination to undermine him gained a political fervour.

Mum and Dad purchased a copy of the curriculum and discovered to their horror we were two years behind. They asked that the education department review the school. The visiting superintendent concluded that I was a disabled child with severe behavioural problems, and that the headmaster was doing the best he could with an unsatisfactory student.

So Mum and Dad took their three school-aged children out of school. It caused an uproar in the district — three children being removed was enough to put the school at risk. Alerted by Mum and Dad's concerns, two other families removed their children and the school eventually closed.

Mum and Dad decided to teach us themselves, so that we could catch up and re-enter the school system at the correct level of our age. Two years' work was crammed into eight months of intensive learning. I remember these months so well: working by the hour on algebra, geometry and long multiplication; listening to tapes followed by comprehension tests to improve my ability to listen; long walks to find fungi which had to be drawn, classified, labelled and written up.

By spring the mushrooms had long gone. We looked instead for the fragile, airy, grey toadstools, the hard, orange wood fungi, the crumpling, white puff-balls. We found lichen and liverwurst and moss, which we also drew and labelled. We longed to find a slime mould — a fungus that can flow along the ground as an animal might, but root and grow like a plant at other times — but we never did.

On these walks Mum would talk to us. I came to see my behaviour towards the headmaster as bullying and to be ashamed. I was a difficult person to teach about such things: a childhood of being taught to do-as-you-would-be-done-by with my siblings had not taught me to extend the courtesy to people I didn't like. But Mum was carefully stripping this attitude from me. She showed me that I could hurt others, had certainly upset my teacher, and I lost forever my ability to imagine other people (even headmasters) as not feeling as I did.

I learned a great deal from this time: empathy, how to listen and that Mum and Dad thought a good education important. All good lessons, but the thing that resounded most strongly for me was this: it was more important to do what you think is right than what other people think is right. When Mum and Dad took us out of school to teach us themselves, even before the school closed, most families in the district had angrily withdrawn their friendship. The community had closed to us — and it was made plain that all would be forgiven only if we kids came back to school.

But Mum and Dad did not alter their decision. Even if nobody understood, even if everyone thought you were wrong, I learned, it didn't mean that you had done the wrong thing. Only time can show whether a decision is right or wrong; and what matters is what you gain by doing it, not other people's criteria of success.

This isolation did not dim our pleasure at being taught at home. It was like the school holidays, it was like being little once again, withdrawing into the safe cocoon of family once more. It was one of the nicest times in my childhood, and I think now the end of this time was the end of my childhood.

4

BACK TO SCHOOL

'No-one can make you feel inferior without your consent.'
ELEANOR ROOSEVELT, *CATHOLIC DIGEST* (1960)

At the beginning of the year I was to turn twelve, we returned to school. Mum and Dad chose Gingin. It had a high school and I would be going to high school the following year. It was too far to travel everyday from the farm, so Mum and Dad had quickly built a little house near the school itself. Mum was to live there with us kids during the week. On weekends we would come home. Some nights Dad was to visit.

The house Mum and Dad had built was very small and square, the ground outside sandy, the other houses close. There were people all around us; the school was a big one, with a teacher and teacher's aide for every year. In my mind the little house came to represent our sacrifice to meet the status quo, for us kids to be at school like other children. I did not like it much, it seemed like a cell in the prison of the little town. Its squareness, its smallness, its creamy walls reminded the other children at the school of something else: they called it The Butterbox.

Attending that school was my first experience of loneliness. For at Gingin the teachers did not like you to sit, eat or play with your siblings. Soon we all discovered that we had to stay 'in your year group' or get in trouble. This was hard to understand, and nor did I understand why it mattered that the other children thought our house looked wrong, but it did. I didn't understand why they waited to be friendly. I did not understand the criteria by which I was being judged; I just knew it was happening. But what were the right things to do? What were the wrong things? In those first few days I found myself remembering an incident of five years before.

A winter's night, I was six years old and the circus was opening for one night only in the tiny town of Mogumber. The vaulting tent, the raked dirt, the bright-faced clowns, the gaudy ponies, real sound lost to music and shouts: it was all just as I had read about in Enid Blyton books. Not the ringmaster, for he was a little man with a loud voice. Ringmasters in circus books are tall and cruel or round and jolly. He did carry a whip, which redeemed him a little in my eyes. He filled in between the acts with his own routines: stories and banter, mother-in-law jokes and games with the audience. As the show closed, he embarked on his final routine: the spotlight moved over the audience, looking for, said the ringmaster, the ugliest little boy in the tent.

With a ringing 'hold it' the spotlight was halted over me. I did not understand at first. The Ringmaster leapt over seats to reach us: 'Freckled, skinny, buck teeth and glasses!' he announced merrily, seizing my forearm and waving it. 'You can't get much uglier than this — a big cheer for our winner!'

I smiled because people were cheering, but inside I felt a crumpling. Mum and Dad were snarling as the ringmaster skipped lightly back down to the ring. Afterwards they told me that the ringmaster was wrong, and that I was a nice-looking little girl, and that who you were was more important than how you looked anyway. And I had forgotten all about it until once again I was in the spotlight, knowing I was judged and feeling that the judgement was not going my way, and that it was being made on grounds that I did not understand.

At Wannamal I had known that we were different, but it had been okay. Each family was different to each other family, and there had been no one else to play with anyway: for a game to be satisfactory, everyone needed to play. Gingin was large enough for children to pick and choose. Soon I learned that, just as with the chooks, someone was at the top, someone else was at the bottom and between the two was a ladder on which every child had a rung.

In the chook-yard the top chook is marked by her comb, which is ruddier. She is the rooster's favourite and the best layer. Mum encouraged us to watch as she tipped the wheat into the old trough for the hens. It would separate into dust and yellow grains, beneath which the top chook would daintily and eagerly bend her red-tipped head to peck, well ahead of the rest. And behind her complacent pecking would come the battle for second place. Feathers would fluff, necks elongate, suddenly I would notice how cold the eyes of a hen can be as they flick sidelong to her rival.

It was more complicated for children than chooks. There were different sets of ranking: one for school, one for attractiveness, one for sport. And boys and girls had separate rankings. The boys did not have a ranking for handwriting — girls did; it seemed to be a marker of femininity. And the ranking would be averaged out and everyone knew who was the top boy and top girl. Later, as other children joined the class, I worked out that the long period of being watched with no offers of friendship, had been necessary for everyone to see where I fitted on each ladder. But the sidelong flicking glances were the same for chooks and children. And just as with our chooks, that top position was rarely assailed; the real competition was for the other rungs on the ladder.

Mum and Dad had taught us well. By the time we reached Gingin we had not only caught up our missing two years, we were ahead of our year in some subjects. I was shortly top of my class in the unfeminine subjects of maths and science. Soon my place on the rankings was set: low for looks and femininity, high for brains, ordinary at sport.

On a farm every child has their special place, a hidey hole, a place to dream and to think. A place to be comfortably on your own. But it was not easy to find in Gingin. In the tiny Butterbox there was no such place, and outside the house were the houses of other people, their dogs, their gardens. Eventually I discovered the school library and found that books were not just for learning or entertainment, but that each good book was a place — somewhere you could go to dream and to find comfort.

My strongest memory of Gingin was not the library or the schoolroom, but the monkey bars. At lunchtime the boys in my class played a game where one person tried to swing across the monkey bars, and everyone else tried to stop them. Boys atop the monkey bars would bang violently on hands, boys underneath would pull the person down by their legs. It was mostly a boys-only game. But sometimes the popular girls would play too. As a mark of favour they would be let across with no attempt made to stop them.

I cannot remember exactly how I came to have a turn at getting across. The idea came from girls in my class first, I think, and was eagerly seized upon by the boys. It's a horrible feeling, knowing you are being set up to fail, knowing everyone wants you to fail. I knew that they wanted to humiliate me: refusing to try would have been humiliating, failing to succeed would be humiliating. It was a way of letting me know that I was not liked, that I was not a proper girl. I stood ready to swing. All around, on the patchy, sandy lawn, eyes were flicking in my direction.

I swung out and from above came fists banging my fingers into the metal. As I had known, I was not going to be let across as the other girls were. And I found myself remembering Uncle Bob, and his words to the doctor became a defiant chant in my brain. I was going to get across. By the time I was halfway across the long stretch of monkey bars, the boys were becoming anxious. They stood up on the bars and began stamping at my fingers. Sometimes they missed, more often than not I would distantly register the blow. I was going to get across. A rock was thrown up to the boys (by one of the girls!) and that was used to bang down on my fingers. Finally, with three rungs left, two boys swarmed down from the top of the monkey bars and tried to pull me off. I kicked violently with my heavy brown school shoes, and kept going.

And I was across. There was silence as I got down from the monkey bars. The girl who had passed the rock up to one of the boys walked hastily away with her friends. 'Bet you can't do it again,' said a boy, but it was a half-hearted attempt. Winners don't need rematches, and he knew it. I began to walk towards the library. 'You're the first person to get across,' called another, as I continued shakily on my way.

Even now I feel proud that I got across; the memory of that steely determination that fell upon me is something I draw upon still. And while I was at Gingin, that incident became my protection: I never could fit the approved model of girl, but I was not a victim either.

The prospect of the weekend on the farm was the best comfort, though. Time and space and familiar tasks and just being with my family; for many years it would be the only place I could feel like a whole person. For at school you are not a whole person; you are not even quite yourself. You become an amalgam of the earliest impressions that others took of you and all your later actions are interpreted in the light of these first impressions, and the character assessment that was first made of you is confirmed over and over.

But at home I felt whole and complex and free. Dad would save the best jobs for the weekends so we could do them together. And Mum would make sure that the old rituals were kept. So at seeding time, when the crop is put in the ground through the night, and Dad needed his dinner brought to him in the paddock, taking Dad his tea would be a whole family affair.

After baths we would dress in pyjamas and over the top would put warm tracksuits. This was the standard procedure in country families for going out for parties in winter, and so even our clothes contributed to the sense of occasion! Into the boot of the car would go two cardboard boxes; in one would be six plastic containers carrying stew and rice with spoons to match, in another would be six containers full of pudding: perhaps apple crumble with custard. There would be fresh-made buns too, buttered and jammed, for we all ate far more than usual on these nights.

At night the farm was a different place, the land before us lit only by the headlights of the car as it rocked gently over the crumpling, steaming soil, the windscreen wipers endlessly catching and directing the rain from the window. Last year's grass and stubble still stood on the paddock margins, gold and white in the tunnelled light.

Dad's tractor would come nearly upon us, lights blaring: sometimes I would have a moment of doubt that he had seen us at all, and wonder at Mum's calm unpacking of boxes as we waited in the car. Dad would hop down from the tractor, open the car door and duck into the car, bringing with him the smell of wet, waiting earth and grain, stripping-off his balaclava and gloves. Then the car headlights and windscreen wipers would be switched off, the interior light would come on; and we would sit in a bubble of light, warmth and comfort, floating in the river of dark rainy night.

Dad was quickly infected by the party atmosphere in the car. He would tell us stories of well-fed foxes following the tractor until dawn, indulging their curiosity now they had finished their serious business of hunting; he would tell us of shooting stars, and of the strange ideas that had come to him as he tracked around the paddock. It is not an easy job, seeding, although it sounds easy enough. Every loss of concentration shows as a bare patch, yet it is a round-the-clock job! Once the rains have come the crop must be put in as fast as possible. By now it was just us on the farm; Gran and Grandad had moved to another property nearby six years before, and for now Dad was on his own. But the crop still went in on time — with no bare patches.

The food would be eaten quickly and half an hour later, Dad would don balaclava and gloves once more. He would quickly confer with Mum on when he expected the paddock to be finished, then Mum would switch on the car lights and in the car we would sit and watch Dad, carrying his new thermos, walk swiftly and steadily over the soil to the tractor. We would hear the tractor's roar and see it transformed into a cage of light, Dad inside just an outline.

The tractor would move off, followed by the inexplicable combine-seeding machine. (I was never able to fathom its multitudes of ploughs and tubes.) We would watch as the tractor departed, taking all noise and light with it. As the world outside went dark, I would again become aware of my warmly dressed body, cuddled against my siblings in the dark, moving car, dry and cosy and fed, ready for bed. And behind us, in the cold and wet was Dad, going on through the night.

When I left home and Gingin Primary School for boarding school, I felt a sudden kinship for Dad: just as he did on those chilly, lonely nights, I was leaving the warm, safe cocoon of family life to go on alone.

When you go to boarding school you leave home. At St Hilda's Anglican School for Girls, I became, as my sister Megan was later to say of herself, 'just another little girl in a grey dress'.

My life became caught up with the life of the school, and although I still worked on the farm at weekends and on holidays, I began to think of myself chiefly as a 'St Hilda's girl' not as a farm girl.

At boarding school you learn to be responsible for yourself: you must keep yourself tidy, organised and cheerful. You must structure your day to match the bells, all while keeping your locker neat, your washing up-to-date, your bed made. I was not good at these things and did not even use my locker (I kept a large messy pile under the stairwell), but the staff were memorably tolerant of my failings. They did little to discourage what the deputy principal called my eccentricity. I have never been quite sure why this was. I think the school's goal was to help people become the people they were meant to be. Certainly, I was not often asked to turn myself into 'just another little girl in a grey dress', although the staff would have appreciated me remembering, just once, to wear my stiff-brimmed hat at the right angle in church.

But while the staff were tolerant, the other girls were not. For them I was not 'eccentric' but different, not hard-working enough to be a brain, not a party girl, not a practical girl, not a posh girl. My lack of organisation must have shamed my friends, for they played a prank that I think must have been designed to embarrass me out of my dreamy ways. It was Saturday, but they told me it was Sunday. How harmless that sounds! I remember a long day in which I became increasingly bewildered.

At eight o'clock my friends explained to me that it was a joke, because I never seemed to know what day it was anyway. They had done me a favour, they said, because at least I would be ready for school on Monday! The prefect-in-charge found me trying not to cry in the bathrooms late that night. 'You've got such a good sense of humour,' she said, for she had played along. 'We thought it wouldn't upset you too much.'

After this I decided to try to be more like the other girls.

At the end of that year, in which I had ardently strained to copy the other girls as closely as possible, I was stunned by a casual remark. 'I don't know what it is, Jo, but you've just got weirder and wierder this year.' Well! I'd tried to be more like them and only succeeded in highlighting how unlike I was. Slowly I began to accept that here, too, where I'd hoped to find people just like me, I remained different. There seemed to be nothing I could do to change that.

There were too many girls at St Hilda's for the ranking system that held sway at Gingin to work. Instead there were groups, held together by common values and interests, and within the groups a turmoil of competition for first place. I was only ever on the periphery of any of these groups. By final year the groupings had begun to dissolve, and there were friendships across the numerous cliques: I liked this last year best of all.

I had made friends at school, but I had still not encountered 'my kind' of people — people with whom I felt as much at home as I did with my family. Did such kindred spirits even exist?

I went to university, where I studied English. It was in the third year of this degree that I suddenly, magically, found my kind of people. And among them I was to find the most kindred spirit of all. The University Science Fiction and Fantasy Association clubroom overflowed with ugly couches, torn posters and books, but best of all, it loudly overflowed with people like me.

Fisherman's daughter, priest's daughter, miner's son, doctor's son — family backgrounds differed, schooling differed — but our aspirations were the same: to live lives that accorded with our ideas of how the future should be shaped. We were political, fanciful, philosophical: lovers of radical science and utopian visions.

In this loud and intellectual crowd Martin was impossible to miss, despite his habitual economy with words. He had just finished his time as a grinder on the South Australian boat in the Fremantle America's Cup. Burnt as dark as he could go (which is very dark, as Martin is a Torres Strait Islander), very muscular and very tall, he looked as much like a handsome bear as a man can. He worked part-time as a bouncer and he very rarely needed to do anything other than frown at an offender. Recipients of a frown would hurriedly finish their drinks and leave.

One day I was discussing a book I'd been asked to review on the university radio station. I was trying to find an analogy for the feeling it provoked in me, a sense that the writer had tried to humble the reader, not in a petty way, but with grandeur and mystery.

'The feeling you have looking at the stars late at night,' said Martin, looking up from his book with a sure but shy smile.

That was it exactly. How suddenly wonderful and complete and terrifying was a world that held such a friend!

5

Travelling Hopefully

*'What do tourists do? … They visit famous monuments,
fountains, old houses full of stones and shutters and
anachronistic lace. They notice a day without duty passes
with the slowness of a dream. They know their existence is
without point. They envy those who go arm in arm, who have
a home to go to.'*

Helen Garner, *The Children's Bach* (1984)

Soon Martin was coming home to the farm with me on weekends. The first day of his first weekend he was sent to repair fences with Dad. On a shared boundary Dad and Martin met a neighbour, who said he had a drilling rig on his property. 'There's a water diviner too,' confided the neighbour.

Drilling for underground water is becoming more and more common in farming life. For although there are ways to read the landscape to guess at what lies beneath, the likelihood of finding water is uncertain; it is as chancy as trying to divine from a face and words what lies in another's heart. As the climate changes, more farmers are looking beneath the earth for what is no longer coming from the skies, despite the fact that you pay whether or not water is found. As the poet Banjo Paterson wrote, 'If we can't get it from the heavens, we'll get it from the devil down below.'

The neighbour departed, and as they repaired the fence, Dad explained water divining to Martin. Water diviners pace backward and forward across the ground, holding in their hands some kind of divining tool — a pendulum or a forked green stick, pulled tight, or a single bent wire. They wait for a tug or a twitch: much as a fisherman waits for the fish upon the line. Where the strongest of pulls is felt, the underground stream is directly beneath, and there is the best place to drill.

'Of course, it's completely unverified and unreliable,' Dad added.

Martin nodded, understanding from this that Dad had no faith in water divining, and that no divining would be happening on Dad's farm, at least.

Martin and Dad returned to lunch, and over lunch Dad told us that the neighbours had a drilling rig and a water diviner searching for water. We discussed which of our own paddocks could do with an extra water supply, and the need for reliable water in the light of Dad's conviction the south-west was going to be subject to increasingly erratic rainfall. After lunch Dad leapt up from the table and announced that he was going to see if the drillers had time to put in a couple of bores on our farm. 'Might invite the diviner too, hey Barb? And cut a stick myself and work alongside,' he added.

Martin stared after Dad in astonishment. 'Your dad isn't a water diviner, is he?'

'Yeah, he is,' I said. 'He strips a forked twig of leaves and he holds it —'

'But this morning he said it was unreliable! He talked a lot about how …'

Mum and I were nodding and Martin's face grew thoughtful.

'But now,' said Martin in a baffled voice, 'he's going to go and divine himself?'

He looked at the lack of surprise in our faces.

'He might have said it was unreliable, but that doesn't mean he doesn't think it won't work some of the time,' I said, helpfully. 'And it's never easy to predict what Dad is going to do.'

'I see,' said Martin, not thoughtfully, but more in tones of ominous agreement. 'Can we go and watch?'

We found Dad striding up and down, grasping the tufts of gum leaves at either end of a forked green branch that was straining so a single branch was pointing to the sky, almost flipping forward to touch Dad's nose. Next to him strode the diviner, holding a bent wire in each hand. Their faces were pulled downward in concentration. The drill rig crew waited patiently.

A shout came from Dad and the diviner together. Dad's branch was now tugging down to the earth, fighting his attempts to strain it up, and the bent wires in the diviner's hand were swinging hard to the left. 'Here,' said Dad to the drillers, jabbing a finger into the earth.

It was the kind of place that would have been chosen without the assistance of divining rod anyway. Above swelled the first rises of a large hill, there were tall trees nearby, and it was granite country. All of these were good indications that there might be water below the ground.

The long metal mosquito shape of a drill is a strange sight on the spring-greened hills of the South West country. It is too angular, too industrial against the soft shapes; and besides, drilling for water seems beside the point in country that looks so happily rain-fed. At that moment when the proboscis drill begins to press down, I always feel an equal pull of distaste and hope.

The drill whines and howls and growls through the layers of rock and clay. The ever-growing mound of different types of earth beside the drill is witness to the many layers that must be pierced to reach the stream that may be there. And always, as the drill goes deeper, the drillers call out the depth — you never forget that you pay for the drilling by the metre. Will they find water?

'Water!' comes the magpie shout from the drillers as the drill reaches 25 metres. But will it be any good? Will it be good enough for stock, or maybe even sweet enough for humans to drink? An old cup is fished out, washed briefly, water is scooped in, and we must wait for the oil and mud to settle before the cup is held out to Dad for first taste.

All our anxiety is refined into this single moment, but it is a short one, for Dad has the most mobile of faces and we can quickly read the news. Dad's eyebrows shoot up, he nods and smiles, his shoulders falling in relief and satisfaction. I look at Martin — his eyebrows are raised too, not in simple pleasure, but in astonishment. The next taste is to Mum and she too smiles in relief. This time the gamble has paid.

Most of the time Martin and I were in Perth: studying, working, trying hard to find a way to move our lives forward so we could live together. Now I see that we met too soon: our only direction was each other and we were not equipped to live separate lives, let alone a shared life. My degree in English suited me for everything and nothing. I had no feeling of life direction, and Martin was equally lost.

Half-heartedly I commenced a postgraduate degree in teaching, but six months later I gave it up. For a while I worked alongside Mum as an occupational therapy assistant (she is an occupational therapist) before being seconded to an acting-management position in Perth. I was doing well, I thought, but slowly discovered that at twenty-one years old I was too young for management. I was relieved when the real manager returned from long-service leave, but I was also out of a job. I began to look for work at the height of the 1980s recession: it did not take long before I discovered that sometimes it was better not to admit to my Arts degree.

My various jobs included law clerk (where I lasted three weeks before being fired for being too different from the other law clerks); telemarketing (one month before being fired); carrot-picking and sorting (I left because there was no escape from the carrots at all: at night I would dream of carrots flowing past on the conveyer belt); and one day at a suburban house whose location I was not allowed to reveal, with telephones I wasn't to answer, writing funny biographical rhyming telegrams that were to be delivered by fat ladies or male strippers or a woman called Madam Lash for birthdays and farewells and bucks' parties.

The business was run by Madam Lash. Madam Lash's real name was Alex, and she was a charismatic, beautiful woman with flashing black eyes, strong black long hair and a very dramatic manner: I liked her instantly. Instead of flying ducks on the wall there were whips, but otherwise it was like any other suburban house: brick and lawn and rich carpets. Alex talked to me about Karma, about making your own rules for living, about what happened to people who crossed her, and how important it was that if men rang and asked for the address of the house, I didn't even say which suburb we were in. It was when she explained the importance of encouraging callers to book extra strippers for bucks' parties as after-dinner entertainment that I finally began to wonder if Madam Lash had another business besides that of funny telegrams.

In the end I lasted just the one-day trial period because my rhymes were not of the right kind. Madam Lash and I parted on good terms, and she paid me twenty-five dollars for trying hard. Afterwards I would see her at the Perth Law Courts, exotic and queenly among the police and lawyers. She would always smile warmly; we would wave at each other, and I would walk on feeling honoured and heartened, all the way down St George's Terrace and on to another employment agency.

But mainly through this time in my life I was feeling disheartened and despairing. At the employment agencies they would ask me what kind of work I wanted — anything at all, I would reply. I didn't mind, I just wanted a job. 'That's not the right attitude,' I was told. 'Think of your skills and match them to a job.' Of course, the truth was that I had few marketable skills. The only jobs for girls like me seemed to be in England: I could work at an adventure camp or as a nanny. Perhaps if went to England I could work and think and sort myself out.

So with Martin and Mum's encouragement I spent the last of my saved money on a six-month return ticket to go to a job at an adventure camp. Each of them talked earnestly to me before I left: the gist of each talk was that they thought I would sort myself out if I was far enough away from both sets of loving, overprotective and overhelpful arms.

With my backpack, my clever clothesline and my four changes of clothes and desert boots, I was trying hard to be a keen, modern and savvy traveller.

I was homesick before I reached Heathrow.

I had six miserable months in England. Now I regard those months as some of the most useful months of my life, but I could find no purpose in them while I was living them. The sight of sheep made me dizzy with longing for the farm. I would be found sobbing in fields. Camp leaders were meant to be happy. The adventure camp management fired me after three weeks for 'contagious misery'.

After that I worked as barmaid: I had that job for the shortest time of all. 'You've got a lovely manner with the regulars, dear,' said the manager at the end of my first night, 'but the language barrier is a problem.' It was true: I could not understand anyone with a regional accent unless they asked for Guiness. And although the regulars did like me, they soon grew weary of ordering Guiness and nothing else.

I waited to be entranced by the old buildings of England, the man-made landscapes, to feel history lapping at the gates of the everyday. The feeling never came. I stood in St Paul's Cathedral, looking at the vaulting, dizzying ceiling but remembering our shearing shed and its starry, night-sky ceiling, like that of every other shearing shed in Australia: the accidental magic of tiny holes in a tin roof. I was learning that you cannot command or anticipate what will speak to your spirit: the everyday details of my own left-behind life spoke to me more than all of the sacred art that surrounded me.

Walking through the streets of London, I thought of Martin. As a fourteen-year old, he'd been set to trail after his little sister Minnie through the streets of London. He'd followed her for hours. London's streets for me were not haunted by Jane Bennett or Lord Nelson, but by a big-shouldered boy patiently shadowing the naughtiest little sister in the world.

I tried nannying. With the family I worked for I went to Cornwall. I fell ill and I was left in hospital when the family returned to London. Eventually Cathi, who'd come to stay often on our farm as a child, now nursing in England, found out where I was. Rightly concluding there was nothing more wrong with me other than extreme homesickness, she told me to discharge myself and come to her.

Often these days people who are unsure of life direction ask me for advice. And this is because I am so very directed, they feel I must know how they can find their own way. And I do have something that I always say. I tell them:

The clues are all there. Try to stand back from life. Look to see what you are naturally good at and feel passionate about, the opportunities you have followed in the past and the signs that will show the way the wind is blowing for you now. Look symbolically at your life, for the doors in your life that have opened easily, and those that have kept shutting. Look for the places and people that speak to your spirit. Remember your favourite games when you were a child; they show you your natural leanings unencumbered by other people's opinions. And finally look for a key, which might be a way of unlocking the right door or just a way of recognising which one is the right door.

But even so, sometimes these words are of no assistance when you are lost. I searched for them and found them and could parrot them but I did not understand them within my heart. If you understand them with your heart, you also know the answers. In the months I stayed with Cathi I did not get quite that far, but I did assemble enough clues to choose a direction.

On the long walk back from the train station to her room in the nursing quarters, Cathi proudly showed me Greenwich. She knew the greengrocer on the corner, the history of the white Royal buildings on the Thames, how many metres we were from the Greenwich mean time line. Her joyous interest in another culture was the antithesis of my limp, homesick, Martin-sick misery. She promised treats of visits of Cambridge, of meeting her friends, of easily finding me work and accommodation. Under the suddenly bright sun, on the warm, hard, cobbled street, but most of all, under the bright, hopeful gaze Cathi directed at me, and the affection in her kind, pretty face, I began to feel some interest in my last two months away from home and Martin.

Very soon I was working as a nursing aide in the Greenwich District Hospital, and I had my own room at the nursing quarters. I was put to work to care for the dying, on wards which did not have that as a purpose, but where people often died nonetheless. I remember particularly the ninety-seven-year-old Cockney who had been a Covent Garden flower girl in her youth. She winked in and out of life once or twice a week. Her heart and breath would stop for minutes at a time, then suddenly she would be back, laughing mischeviously at us. 'Not gone for good this time, my loves,' she would say, a shining behind her pointed, wrinkle-laced face. 'Thought I had, didn't you?'

'Nelly, is there anything where you go?' I asked when the opportunity offered.

'Light,' she said, 'light and joy. But I keep coming back for that telegram from the Queen. I remember her mum coming to our street in the war. We were just about the same age, and she gave me such a look; she understood how I felt. That's why I want my telegram.'

There was the old man with one side of his body lost to his control, and part of his mind too. I improvised and made him a newspaper holder for he enjoyed reading, although he could not speak, and he smiled at me. One day I returned to find that he had died and I remembered that the day before his eyes had blazed a protesting goodbye at me as I walked from the ward. Was he angry at dying? Was he angry at me for not saying goodbye properly? How I wished I had known what I was reading in his face, and known how to respond.

Cathi soon began to insist that I should have some fun as well as work. 'Go somewhere,' she urged. 'Europe is so close.' I prevaricated, with the secret intention of going nowhere in order to save money. Cathi was ruthless. She organised a trip to France, paying for my bus and ferry tickets herself and finding a friend to take me for a week to Taizé.

Her plans were nearly stymied by my managing to lose my passport and the only key to my room days before I was to leave. Cathi took me to the embassy, to the passport office, and just an hour before departure my new passport arrived. The room key was another matter. We searched her room, the outside street, any room I had ever entered. We then broke into my room from the outside third floor window and searched that thoroughly. Cathi was going to have to request that another lock be fitted to the door.

Taizé is a monastery near Lyon. In summer the countryside there seems to be all burnt umber hills and dry grasses. On green-shuttered window sills set into terracotta cottages sat pink geraniums in orange pots. Taizé's accommodation is more a camping ground. Taizé is a monastery of reconciliation, and the monks believed that people meet more as equals if simplicity is the rule and they follow the same pattern of meals and devotions as the monks. There were twelve thousand people camping there with mattresses bumping together. Every day they would stand in long lines for the daily breakfast of yogurt and a breadstick and hot chocolate. They would sing and be silent together in the large flat space of the chapel.

At Taizé I asked to see one of the Sisters. Somehow, superstitiously and foolishly, I had come to hope that someone of spiritual authority could magically reveal to me what I should do. Perhaps such a person could hand me a key by which to understand what to do with my life? The Sister was very thin; I remember nothing else about her except her increasing bewilderment and indignation at my request.

'Only you can answer this,' said the poor woman, flummoxed by being treated as a clairvoyant. She smiled at me dubiously. 'Would you care for me to pray for you?'

I returned to Greenwich with just two weeks left in England, feeling that I had gained nothing in my miserable months away from home. On my last night, as we returned from a film (Cathi's last treat), walking on the hard street back to the nursing quarters, the moon full and the night soft, I became aware that for the last few steps, as my right foot touched the ground, there was a soft metallic click — something had attached itself to the sole of my boot. 'Jo, what's that noise?' said Cathi at the same moment.

Without thinking I responded: 'It's the room key I lost.' And it was. Turning up my foot, still wearing the desert boots in which I had left Australia and worn to France and back, I found on the sole of my boot that very same key stuck on with chewing gum. We began to laugh and dance together on the street; the soft night was suddenly happy and bright with hope. For the symbolism was inescapable: I had thought I had lost my key, and yet there it was; it had been waiting for me on the street.

Very late that night as I sat listening to London and looking across to the Thames, running black under a light sky, I felt as separate from my everyday life as if I had gone a century forward in time. Jubilantly packing for home, I planned the next few years. I would gain every skill I could: never again would I be without work. Some time Martin and I would get married. There would be children. I would trust that I would choose the right direction, that the knowledge would be waiting there in me, like the key that had waited on the street.

And as I planned, I felt a tugging in my palms, as if gentle fingers were drawing me forward. This feeling was, I realised joyfully, how my intuition spoke to me. Perhaps this was how Dad felt, holding the diviner's rod. How hard it is to trust such instincts, to trust life, I thought. And I wondered why I had needed to travel so far to discover something that must have been waiting for me, like the key on the street, all along.

6

Going Home

'Six years I've been in the city and every night I dream of the sea. They say home is where you find it; Will this place ever satisfy me?'

Neil Murray, *My Island Home* (1985)

I returned home with a plan. Looking at the doors that had opened easily for me, feeling drawn to the task of helping others find meaning in their lives, and not forgetting that one of my favourite games as a child was doll hospital, I applied to study occupational therapy. This is not an easy course to gain entry to, but amongst my many dismissals I had collected two very good references from working in hospitals: both could have been written to impress that particular selection panel. I was in.

Now it was suddenly easy for me to find part-time work. I was offered a research assistant position at the university, and another job working with disabled children. Before I had been like a wool-blind sheep in a drafting race, persistently slamming my head into the gate barring one direction, unable to see the wide open entry to another yard. It was hard to believe now how very difficult it had been just a year ago.

Martin and I decided that we would get married at the end of my first year of study. I would be twenty-four and Martin twenty-five. Although Martin was yet to find the right path, we were confident that he would and we were tired of waiting: it was time for a leap of faith. For one year I moved back into the town house that Mum and Dad owned in Perth to live with Steph and Megs. All of us were studying; Steph was in the final year of her degree, Megan was part-way through.

This was to be our last year of living together, for not only was I getting married, Steph was too. Friends had often predicted that I would marry someone thin and mercurial and intense and Steph someone big and gentle and humorous. But our friends had it backwards; it was me who needed someone like Steph and Steph needed someone a bit like me. Bradley was a brilliant student who had graduated top of his year and he was embarking on postgraduate study. He had so many ideas about so many things he had to keep notebooks to keep track of them all. As a hyperactive toddler he'd quickly worn a deep track around the Hills hoist to which his mother had tied him: no one meeting him at twenty-two needed to ask what had caused the exhausted woman to hit upon that idea.

Although the boys were often there on weekends — Martin cooking and listening, Bradley talking fast and straightening, Kynan out of boarding school and eating, and maybe one of Megan's court with flowers or food — it was ultimately a girls' house. It had an air of shabby chic. On the dining table would be placed a neat bunch of pink rosebuds, Steph's from Brad, crisp and symmetrical. But underneath, with neither crispness nor symmetry, would flow one of Megan's dark-coloured, whorling and flowering oddments of material. Steph's neat bows held back the curtains, but atop the pelmets would sit Megan's favourite rocks and crooked half-used candles.

Martin and Bradley considered themselves part of the family after four years and they found the same things funny. In particular they liked to tell stories about the Jacksons to each other. This was probably because Steph and I told stories about each of them to the rest of the family. The day Dad saw the shadow of a spider in his reading glasses and threw them to the ground, where they smashed, then realised that it wasn't a spider but his own eyebrows he had seen was a very happy one for Martin and Brad.

But most of the time it was just me and my sisters. Living together, we three girls found the old rhythms and patterns of sharing childhood jobs were with us still. Folding the washing had been a mum-and-kids job at home; the youngest had always paired and, with little hands, tried to roll the socks together. Megs was the youngest in the house so pairing and rolling the socks was her job.

Unfortunately, she was at that age when the wearing of matching socks was an anathema. Her black boots were painted over in swirling shapes with nail polish; one glittering shoelace was silver, the other violet. Above she wore a brown and orange flowered skirt with flowing crinkly lines and with all of this, a blue shirt with a collar she had decorated in blue and green crystals. Matching socks just did not work with an outfit like this! And if Steph and I did not supervise her, none of our socks would match either, for she would often borrow just one and vanish out the door.

The special powers of cheering and healing were in that house too: there is often some miraculous talent for changing another's mood that is possessed by one sibling alone. If Megs was grumpy, I could do nothing but empathise, but this brought no cure. Steph could make her laugh against her will.

Megan, pale and pretty and peevish, would walk in. A cup of coffee would be soothingly offered. A snappy, unsoothed reply received. Steph would make puppets of her hands.

'Mmph?' the right hand would inquire of the left, somehow meaning 'Would you like a cup of coffee?'

'Mrrup!' the left would grumpily respond.

'Mmm,' would croon the right, in sympathetic tones.

But the left hand could not leave it there. 'Mrrup! Mrrrrgggrrr!' it would snarl and begin biting the head off the right with savage little nips.

Megan would shake her head fiercely at Steph and try to regain her mood, but it was of no use, the puppet show had won and Megan was overcome with reluctant giggles. My moods could be overcome when a sibling assumed a rock-like calmness (Martin's habitual manner, in fact) or by the making of lists. Steph's bad moods required her to be answered as firmly and as fiercely as she herself was feeling — trying to placate her only made things worse.

Slowly we began to ready the house for the two weddings. Mine was to be first and I was determined not to use an anonymous venue, a place to which I had no emotional bonds. I wanted a wedding that was built out of my everyday life. Steph agreed and, rather more practically, also felt that it would save money in the long run for Mum and Dad.

The sandy backyard — full of weeds and bricks, the indigo trumpet flowers of the glory vine trailing over all, a dignified grasstree standing solitary, scattered with the remnants of outside fires and the chairs left from previous parties — was to be transformed. Megan watched sadly as it was paved and tamed; but soon the long garden beds placed alongside each wall were responding to her anarchic gardening gift; among the white wedding petunias were green beans, and the glory vine was soon climbing the walls once more.

The house was repainted, our exams finished, Gran had finished making our dresses. The day had come. As we dressed, the whole family together in the little house, Dad became peculiarly mournful. 'It's the last time,' he said, 'the last time we will all be together like this, getting ready as a family.' I reminded him of Steph's wedding, just a month away, but he remained grave. 'It's important,' he said, 'to recognise when things have changed.'

Things had changed but the change had begun a long time ago — four years ago — when Martin and Brad had first started to come home. They had woven themselves into the fabric of the family: where would family storytelling be without Steph's stories of Brad? We had all loved him since Steph had naughtily confided to us the story of his inarticulateness when trying to say how much she meant to him: 'Steph to me you're just … worthless'. ('You mean "priceless", don't you?' Steph had asked, just to be sure.)

The weddings were done. Ours was informal and almost indistinguishable from the parties we had so often held. Steph and Brad's formal. On each table, instead of flowers, there was a cornucopia of fruit: red globe grapes, Sicilian strawberries and cherries from Brad's parents' cherry trees. Then each of us had moved out. The little house was Megan and Kynan's now.

Martin and I ended up renting a house just streets away from Steph and Brad. Our house had been built in the 1930s by someone who disdained right angles, and over time the majority of the house had sunk away from the big stone fireplace so all the floors tilted down. On the door there were six peacocks, the windows were of stained glass and the bath had gold clawed feet. Life was good there; psychic friends often told me they could feel a 'happy presence' in the house: I wondered if it was simply the echo of our own happiness.

But four years later I was becoming uncomfortable in Perth. It was as though the time in London had oversaturated me with city life. The city skyline which had seemed so exciting was now barren of meaning. This was despite my good marks in my study, my part-time jobs that promised a further choice of good careers either working for the *West Australian* newspaper as a freelance journalist, continuing to help design multimedia tools as a research assistant, writing curriculum and lecturing for another course at Curtin University. Martin, too, was studying and working part-time, building an electronic publishing business with friends. I knew he felt just as lost as I did. Steph and Brad's departure for London, where Brad would do post-doctoral work, only made us more restless.

More than anything we wanted children, but I was scared of ending up a mother in an anonymous suburb I felt no connection to. Martin was uninspired by the prospect of a life seeing his children only in the evenings, shopping on Saturday and sleeping on Sunday. He hoped that working on the Internet would mean he could be at home with them a little more. We were happy for now, but we knew that we could not be happy for much longer. I was beginning to dread graduation and 'growing up'.

The year before, Martin had badly injured his Achilles tendon playing basketball. All the physiotherapy and care in the world had made no difference. His calf muscle would have to be removed and rolled up to become a new Achilles tendon, said the specialist, if he was ever to walk without a limp, stand on tiptoe, run or jump. Two massive haematomas had blocked healing; they would need to be removed too. Martin had lived over a year without sport, unable to ride his bike, play soccer, row, or play basketball. It was unimaginable for a man who had once been a member of West Australia's King's Cup rowing crew.

It was halfway through this year, when I was twenty-seven and Martin twenty-eight, that the invitation from Minnie came. Martin's little sister was fulfilling her dream of exploring the other side of her heritage, having grown up in suburban Perth away from her mother. Now they were living together on Thursday Island. Minnie was working for the Torres Strait Regional Authority. Martin's brother, Paul, whom I had never met, was crayfishing in the outer islands, having left Perth as a teenager.

'Come and see us. Come and meet the rest of your family!' Minnie said to Martin. For Minnie had been lost once too. In her island family she had found out more about who she was and where she'd come from, and this feeling of coming *from* somewhere had made it easier for her to work out where she wanted to go. She was sure that meeting the Island side of his family would help Martin.

I had met Martin's mum just once before; she had come to Perth and stayed with us for two weeks. We had picked her up from the airport, this extraordinarily young woman who looked like Martin. She was carrying a traditional ornamental boat. She walked up to us, hugged Martin, hugged me and said firmly (while weeping), 'You call me Mum. I love you.' Often she would be crying as she laughed, as she spoke of hardships and good times, as she told stories, as she gazed at Martin and thought how long it had been since she had last seen him, and how soon she would be going home. 'Don't mind me,' she would say, reaching for another tissue, 'I have soft eyes.'

It took just two weeks for every person on our long anonymous street to begin to greet her. While we were away at university, she would somehow manage to have adventures: finding money and returning it, persuading the fishmonger to locate a traditional ingredient for her, making friends with the lonely, very old man next door. At night she would cook for us — Island cooking, and I finally understood why Martin cooked the way he did. He'd no memory of learning to cook, but he must have watched his mother very closely as a baby sitting on a bench, for their rice and coconut dishes were identical.

The two of them were both different and alike — as if they were an introverted brother and an extroverted sister with the same family ways. It was from his mother, I realised, that Martin had inherited his extraordinary ability to decide for himself. It is not that they fight against the opinions of others; it just never occurs to either of them that other people's opinions should in any way influence their own.

In an introvert such a character trait can be missed, but in an extrovert it dances on the outside of their skin along with every other quality. And Martin's mum seemed always to be dancing; her teasing grins were paired with a little two-step manoeuvre, her laughing shake of her head was graceful — as if it was part of a traditional dance. I had never met someone who used their body so. It was cultural I told myself in envy. But I was not to meet another person with that quality again; at least, not until my son Tim was born, for he has it too. When she went home, it was not just Martin and I who missed her. Our long street would never be anonymous again. Until the day we left, everyone asked how Gladys was and when she might come again.

Thursday Island cannot be reached directly by plane. The airstrip is on Horn Island. From there it's a bus to the ferry and a ferry ride to Engineers Wharf on Thursday Island. Minnie had told us all of this: 'It doesn't take long. An hour after you land on Horn, you will see me!' We climbed from the plane to find a little airstrip. It was a typical outback airstrip, I know now, but it was the first such place I had seen. Beyond was a low jungly tangle of trees and orangey vines. The air as we climbed from the plane was not tropically moist, but simply hot.

Most interesting of all were the people — some professionals, Torres Strait Islanders and Europeans, wearing warm-looking working clothes, ready to travel down south. But mostly people wore clothes I thought of as 'Queensland clothes'. Brighter and lighter than the clothes of Western Australia — the clothes I was uncomfortably wearing. Faces were patient, clothes loose and patterned with soft, bright, geometric shapes. I was yet to learn that the Torres Strait is halfway country, the Torres Strait Islanders counting cousins on both mainland Australia and mainland Papua New Guinea. It felt like a new country, an Australia I did not know. Everywhere was the Torres Strait flag, based on the dhari, the warrior head-dress of white on green and blue, on T-shirts, bags, walls and vehicles.

On the ferry, Horn Island behind us and Thursday Island ahead, I saw better than I had from the plane that Thursday Island sits within an archipelago. All around are the inner islands of the Torres Strait. Prince of Wales, Friday Island, Hammond Island, Wednesday Island, and more in the blue distance — blue granite outcrops ornamented with grey-shelled crustaceans, white sand and long needle-leaved trees and tangled vegetation within. Everywhere was blue: the spreading radiance of the sea colours the light. Closer and closer ahead was Thursday Island. White buildings stood on the foreshore beyond the white sand, the white sails of the giant wind generators waved on green Milman Hills, and everywhere there were houses.

We stood together on the ferry as it touched the wharf near the huge netted shifting pile of luggage on the top deck. At the tip of the wharf small children fished with lines and buckets. Tethering ropes radiated out to the big crayfishing boats and, closer to the shore, the little silver 'tinnie' dinghies. The pile of luggage was plopped onto the jetty, to be picked over by passengers and officials alike then distributed, some of it into small white utes which reversed dangerously and rushed past us and out onto the island itself. In the blue bouncing light only the pylons which anchored the jetty and the island beyond looked still.

Carrying our luggage, we walked slowly (for Martin could no longer walk fast) down the jetty. Before us was a bitumen road, skating the curves of the harbour; its sides fell sharply away to the blue granite and gentle wash below. Taxis went by; we were to discover that nowhere on Thursday Island is more than a five-dollar taxi ride from anywhere else, and the drivers are kept busy with little swooping trips around the island. Then the biggest panel van we had yet seen came towards us. It slowed confidently. Inside was Minnie, her golden jewel-cut face glowing; her eyes alight with pleasure and some minor mischief. 'We'll surprise Mum!' she said.

Martin's mum found us waiting when she came home and instantly began to cry with overwhelming happiness and shock at our appearance; she also scolded Minnie for the surprise. A little later she revealed that in fact she'd heard already that we had arrived from lots of people: a tall handsome Maori, they'd said, and a small white girl.

'And I told them: "That's no Maori, that's my boy!"' she said.

That night she examined Martin's leg — the wasted calf, the lumpy tendon, the painful gastrocnemius muscle. From her bedroom she took a little bottle of white fluid. 'Whiteflower,' she said, massaging it in. It smelled like eucalyptus. 'It will heal you, son. I rub it in every night.'

In Perth Martin's mum had been extroverted. In her own place and with her own people she was much more so. Walking down the main street, she waved and laughed. People called her over, she told stories, they laughed. She introduced us to everyone she saw, most of them cousins or aunts. I learned that I was to introduce myself, for my mother-in-law could not say the name of those who have married into the family; it's a mark of respect. In Perth it had been fine to use my name, but here it was not. At first I was wondering if she had forgotten my name, such was her air of gentle puzzled waiting as she looked to me to introduce myself.

The speed of her fluid changes to the right cultural practice was dizzying, and I learned to watch for the quick shifts of persona and manner, and very often, language. For each island has its own rules and ways: they are subtle differences but important ones. Martin's mum speaks five different languages fluently and understands all that are spoken throughout the Torres Strait. Martin, too, found himself understanding words and phrases here and there.

At the end of the first of these promenades she said to us earnestly: 'But we will go to Yam. There is not much family here for you to meet. On Yam everyone is family. But tomorrow we will go to Friday Island with these people,' she said, one arm around Auntie Mokea. 'They come from the same village as your great-grandmother, son, so we camp together.'

That night a boat of crayfishermen returned from a two-month stint at sea; I fell asleep hearing the excited voices of children on the shore-front. Martin's brother Paul's boat would return in another week. Out at sea the Torres Strait Islanders catch crayfish. The fishermen work in two-man teams, a dinghy driver and a diver. The driver must watch for the bubbles coming to the surface, and watch for the tiger and reef sharks who are equally keen on the painted Queensland cray.

The next day the returned crayfisherman and their families, and us too, packed tents, swags and food, ready to holiday for a week on Friday Island. Friday Island is mostly uninhabited as there is little water and, by consensus, it is left mostly for holidays. The camping ground was a bay with white coarse sand, small Tuesday Island in the distance and blue sea ahead. To my delight I discovered that the long-needled, leaved trees were she-oaks — the nut far larger than at home, the tree itself bushier and deeper green, but the rushing sound as the wind moves through, that friendly evening whisper of my childhood, just the same. Ropes were tied from tree to tree, canvas hung over, and tents pulled wide by stakes in the sand.

Sky and sea grew slowly dark, lanterns were hung in the she-oaks, and for every tent there was a fire. At ours Martin's mum cooked cray tails, pumpkin, coconut rice and pumpkin tips. Pumpkin tips are the tendrils of the pumpkin vine. The fibrous top skin is dexterously stripped away and it is eaten as a green vegetable.

Men were always served first. I protested privately at this to Martin, but he asked swiftly, 'Who is given food first at your house?' And of course, it was always Dad, for he had worked hardest and needed the food most. This country was not as strange as I had thought, for I had grown up inside one kind of primary industry and this was life lived around another.

Days were spent looking for food, searching for mud crabs in the mangrove mudflats, prying mussels from the black rocks, fishing from dinghies. A place is chosen, the boat anchored, and the fish leap to the hook. Around us jumped flying fish and green turtles swam by with a strained and reproachful air. These are not safe waters for turtles, as they are hunted in the Torres Strait. Around our lines came manta rays who prey on turtle, skiting and skooting and swooshing as if flying from the top of a circus tent.

The children were always busy too, helping in the hunt and taking pride in every catch. From each little face shone the confidence that comes from feeling needed. Fathers lavished gentle attention on their children; they were carried and cuddled and told stories. At night there was dancing, and the children's attempts at traditional dancing were egged-on with delighted cries from their parents.

The food was shared. Before cooking it was divided according to need. After cooking Martin and I would be conducted from camp fire to camp fire to taste and be told the names of each dish in at least five different languages. 'Try some turtle, son. Auntie Evelyn cooks it well.'

'Can my big boy ...' and here Martin's mum would always giggle, for Martin towered over everyone, '... try a little of your mud crab, Anna? Eee, a big one! Morgan, is this the one you caught?' She would say to the only boy of the family, 'You going to be great hunter. Thank you, my dears.'

Then it was time to go. The camp was packed away, the sand and the she-oaks and the sea looked as they had on our arrival. One cray boat was leaving, another arriving. And on the boat docking would be Paul ... But he wasn't. Instead there was a message to come out to Warrior Island, a sand quay on the middle of a reef. He would meet us there in two weeks time. Warrior lay just beyond Yam Island. 'Aaah. Paul wants you to come and meet the family on Yam,' said Martin's mum. 'I was taking you anyway, but he is making sure.'

'Paul wants you to see how much they respect him on Yam,' corrected Minnie naughtily, for Martin had last seen Paul as a troubled teenager. Paul had not been able to find his way in suburban Perth. He had been lost until he had rejoined his mother and begun diving for the Paspaley Pearling Company in both Broome and Darwin. Now, of course, it was Martin who felt lost in the suburbs, and Paul who had found his way.

Yam is a five-hour dinghy ride away from Thursday Island. Paul had arranged for his good friend's cousin, Waiben Wosomo, to take us to Yam. The dinghy we were to travel in had been borrowed from Uncle Charlie, Martin's mum's brother. In fact, Uncle Charlie is a cousin–brother to Martin's mum; she was adopted into their family. It was explained to me this way by Martin's Auntie Sue:

Mangroves grow in families. The trees near each other in the swamp are closely related. But if you pick up a new tree, a shoot, and carry it and place it away from the rest of its family, it will do better. It grows faster and stronger. It is believed in our culture that sometimes it is of value to give a baby to another family, and that the baby will do better there, grow faster and stronger too. You don't know if you or a big sister or any of your siblings are adopted. It is kept secret, and only when you are an adult, perhaps forty years old, will you find out. Gladys was adopted into our family — her mother was my mother's sister — and she was very sick when Gladys was born: too sick to care for her. Gladys was weak too. But my mother, who is a nurse, cared for her and Gladys came to be her baby. We younger children did not know for years; she was just our wonderful big sister, like a second mother to us.

So Martin's mother has two sets of siblings and she honours her connections to each family. It is very complicated for a new in-law from another culture. I sat down one day with her to try and map out Martin's family tree and write it down. Some grandfathers had two wives, some cousins had been moved from one part of the family to another as babies: soon I was hopelessly lost. But I could see one thing: Martin had family on nearly every island of the Torres Strait, and was closely related to nearly every person on Yam Island.

Into the dinghy we went. We took no map, for Waiben knew the way well. He would navigate by island and once we reached the open sea, by stars. It was two o'clock in the afternoon, the time carefully planned so that it would be dark for the final part of our journey, when the stars would tell us the way.

The dinghy motor made conversation difficult. I sat holding the side of the boat with one hand, my hat on with the other. The day was a little cloudy, and I watched the clouds and the sea, and looked for the islands that would guide us. I was always the last to see them. In teasing consolation Martin's mother called to me: 'Don't worry, dear. We are Eagle clan.' I understood. It was not that my sight was so bad; it was just that theirs was so very good! (Later I discovered I was being teased indeed, the family is 'Umai', or dog clan.)

Once in the blue water I saw a coconut floating by. Some islands were inhabited, many were not. Some were just black rocks, home to birds alone. One of the largest had once had family living there, explained Martin's mother, but there had not been enough water and they had returned to Yam.

We threaded through two islands. Out of sight was another and the direction taken to navigate through the first two had set us straight on course for the third. Once we stopped the boat to refuel, and I realised how very rough the sea was. I sat there feeling sick, longing for the engine to start again, my eyes fixed on the islands behind us. Martin was sucking the fuel up the siphon. Later when I told him how sick I'd felt, he said, 'Yes, and you didn't get a mouthful of fuel!'

Low in the sky the sun was lemon-coloured. It fell behind a rag of tangerine cloud; the blue world was suddenly flooded with rosy light. And I felt the world turn, for when you can see nothing but sea the horizon is not quite flat: it seemed we were on the cusp of the world's turning. Tangerine faded to amber. The sun dripped through one cloud, then another, honey-gold light trickling slow. Finally the earth's turning took it out of sight, down past the curving horizon. The world was flat once more.

We travelled on in the darkness. Waiben was using only the stars now. Suddenly we were docking at a short jetty of white stone and wood. 'This is Yam, son!'

We climbed slowly out, walking down the sand path from the jetty into a little village of houses, highset and like many Queensland houses, painted white. It was eight o'clock.

'Hello!' called Martin's mum as we walked among the houses. Martin and I were awestruck by the low tropical gardens bordered with large shells, the white path leading on through trees and houses, children's voices protesting bed, the soft wash of music and cooking smells. From beneath one of the houses a woman appeared, carrying a basket of clothes. The area under the houses was laundry and bathroom.

'Gladys?!'

'Yes, it's me,' said Martin's mum; she was giggling.

'Aaah. Paul said maybe!' said the woman.

There were introductions.

'And this is Martin's woman …'

'… Jo,' I said, holding out my hand and smiling. We had it down to a fine art, now, Martin's mum and I.

'Come, we go to the house of your *maate* for a cup of tea and cake, son!' said Auntie Riana.

Maate is a curious word. At first I understood it to mean great-grandmother, but it is more than that; it is a word which honours the relationship of great-grandchild and great-grandparent. Only the great-grandchildren can use that word to address their great-grandfather or great-grandmother.

Of course, in Island culture a child may have several *maates*, as the brother and sister of the actual great-grandparents and the wives and husbands of those siblings all stand in that relationship. In fact this lady was the wife of Martin's great-grandfather's youngest brother. Nonetheless she gazed with joy at Martin, calling her husband out of another room. Together they sat and looked at him, exclaiming in excitement.

'Photo,' was the one word I knew. From a drawer a very old photograph was taken, handled as if it were gold. This was a photo of this great-grandfather's father, Martin's great-great-grandfather. He had not been young when it was taken, but I could see how very tall he was, towering over the other men in the photo. The photo was faded black and white. Martin was much heavier after a year without sport than his great-great-grandfather can ever have been, but the resemblance was unmistakeable. Martin looked more like this man than he did anyone else.

During the day we walked the long beaches, collecting shells with the children; many of them were aunties and uncles to Martin. Martin was walking without a limp, I noticed suddenly, even when carrying a heavy five-year-old uncle and walking in sand.

At night we stayed with the family of Arthe (uncle) Dick, one of the happiest men I have ever met. He sat holding his new baby, a toddler leaning against him, and frequently reached out to touch and smile at his three other children. He talked a little to us of the dangers of crayfishing and how very glad he was to come home to his family each time.

One morning I woke late. The family had long left their white-stilted house for school and work, but from their little ghetto blaster came an Island woman singing a song I'd not heard before:

Six years I've been in the city and every night I dream of the sea.
They say home is where you find it;
Will this place ever satisfy me?
For I come from the salt-water people
We always live by the sea.
Now I'm down living in the city …

The yearning song blew through the house, through my head and my heart, and I lay very still.

7

THE ROAD LESS TRAVELLED BY

'I shall be telling this with a sigh
Somewhere ages and ages hence:
Two roads diverged in a wood, and I —
I took the one less travelled by,
And that has made all the difference.'
ROBERT FROST, *THE ROAD NOT TAKEN*

Paul had arrived the night before, and he and Martin talked late into the night. He looked like any of the other young Island crayfisherman, but his voice was courteous and soft and Melbourne-accented.

The next day he was to return to Warrior. 'Please come with me,' said Paul, 'Mum can cook for us. You can come out in the dinghy with me while I dive for crayfish.' He wanted to show his brother what he'd done with his life.

Warrior was not far from Yam Island. 'Shaped like a triangle, with a few palm trees and a couple of shacks, a river running through, it's very nice,' said Paul, from the back of the dinghy as we left Yam. 'Lots of crayfish. I'll get us a couple for dinner.'

The long time apart had been bridged, but there was still constraint, I thought, between the two brothers. Perhaps it was born of all that gentle courtesy, for Martin was every bit as polite as Paul.

The water grew shallower. A little way ahead was the sand quay, so low above the sea that the coconut palms and shacks looked like miraculous survivors. Indeed, no one lived on Warrior in the winter months. Paul stopped the boat.

'See that rock? There'll be a couple of big ones there. I'll just get on my wetsuit.' He struggled a little with the zip at the back of his wetsuit.

'Help your brother, Mart!' said their mum.

The picture of Martin carefully zipping up his little brother is the one that has stayed with me most from this time. For it was after this that the constraint vanished. Their mum had cleverly evoked their shared childhood — they were back to being brothers again.

We stayed two nights at Warrior, then went back to Yam, then back to Thursday Island. I remember those last days as flashes of palm trees, a suddenly grey sky announcing that the 'Wet' was coming. I remember Martin's mum crying over each little milestone on the way to the morning we would leave: the last time she would wash Martin's clothes before he left, the last crayfish dinner. I remember trying to say thank you adequately to Minnie.

Then we were hugging goodbye on the jetty and suddenly we were back at the outback airport on Horn Island. It had been five weeks. For those five weeks I had not thought at all about what would happen next in our lives, but now, suddenly, I had. We were going back to the city, but I knew now that this life would never satisfy me. 'Did you miss Perth?' I asked.

'No,' said Martin.

'Do you think I should try for that job-share position with Mum?' I said, as if I'd been thinking this for days, although I hadn't been, 'ask Mum and Dad if we could live on the farm, bring up our children there?'

'I could drive to Perth some days,' said Martin, 'but most days work from the farm on the Net. Let's give it a try. Ask your mum and dad.'

The decision was made. We returned to Perth with this future in mind, a destination as clear to us as if it were an island we could see ahead.

At the end of that same week, back in Perth, we were once more in the office of the specialist who eight weeks before had told us that Martin would require radical surgery to repair the Achilles tendon in his right leg. At his command Martin stood on tiptoe, jumped and finally hopped on his right leg.

'I'm having difficulty believing this,' the specialist exclaimed, shaking his head and grinning. 'Surgery would not have given you this good a result.'

He consulted his notes. 'The injury occurred over a year ago?' he asked. Martin nodded. The specialist held up the ultrasound images to the light. 'These haematomas should have made what I'm seeing impossible. And there was only thirty per cent of the original tendon left!'

He laughed.

'It's a miraculous result. What have you been doing?'

So Martin told him about the nightly massages with Whiteflower, about eating crayfish, about travelling, about meeting much of his family for the first time.

'All of those things would help,' said the specialist, 'but none of them can explain this.' And he leaned forward to tap Martin's calf as if it were a talisman, looking as happy as if it were his own work. But it was Martin's mum who had been the healer. And I wonder now if perhaps Martin's leg healed in part because the road he was walking had changed, both behind him and before him.

The occupational therapist Mum worked with in Moora sold her farm and moved away and soon I took her place. Martin and I began a half-life, working both in the country and Perth.

I remember the first day of work with Mum with awful clarity. My first job was to make a splint. Splints are mostly made of thermoplastic material, which is very drapy and sticky when heated. It dries quickly to make a hard supportive shell for a sore finger, joint or limb. I had always been an ordinary splint-maker, and that was with the state-of-the-art facilities available at the school. I looked at the manky old frying pan Mum used for heating the material (surely I remembered it from childhood?) and her hairdryer for making small changes after the rest of the plastic had dried. At school it had been stainless steel extra-wide splinting pans and heat guns. I looked at the client — a shearer who had worked so hard that the sheaths through which his tendons ran had become scarred with overuse.

He extended and flexed his wrist, and I could hear the tendons squeaking like hawsers under strain as his hand moved up and down. I stared at him in horror. Clearly I had to stop his hand moving in one direction at least and give the tendon sheath a chance to heal.

I measured the splint, listening to the client; he had once been to Mum and Dad's farm to shear the sheep. 'I'd certainly like to have my name above the title deeds,' he said smiling. 'Think your Dad would sell it to me?'

He was trying to put me at ease, but unfortunately this comment could have been calculated to distract me. For I had come to see that Dad would have loved to sell. The adventure of the farm for him was over and he wanted something new. But first Kynan had to be given a chance to slowly buy the farm off Mum and Dad by working it, in the same way they had bought it from Gran and Grandad. And us girls, too, had always been told that we could come back to the farm and work for our share. This is becoming common in farming families. Once upon a time the family farm was gifted to the sons alone, and the daughters gifted any off-farm assets. As farming grows less profitable, more and more farmers must sell the farm to the new generation to pay for their own retirement.

I looked down at the long, hairy, squeaking forearm of my client in despair. Would his hair get stuck in the sticky material? I had only ever practised on the much less hairy arms of women. I lathered the barrier cream onto his arm. And the splint that was required was a very long one indeed: would the splinting material even fit in the pan? Mum came to help me. Soon we had the warm plastic draped on the client. Mum went back into the office, leaving the final adjustments to me. I picked up the hairdryer and began, but shortly it stopped working.

'You have to wave it about once it gets too hot,' called Mum from the office.

'What about the splint? If I'm waving the hairdryer about, it's not going to be heating the splint,' I said, trying to pace my words so that the panic would not show to the client.

'You have to wave the splint around with it,' said Mum very reasonably, but I could see a half-smile on her face. 'I told you the equipment here was difficult to work with. You told me that at the school they said it was important to adapt to your workplace. I've been adapting.'

I stood there and waved splint and hairdryer back and forth together: on my way to being a proper bush therapist.

The little town of Moora in which we worked is advertised as the Gateway to the Wheatbelt; and indeed, to its north, east and west are the wheat farmers on their large flat acreages. Like every wheatbelt town, Moora is built on the railway. Once a year the grain silos fill with wheat, but all year the trains run, taking the grain down the line to Fremantle and the boats.

Mum and I worked out of a beautiful little community centre, built by the people of Moora themselves and still kept in flowers and cups of tea by their hard work. Although, it was built by Seniors for their own use, no occupational therapist had been consulted about design, so the two toilets were not suited for elderly clients with sore, arthritic knees and hips. Mum had modified one with an ancient over-toilet frame. This device is four-legged and crouches over the toilet, providing a much higher seat to sit on, and rails either side to push up on.

If I install this device now for clients, I always explain the importance of providing a continuous surround between upper and lower toilet seats with the following story:

> It was my first day of work. Minutes before I was to meet my new boss, I needed to use the toilet, but the only one available had an over-toilet frame just like this one. I was in a hurry and did not seat myself properly. The stream went down, caught on the lip of the bottom seat and was neatly directed all over the back of my trousers.

It is a good story to tell, because clients laugh and also feel reassured that someone my age can have accidents. Honesty breeds honesty, and you always need to reveal something of yourself before asking a personal question, which in my job is all the time! I'm pleased I've been able to turn this incident to good account because I was not so sanguine at the time. Aghast, I called Mum in for help, forgetting in my upset how much she loves to laugh.

Eventually she was able to find me a mop and advise me that the hot day would dry my trousers before I reached the hospital. It did, but there was still, faintly but definitely, The Smell. So I shook hands with my new Director of Nursing in a way that I could see struck her as odd. Keeping my legs outside her door I leaned in from the waist, bending almost to a right angle, and holding out my hand as far as I could to reach hers and briefly shake.

Those first few months after graduation were months of learning. About the job, but also about all the places in which I had to work. We provided therapy services to nine shires, and the thirty-five towns within those shires — from true inland wheatbelt shires, to a line of shires down the coast, to the mixed wheat and sheep country south of Moora, and even shires that bordered Perth's outer suburbs. It was a huge area. Each town is different, each has different stakeholders and networks. I had to learn them all.

But it was not the people in each town that daunted me. It was finding the towns. As a little girl I ate a thermometer (to stop Mum finding out that I had bitten it in half), and I have heard that eating mercury destroys the navigation centres of the brain. Or perhaps my not being able to see well from an early age had left me unable to navigate. Whatever was responsible, my problem with reading maps and remembering landmarks was the biggest challenge in my new job. So the sight of the little welcome signs trotted out in advance of a country town always filled me with joy. There was the Lions sign, the Apex sign, and then the Hazchem sign. The Hazchem sign was not one I remembered from childhood, and I assumed it was the welcome sign of another beneficient society. 'Hazchem' sounded to me like a word for 'hello'. The society must be an ethnic one that had only recently reached the bush. Writing 'hello' on a sign seemed to me a particularly friendly thing to do, and so whenever I saw that particular sign I would say 'Hazchem' right back.

It was not until I was travelling with Mum one day (she had challenged me to navigate while she drove) that I discovered that I had the wrong idea completely. As we'd entered each town on our way to the little town of Dowerin, I had said 'Hazchem' under my breath. Mum looked at me curiously. We reached Dowerin, and I'd only had to be prompted once! As I saw the Hazchem sign for Dowerin, shiny red and welcoming, I said very brightly back to it, 'Hazchem!'

'Why do you keep saying that?' asked Mum, quite intensely. She'd obviously been wondering for a while and she is a person who has to know.

I explained.

Mum made a choking sound and pulled the car onto the side of the road so she could laugh in safety. When she finally regained control, she explained about hazardous chemicals and Worksafe signage requirements. I never said 'Hazchem' on entering a town again, but for quite a long while after that Mum never missed.

My navigational ability was also hampered by the pictures outside my windscreen. In middle spring, when the sun is shining, the wheat crop takes on an extraordinary colour that is neither blue nor green. Crème de menthe green, or appley-aqua, or perhaps the bluest shade of jade? It is quite indescribable. Looking at acres of it did something very satisfying to the inside of my head. It was like hearing a vast harmonic chord or eating mango — all my senses would be bound up and satisfied just by the sight of the new wheat crop under the sun.

I am sure I found more jobs to go to in the wheatbelt shires in the middle of spring. In late spring and early summer I would find myself working more along the coast, where the sandplain wildflowers were at their height. From the side of the road they coruscate and snap and twinkle and soar. Even if you look at them closely, stop the car, and get out to go and just stand and look at one flower, the firework resemblance remains. A banksia is made up of thin streaks of colour leading to a bright burst of that same shade intensified a hundredfold. There are flowers curvetting like catherine wheels, little pops of bright colour low to the ground. The wattle explodes like the heaviest shells to cascade down in white and yellow. I imagine insects dazzled and frantic amongst a never-ending bombardment of scent and colour. We can only feel the echo, but that is enough.

In the dry months I loved to work in Dandaragan, for there the water table has risen above the ground in many places. Although this is a sign of land degradation, in late summer it means there is still some green among the dry yellow paddocks.

No one could manage this better than the progressive Dandaragan farmers. I knew that one day those summer patches of green would be gone. But to me at that time they said water and renewal and spring on the hottest, longest days of the year.

In late autumn and early winter I loved my own country best, though the rain on the windscreen and the first green on the hills made any trip good. But this had been my favourite time as a child, and so it remained.

I liked to pull back the lifting clods of earth to see the seedlings, still yellow and coiled, waiting for a little more rain and a little more warmth to push through to the world. I liked to watch the mites, black and red-legged in the puddles, moving apparently without volition in the tiny currents of water. I liked the first winter meals of stews and jacket potatoes and starchy puddings, the fires in the house, the dark mornings and early evenings. Best of all I liked picking mushrooms.

Only if the season broke early would the lacy white mycelium underground push mushrooms into the world above. An early season confers many benefits to the farmer, but in these days it was the mushrooms I cared most about. There were at least four different kinds of mushroom to find. The first were the most fragile — fairy-thin with a delicate taste. Then came the big bold button mushrooms. No matter how large, they barely opened, though on the very largest the membrane between stalk and cap would be strained into transparency. Then followed large sturdy field mushrooms and finally the huge strongly smelling horse mushrooms with their glossy purple gills and thick bulging stems. The horse mushrooms were not found in rings like the other mushrooms but just in groups of two or three at the base of certain trees, and only in the wettest years.

Mushrooms are wonderful to pick alone, but better still for picking with family. Carrying butter knives and empty containers — not too large, as optimism of that kind seems to scare them back into the ground — and walking calling-distance apart, we would watch each other for the run and crouch that indicated mushrooms had been seen.

Sometimes it would not be a mushroom at all but an old gum leaf, bleached silvery-gold by the sun, and looking teasingly like the soil-dusted silvery membrane of an early mushroom, pushing up through the thin dry straps of last year's grass and this year's new green. But eventually a ring would be found, with some mushrooms too old and wormy — their umbrella shape weather-wrecked — and some too small for picking, just pushing through to the surface. But there would always be some that were perfect, and we would press down into the dirt, past the springy resistance of the grass and slice precisely through the stem. With gentle fingertips we would dust the soil from the cap and lift the mushroom to place it, stem down, in our container. Mushrooms placed neatly together are every bit as satisfying a sight as brown eggs in a basket.

At home we would lovingly wash them, showing each other the very best one we had found and deciding on the very best one of all. Some would be cooked and eaten straight away, grey-brown mushroom gravy over toast, but most would be cooked to freeze. If it was a good year, if we were careful, we could have some mushroomy stew every week of winter. But the good years were becoming rarer, and in the poor years instead of mushrooms there would be toadstools. In a good year I could ignore the toadstools and just glory in the mushrooms, but in a bad year I would regard the toadstools with resentful eyes. If I saw one I would squash it.

Of course, insufficient mushrooms was not as important a consequence of a poor season as no crop or no feed for stock. On the farm we could see the climate change so long predicted for the south-west of Western Australia coming to pass. There weren't as many rainfall events, and those events were more severe, increasing the likelihood of feed damage and erosion.

Dad totted up the rainfall figures for the last twenty years. They showed a sinister decline. We continued to look for artesian water and to find new ways of harvesting the rain that did fall. But bores and dams are not cheap to build; neither solar cells nor diesel-fuelled pumps nor tanks are cheap to buy; nor does maintenance come free. Water is expensive in the bush, and we needed it not just for living but for livelihood, and the finding of it was getting harder.

Fuel prices were rising too. In fact, all costs were rising but not the 'farm gate' prices for the things we produced. On our travels from one town to another Mum would eagerly look at other farmer's paddocks. What were they growing? What stock were they grazing? What stock were they feedlotting? She was always looking because Mum and Dad's ability to make lightning changes in enterprises, always six months or so ahead of market trends, was what had put four children through boarding school. If a lot of people were doing what we were, it was time to think about a change.

The qualities of innovation and flexibility that characterised my parents as farmers characterised my mother in the workplace too. In truth, nine shires were too many for two part-time occupational therapists, but Mum was very good at developing ways to duplicate our time. I learn by writing, and everything Mum said to clients — the way she networked, the systems she set up — I carefully documented. I had not done this for any purpose except my own learning, but Mum began to think on how this skill could best be put to use.

Until I had children of my own I didn't understand purposeful thinking. For when you have all the time in the world, the ideas just come; there is no need to set aside time to think. I was baffled by Mum's habit of saving problems to 'think about in the middle of the night'. Why would you do that? Why wouldn't you be asleep? Yet I couldn't doubt the results of her thinking time.

My writing on the children we saw became a database from which we could print reports and home and school programs. This one innovation gave parents and teachers customised information about a child but saved hours of our time. I wrote curriculum and taught occupational therapy assistants who Mum then employed to help particular clients who needed the intensive help we didn't have time to give. I was proud of these innovations: I had no idea that the real revolution was waiting.

Kynan finished university and within days of leaving he and Mandy joined Mum and Dad on the farm.

Mandy had long been learning the farmwork by coming to stay most on holidays and she was quick to gain skills in a world that was very new for her. As Mandy is a very small person, she would borrow the farm clothes we had worn as children, and go out to move stock or work in the yards or help Kynan fence.

Mandy is a speech pathologist and soon she had begun work for the same health service as Mum and me. Jacksons at home and Jacksons at work! But Mandy did not allow herself to be swamped and quietly began developing her own ways of dealing with nine shires and thirty-five towns and many kilometres of travel. It was more cost-effective to travel together, so we did. Soon we discovered that a child who needed to see a speech pathologist almost always needed to see an occupational therapist too, and vice versa. Shared programs were developed, making it easier for parents and teachers, and children got better faster.

There were too many children reaching school who were not ready to learn. Later they would be referred to us with learning difficulties, behind in their schoolwork and often behaving badly. This is what we might tell a parent or a teacher of such a child:

Imagine starting school with your body not strong enough to sit for hours on a chair. On the hard seat you sit and you are not comfortable. Your back muscles are tired and you begin to shift endlessly in your seat, trying to get comfortable. Soon you are so tired you cannot listen to the teacher any more. When you are called upon by the teacher to demonstrate your knowledge, you have nothing to say or to show. You know the teacher is disappointed in you. Later when your mum and dad hear, they might be disappointed in you too. Disappointment is the hardest of all emotions to bear; it is an esteem-eater. You feel hollowed and hopeless and angry in the face of the disappointment of adults. How much easier to bear is the anger of adults, rather that than the scourging, discouraging lash of disappointment. So next time you are asked what you know, you are perhaps rude, or perhaps you poke Susan-sitting-next-to-you. The teacher might be angry with you, but you have allowed her no opportunity for disappointment. Her anger is far easier to tolerate: you have found a way to cope with the worst consequence of your learning problems! But you are still not able to learn.

These were the children who might be referred to us at eight or nine years old. Therapy might be able to correct the underlying difficulty, but those four years of school are much harder to make up. Mandy began to search for a program that aimed to help children before the problems began — something that would stop the whole sad cycle. Eventually she found one. It was a speech pathology program where children in the earliest grades were screened for the skills that are required before you can learn to read or write. Teachers and therapists worked together to develop whole-class games and activities to develop any missing skills and ready the children for reading and writing. Swiftly Mandy modified this to include occupational therapy, believing that a combined approach would be better still. The resulting program has since been acknowledged as being at a State level of excellence. Yet Mandy and Mum were twice refused the opportunity even to trial the program. After the second refusal, Mandy simply waited a discreet length of time then began work. When the program proved successful, she informed her manager, just as if permission had never been denied. And, keen to take a share in the praise coming from schools and parents, our manager, the Director of Nursing, also acted as if she had long given her support to the program.

At home Kyn was trying to reconcile what he knew about making money from cropping with working alongside a father who had grown to loathe chemicals. I have met many farmers like Dad. Over the years they have learned to detect the disturbing incursions of artificial chemicals on the pathways of the body. Of course, there is a threshold and for years nothing is felt.

'It's so safe you could spread it on bread,' says the young farmer. But eventually the threshold is reached, and the farmer finds that he has to force himself to touch the chemicals. One day he can no longer even do that. Dad could still make himself handle and apply chemicals, but having to do so disturbed him more and more.

And philosophically, Dad believed chemicals were wrong, damaging to the environment and therefore unsustainable. Kyn would respond that organic farming was just as unsustainable, for there is nothing less sustainable than an enterprise that does not make a profit. In his view the price paid for organic products was simply not enough to cover the extra labour costs and lost productivity. My views would swing widely as both were very convincing and, in fact, I was convinced by both of them in turn. Surely there was a way to reconcile this debate?

Kynan might be more comfortable with chemicals than Dad, but his attitude was not relaxed by any means. Once I took out morning tea to him while he was spraying. Everywhere the pink marker foam rolled: it was there to show where the chemical has been sprayed and on the brown seeded earth it has an artificial prettiness. There was an unpleasant stale smell masking that of the turned-over moist earth.

'Thanks, but I'll come in next time,' he said. 'Just keep out of the paddocks right now, okay?'

For the baby Martin and I had wanted for so long was on his way. Just months before, Minnie had come to Western Australia for a visit. And with her was a three-month-old surprise. Kaylee was golden and plump, placid and smiling, with almond eyes and black hair.

What changes Kaylee has wrought in the world! By her second visit, when she was three, Martin's mum and dad, long divorced, had begun speaking to each other again. They ate meals together. Both were determined that Kaylee would have grandparents who were on friendly terms. But on this first visit her impact was even greater because after washing her, holding her, and playing with her, Martin and I decided that we could wait no longer for our own baby.

Tim was born just ten months after Kaylee's visit.

Martin had asked Mum to stay and support him while he was supporting me, but at the birthing centre Mum had suddenly looked around at the assembled family and asked that someone stay to support her! Everyone did. Kynan and Mandy, my sister Megan and Dad stayed through a labour that ran well over two days. In the fifty-fifth hour, Martin holding me and Dad coaching, Tim was finally born, golden and scowling, his fists held tightly and his legs crossed as they would have been in the womb.

Afterwards the midwives came to tell me that they had never seen a family work together the way mine did. I said it was years of working as a team to move sheep and cattle, which I think is true, but the midwives thought I was joking. 'You tell your family that they were incredible,' they said. 'It was a real privilege to be a part of that kind of teamwork.'

What a strange place for a baby is a hospital! Not the labour room, for that is filled with family, but the long anonymous wards and the multitude of private rooms. No sooner did I have my baby than I wanted nothing more than to take him home and discover which of his new clothes would suit him best, which was his favourite place to be, and what kind of music he liked most. There is a phrase 'growing up kids' used to describe parenting. A hospital is no place to grow a child. You want to plant them in their home ground straight away. But what was home ground? Martin and I were still living in two places. It was time to finally choose: take up the offer of joining the family on the farm or return to living in the city.

It was the thought of working alongside each other, keeping Tim with us, growing him up in an environment as rich in family and natural beauty as the Islands, that appealed most. We would learn how to be farmers and join Mum, Dad, Mandy and Kynan on the land.

8

PIECES OF GOLD

'If you pour pieces of gold into a hand which is full of stones, the gold will fall off. You will first of all have to give up something of yourself in order to make room for something new.'

BODO J BAGINSKI AND SHALILA SHARAMON,
REIKI: UNIVERSAL LIFE ENERGY

My life was taken over with the very important job of watching my baby. I did not want to miss a single moment of the tiny daily changes in his face: the black eyelashes a little longer with every day, slowly crept out from under the deepset tight-shut eyes. As he slept, his little face would quiver with emotions that surely there had not been time for him to feel: wicked humour and stern reproof, curiosity and defiance. I loved the greedy expression he had on awakening and the approving grunts he made as he fed. I did not want to miss the sight of the tiny, wide-palmed hands lying loosely on the striped cardigan, the long baby legs encased in leggings, the dear blunt nose and the bearish little brows and head.

At night Tim slept on his father's huge chest, Martin lying on his back, absolutely still. I could not miss watching that: the tiny baby cradled between two large brown hands. Martin, even sleeping, looking as if the world owed him nothing else now he had his baby.

I remember the first real smile very clearly. Around the dining table we sat, me holding Tim, Martin, Mum and Dad. Suddenly Tim made a little wooing sound, and I glanced down. He smiled hugely, clearly delighted that I'd looked at him just as he wanted me to. I remember the feeling of being lit up with amazed joy. For minutes we just smiled at each other, my baby and I.

Then a blowfly hummed in the early summer air, and Tim turned toward the sound. I looked up; Mum and Dad were looking as joyful as I felt.

'Did you see?' I said. 'Did you see him smile? That was the first real smile.'

'Actually, we were not watching your baby,' said Mum.

'We were watching our baby smile at her baby,' said Dad.

'So we got to see a different kind of first smile,' Mum explained.

'I was watching Tim,' said Martin. 'Can I have him now?'

For a little while, the world shrank down to just us three: Martin, Tim and I. For a long time we had been two, but three was more satisfying by far. We are commanded to polish the passing moment as if it were a jewel, for it is all we possess in the world. How hard that is to remember! A baby of your own is the best polisher, and in Tim's hands the passing moment was slower than it was in ours; his smiles and excitement gave it a lustre we could not. All we had to do was let the moment be his.

Tim became my constant companion. We took him to work, Mum and I. When he slept I wrote reports. When I visited clients he came too. I had unwittingly shaped my skills so that I could work with a child alongside. All this was possible because Tim was the most well behaved and personable of babies — and sometimes it was he who was the therapist and not I.

I had been referred an elderly lady who had a very sore leg after a fall. The doctor had asked that I try and reduce the swelling in her leg and foot. Joyce was a community treasure.

At ninety-three and with greatly reduced vision she continued to bake constantly for a multitude of fundraising endeavours. On more than one occasion a cake from Joyce went to the doctor's surgery, and no health professional in that community felt unappreciated. With the cakes would go the words, 'For all your hard work'. Was it any wonder that the staff turnover was so low? And Joyce's cakes were the lightest, sweetest and creamiest of sponges; there was nothing in them that could weigh heavy on the stomach or the soul; they were the culinary embodiment of their maker's intention: to lift your spirit!

I walked, carrying Tim, to Joyce's flowery and cushioned apartment. There were no rugs upon the floor for that would not have been sensible, and Joyce was always determined to stay well. She had once showed me her tilt table, on which she lay upside down daily to rejuvenating effect! I loved this opportunity to look into elderly people's homes and their lives for, by that stage of their loves, what has spoken to their spirit is displayed throughout their home. It might be pictures of Elvis and a record collection, or a lifetime's worth of painstaking embroidery or carving, or books from floor to ceiling, or an altar built from family photographs. And I like to look at their face among their favourite things, for by then the face, too, is a construction of the spirit within.

Joyce's face was lively and sweet, creased equally by concern and humour. Her hair was as creamy and fluffy as her sponge cake. Even though she could not see well, her eyes would look intensely into yours as she enquired into your health.

'How are you really, Jo? You must keep up your strength, as feeding takes more out of you than pregnancy. Porridge every morning is good. Peanuts too, you know, they used to call them mother's nuts. But this beautiful little fellow is really doing well!' And she would laugh and Tim would laugh. It was always a little difficult to turn the conversation to the subject of Joyce, but eventually I would find out how she was and how I might help.

On this occasion I set up footstool and chair, admonished her to stay out of the kitchen and off her feet, and finally gave her a massage to move the fluid from leg and foot back into the lymph system. Where to put five-month-old Tim? Joyce was lying on her back, and I gave her the baby to hold, chest to chest. For a few minutes his head was lifted up, peering eagerly and curiously at this face up close, Joyce looking and talking happily back to him. I concentrated on gently sweeping the fluid up under the delicate old skin. When I next glanced up, Tim was asleep; Joyce holding him close, an expression irradiated with a look of tender peace.

Afterwards she always said that she was sure the massage had helped, but it was having the baby fall asleep on her that had really done her good. Like a baby, Joyce had a genius for polishing the passing moment.

Our baby brought meaning and joy to our lives, and something else too that was not so easy to live with: fear.

The voice of fear nearly always asks questions. 'What if ...' is how these questions began. What if my baby stops breathing? What if my baby falls off my sofa? What if ...?

Now, I am used to the fearful current of thoughts: they have become like a good angel who speaks to me of the welfare of my children at moments when I am busy. But at first this fear, this sense of having become hostage to fortune in an entirely new way, seemed unendurable. It took me a little time to learn that it was those thoughts that helped me keep Tim safe.

And there were other 'what ifs' too that went beyond the short-term and safety. Now we were part of the farm business, the fear that it would not rain and concern about rising costs were the demons that plagued us. I felt besieged by the adult world as I had never done before. What if farming was the wrong path for Martin and I? What if, in our inexperience, we made mistakes that would cost not just ourselves, but Mum and Dad and Mandy and Kyn dearly?

For learning to farm is very hard indeed. Kynan had been able to learn farming as he grew. Martin's sporting and business background gave him strength and endurance, the mental discipline to work hard and long and a wary, bottom-line mind. He had the raw ingredients, but none of the skills. For a farmer, like a bush therapist, must specialise in many things.

Stockman, builder, mechanic, agronomist, businessman: the farmer must be all of these, and each role has innumerable skills that must be mastered. As stockman the farmer must be able to read the land to see if there is enough grazing for the stock it carries; know the different water and feed requirements of his stock; diagnose and treat deficiencies, diseases and injuries; move stock without distressing them; know when and how to fix a fence or move a fenceline; and see potential hazards for the stock and know how to fix them. A good stockman is observant of the interaction between animal and environment and knows why, how and when to intervene.

Each role, with its different skills and knowledge, Martin had to acquire, while at the same time doing the work of the farm that had to be done. As the least skilled man, the least skilled jobs were allocated to him: he spent a lot of time at the end of a shovel! Then he learnt to repair fencing, then to make fences. Dad would say to him, 'You have to think like the animal you are building the fence for. You have to ask yourself whether or not the fence would stop you.' It is hard not to laugh when you are asked to think like a sheep, and Martin did, but he also did his best to see it from the animal's point of view. He discovered that a fence for a Merino sheep is different to that required for a Poll Dorset. The long-legged Merino has a nervous and pessimistic temperament; it sees a fence and thinks 'too hard'. But the short-legged Poll Dorset is optimistic and experimental; it will try to barge through a fence and look for gaps to exploit. Fences for cattle, and the different breeds of cattle, need to be different again. Martin's fences steadily improved, as did all his skills. Now it is hard to believe where Martin began, so skilled is he just six years later.

To the usual swag of job roles that we all had, Dad and Mum added a new one: horticulturist.

'We've got to get out of bulk commodities,' Dad had declared, in one of the many discussions we had in the light of increasing costs, less rain and unchanging prices. The bulk commodities he referred to were crops — wheat, faba beans and canola. 'They take too many nutrients from the soil, and the dollar returns aren't large enough for us to put back what we've taken out. We're just exporting our capital asset, and one day there will be nothing left.'

'Crops are a reliable income,' said Kynan, 'and we need that right now.'

Martin nodded.

I was pregnant again, and Mandy was pregnant too: her baby due to come six months before mine. Ability to provide a secure income was at the top of Kyn and Martin's lists. Dad was looking further forward to the need to ensure that the soil could still grow food for generations beyond this one, stretching out of sight. Of course, as a young father his first concern had been for his children, and he admitted that but now his perspective had changed and he could not change it back.

We sat silent in face of this seeming no-way-forward.

'Surely there are ways of finding a reliable income from products other than bulk commodities?' said Mum into the silence. Mum has a gift for hope and new ways of seeing, as if she is always standing a little further down the road from the rest of us, holding a bright lantern. Our silence changed in colour — green and blue instead of red and black.

'Take wool,' suggested Dad, 'that's the kind of product that I like. When you sell wool you are exporting the minimum amount of nutrients off the farm. And you get a good return most years.

A minimum of five dollars a kilo. Now we can't just do wool, but we need to aim for products that meet those criteria: exporting as small an amount of nutrients as possible for no less than five dollars a kilo return.'

'So what would we do? Aquaculture?' asked Martin hopefully, and then, even more hopefully, because he loves feedlots (where animals are fattened by regular feeding): 'More feedlotting?'

'Value-adding?' chipped in Mum, meaning that we could refine our raw products ourselves. 'Or a tree crop?'

'It's going to take a while and a lot of dollars to set up anything new,' said Kyn, pragmatic in the face of Dad's visionary zeal. 'In the meantime, we need crops!'

Dad's green eyes lost their zealous glow, and he glared at Kyn. We could all see the old and pointless argument about chemicals was about to reignite.

'No kicking, no biting!' piped up Tim from his highchair, looking at his grandfather and uncle in concern. Martin, Mum and I choked.

'You are a clever boy, Tim,' said Mandy warmly, but also allowing a warning to Dad and Kyn to sound in her voice. 'No kicking or biting. Uncle Kyn and Grandad know that you can be nice to each other even when you don't quite agree.'

And soon we had our way forward. The crops would continue, but slowly we would plant trees, olives and avocados and mangoes, and move into horticulture and feedlotting as our long-term operations. The manure from the feedlots would be recycled onto the trees, reducing our dependence on inorganic fertilisers.

But a big problem remained. In winter there would be enough rain for the trees planted in our orchards to grow. But not in summer. And there was not enough water under the ground to both irrigate the trees and water our stock. Although there was water nearby which we could purchase, various government departments seemed determined to suffocate our ability to buy water from the owners: not with deliberate intent, but simply with ever-multiplying red tape.

Where could we get the water we needed?

Kyn's special area of study at university had been water harvesting. With a grandfather well ahead of his time on contour banks, water harvesting was a natural interest because it too uses contours and channels the land to direct water that would otherwise run off into dams. His final-year project had been to design a way of harvesting water on the farm from granite outcrops and roads. Now we put his plan into action. One large dam went in. A year later, after walking miles, Mum and Dad located a site for another even larger dam, and that dam too was built.

We had acted as fast as we could because new legislation was looming. This legislation was designed to regulate water harvesting. Its aim was to protect wildlife and town water supplies as well as farmers further down in the catchment. Behind the legislation was the philosophy that even if the rain fell on your farm, it belonged not to you alone but to anyone who might benefit.

While on first reading I could appreciate this ideal, very soon I began to question the logical base of this philosophy. It is generally agreed that much of the run-off from one farm to another is the result of land-clearing. Planting trees and revegetation are encouraged and viewed as land care. But collecting and storing the water and using the stored water to irrigate tree crops (from which the farmer can derive an income as well as improve the land) is not. And yet both reduce erosion and both result in an increase in trees and biodiversity. Coupled with government policy that keeps food prices artificially low, it seemed to me that somewhere in government there was an ideological distaste for making money from the land.

And while I could see that this distaste for farming might stem from a love of nature, it spoke more to me of a forgetting of what we are — animals that need food like any other. Unlike other animals, though, we are divorced by setting and disance from what we are really buying. In the shop the packet of pasta does not remind us of the paddock in which it grew, the water and soil which nourished it, the mines from which came the fuel and metal with which it was processed. We think instead of the cultural connections, what else to buy with it to make a meal. The means of production and the land from which it was produced can be ignored even as we eat.

Australian food prices are kept low by the government in the interests of political stability. The mechanism by which this is achieved is a simple one — should the price to the consumer of any basic food item rise unacceptably high, the government imports that food from elsewhere. (Most often from a country that subsidises its farmers.) While this is great for the rest of the population, the farmer is left to contend with rapidly increasing production costs but prices for his products that change only marginally. The bottom line is that the farmer has no money left over to care for the land. With this in mind, I appreciated Dad's passion for growing products that took less from the soil and earned more, so that there was money enough to care for the land as well as make a profit.

This distaste for farming is not a universal feeling. In the middle are people who do not care either way, and at the other end of the scale is the 'foodie'. How I love these people who love their food! The ones who watch the cooking shows, who want to pay good money for their produce and know that it will go to grow more, and to keep the land in good heart. How I love to watch them shop, their animal natures proudly on display. There is the young mum, encouraging her baby to sniff the rockmelons and help her choose one; the woman gently stroking an apple to judge its crispness; the hungry admiration in the eyes of a young man as he looks at the unscaled fish, fresh on ice.

Foodies and farmers are kindred spirits, and the prospect of growing food for foodies excited us all. Our avocados and mangoes were not yet in the ground, but our olives were.

Together we had learned how to plan an orchard. We discovered that the first step was irrigating; planting comes second. We found that olives, contrary to every manual we read, like lots and lots of water. We never did kill one by drowning. We learned to feather out their roots as we took them from the pot to make sure that they were not in too deep, nor too shallow. Suddenly, what had been good feed was now pestilent, olive-strangling weed, and we learned not to leave the weeding too long. Planting trees for land care is something we had always done; we were amazed to discover how much more exciting planting the olives was, how much more meaningful.

This was not the only learning I needed to do. Although I had grown up on the farm, there were many holes in my understanding. The farmer's wife has a slightly different role to that of the farmer. She is the sounding board and so she must be as well informed as the farmer, and collecting information from anywhere she can is an important job. She listens to the radio; she talks to other people. Then she must think about the information she has collected, evaluate it for quality and think about how it might be applied.

Mum talked to me and Mandy about this as we walked along with Tim, and now Lachlan, in prams. At any stage these conversations might be interrupted with the need to attend to our sons. So one moment we might be learning to examine fences for the tell-tale scraps of wool which indicated an illegal Poll Dorset thoroughfare in a fence, and the next singing together a drowsy wandering song to put Lachlan to sleep. In the warm summer evenings our voices seemed to rise then be lost among the treetops. The children would turn from watching the dogs dart and play ahead or look to the treetops, as if following the sound with their eyes, to watch the black cockatoos settling in the trees.

No walk was complete without the dogs, both pet dogs and working dogs. On some farms, working dogs live much of their lives whirling and barking on the chain, let off only when they are needed. They have names but they are nearly as anonymous as the stock they work. If there are pet dogs, they belong to the women and are confined to the house. They might be different species, and each kind of dog knows their place.

But our dogs never seem to know their place, perhaps because they are allowed to see how the other half lives. For each of our pet dogs wishes to work and each working dog longs to sleep inside. There is something endearing in this yearning for another life. It is hard not to sympathise with the pet dog's desire to help — the ride in the back of the ute, the thrill of the boss's praise for a job well done, being allowed to join in the activity of the shearing shed — how hard it must be to be denied these! And the working dog longs to be loved without conditions — the best scraps from the kitchen 'just because', the first pats from the baby — this is a life of privilege, of closer engagement with the beloved family.

On walks the pet dogs would scout proudly ahead and the farm dogs would linger near the people, chasing affection that would nurture them through their night outside. At the start of every walk they had to be acknowledged and patted, and only then they would join the scouting party ahead. Once the work dogs had been satisfied, the children settled, then the teaching could begin.

Mum taught us the old saying, 'The best fertiliser is the soil on the farmer's boots'. It's a way of saying that it is by walking around a property that a farmer knows what has to be done. And this is part of the role of a farmer's wife too. So she might be pushing along a pram, but all the time she is looking with the eyes of a farmer. Mum taught us to pick up wire whenever we saw it, to save a tyre from being staked — and thus the men's time spent repairing the tyre. We looked for Paterson's Curse, a purple-flowered weed, and rooted it up. Whatever problems we saw had to be reported back to the men: an overflowing trough, a steer half-out of the feedlot, a sheep urgently biting its backside. For these are all potential threats: the wasting of water, a breakout from the feedlot, or a blowfly strike in the sheep.

If something had gone wrong on the farm, we would also use these walks to discover why it had happened. What did Dad say about it? What did Kynan say? What did Martin say? For almost always the problem was caused by a difficulty in understanding, not in intention. Father and son misunderstood each other rarely, but between father and son-in-law an abyss sometimes yawned. I began to see that Martin's misinterpretation of Dad's views on water divining all those years ago had been a strong indicator of the difficulties to come.

'You going to move those rams now?' said Dad to Martin at the end of a long day. 'That's good. You'll need Noni.'

Noni is a half-dingo sheep dog. A visiting truckie had said to Dad, 'You see that dog? She's a good little worker, but I'm giving away trucking so I'm going to shoot her tomorrow if no one will take her.' Dad took her.

'Yes, I was planning on taking Noni,' replied Martin.

'What about Wanna?' said Dad.

'What about Wanna?' returned Martin, meaning, she'd be hopeless on a job like this and I'm not taking her.

Wanna was Dad's favourite dog. She'd been bought as a worker but had decided that she wanted to be a pet. If taken out on a job, she was likely to ignore the sheep and try and play with Noni because Wanna loved other dogs just as much as she loved people. She saw sheep-work as an opportunity for a delightful game with both people and other dogs: sometimes you barked at the sheep but mostly you barked at people and other dogs. The sheep were there to run around and through, and they added zest to the game. Often when you did this, the people got very excited, and screamed a lot at you. (You were not sure why they did this, but you hoped it meant they were having fun too.)

'She'll want to come,' said Dad, meaning, you'll have to tie her up to prevent her following you.

Martin had intended to tie Wanna up. Now he heard Dad telling him to take his favourite dog on an outing.

'Right!' he said, somewhat savagely.

Dad was astonished when he saw Martin departing from the sheds with not one but two tails wagging merrily from the back of the ute.

Martin and Dad were very surprised to hear from Mum and I that at all points they had agreed about what should happen. They vowed to repeat back what they had heard to each other in an effort to prevent more such misunderstandings. But as soon as they were tired, or worried, or busy it would happen again. The relationship was saved only by the grace that comes from mutual goodwill.

There were nine of us on the farm at this point. Gran had joined us on the farm a year before, arriving, snail-like, with her own little house that she then adjoined to Mum and Dad's. Gran and Grandad had retired to the coast, but Grandad had died some years ago, and now Gran felt there were few years left in which she could live safely alone. She decided to move to live with us and seek the support before she needed it. Gran began to call her time away from the farm 'long service leave'. It was now over and she was back.

When Sam was born, it was Gran who drove every day to my house to hang out my washing. When I remonstrated, she replied, 'I'm collecting brownie points; one day you can pay me back.' With Sam's birth there were ten of us. We were becoming ever more uncertain of the way forward and the financial viability of the farm, and yet growing in numbers all the time.

When Sam was three months old, Mum and Dad went on a working holiday to look at irrigated orchards in South Australia. Much of the land that is irrigated there is semi-desert country. There they noticed that where there was a good artesian water supply, low rainfall did not matter. Indeed, reliably low rainfall meant less damage to delicate fruit crops.

It was on the afternoon of their return in late winter, on the verandah of my house, that Dad outlined to Martin and me the radical new vision he and Mum had dreamed up: to sell the farm and lease cheap land instead — station country with an abundant water supply. A station like Austin Downs.

'It would be a better return on capital,' Dad said to Martin, and as I handed a second cup of tea to him he remarked casually to me, 'You could teach the children yourself through the School of the Air.'

'We will look at it all very carefully,' he said to us both, on finishing his tea, 'and test the water and test the soil and do our research, but there comes a time when you just have to jump, to make a leap of faith, if you like. I think that's what it's time to do.'

After he had gone, I sat looking down at Sam's head, fluffy with new soft hair, as he slept on my knee. Sell the farm! It was too big a concept. I tried to break it down so it made sense to me. Sell Montevid Paddock, sell Ram Paddock, sell the sheds and the houses. Still too big. Sell Halfway Rock and the wattle that grew from it. Sell the Mud Patch. Sell the shearing shed. I would not be able to take my little boys to these places anymore and share with them my childhood.

That night Martin spoke admiringly of the boys from stations he'd known at boarding school: their self-possession and their confidence in their own skills. Those skills were something

Martin had discovered he was lacking. Two years before, we had gratefully accepted the invitation to join the family business, but if you haven't grown up on a farm, doing even the easy farm jobs is difficult! I could see he was dreaming of our two little boys growing up into just such competent and confident young men. That night Martin and I talked some about Dad's idea.

I reminded myself that the boys could have a wonderful childhood somewhere else. And it was their childhood that I must be concerned with, not mine. We would sell the farm, and I must be ready to help in preparing it for sale, and for packing it up for, in spite of agreeing with Martin that it was unlikely to happen — just another possiblity — I was sure we would go to Austin Downs. As Dad had spoke, there had been a faint tugging in my palms. Not since I had left England for home had the sensations been so strong, and I knew it presaged another journey.

Later that night I found these words in the book Martin had given me for my thirty-second birthday:

> If you pour pieces of gold into a hand which is full of stones, the gold will fall off. You will first of all have to give up something of yourself in order to make room for something new.

Perhaps we had held onto the farm for too long. Perhaps it was time to let go, to move on — time for a new adventure.

9

From Farm to Station

*'When we remember we are all mad, the mysteries disappear
and life stands explained.'*

MARK TWAIN

First we put our farm on the market then we went, all of us,
to see Austin Downs. It was August, and the farm was at its
most beautiful. The visiting Mountain Ducks brown and
black, the new lambs white, the Cape weed blossoms yellow, like
ornaments placed on the green.

We left very early on a white morning and drove in convoy up
the Great Northern Highway through wattle and wheat country,
the gold of the wattle competing with the dawn ahead.

Between the cultivated farmlands and the uncultivated
rangelands is Wubin. Wubin is a border town. It is here that extra
trailers are added to the road trains, growing them into the four-
trailer-long monsters that are seen in the north of Western
Australia. Here they warn you of the kangaroos and emus and
goats and cattle on the road and suggest you refuel now, as the
next town is 160 kilometres away.

We ate breakfast together at Wubin. We were all high on the
first step in our new adventure, faces bright, making lists of what
to look for and what to ask. Just a few kilometres out of Wubin
the station country begins. There is one last paddock and beyond
its fence is uncleared land.

Only Martin had not seen this type of country before. Mandy

had stayed on a station in wildflower season as a schoolgirl. Mum had lived on Gabyon station as a very little girl, and Dad had always loved this area; each twisted tree is to him a thing of beauty. As children Kyn and I had both visited the station country. I remembered the hypnotic quality of the landscape: the details are different, but the look of the land stays the same over hundreds of kilometres. Occasionally there is a fence. Sometimes a windmill. But mostly just small trees, bushes and grasses. Your eyes hunt for same and different, as they do with any repeating pattern. It is nothing like the stop-start visual impact of a city, or even of farmland, with its fences, sheds, silos, patchwork of cropping and easily seen stock and farmhouses.

The winter season had not been good, and a good winter season is needed for the famous West Australian wildflowers to grow, but I still had not seen anything quite like this. As we sped past, the colours blurring, I felt as if I was travelling underwater past coral outcrops.

The bright flowers seemed embedded in the solid rock outline of the bushes. The colours of flower and leaf are reef colours too, soft and bright. And sometimes the scarlet Sturt Pea flashed, ribbed with black, as startling as an anemone fish against the softer colours of the other plants.

Meteorologists predict that the Murchison region (into which Austin Downs Station falls) will see fewer winter seasons; more and more of the annual rainfall will fall in the summer season. And the rainfall figures for the last twenty years, which we had spent hours studying, were in line with these predictions. We had concluded that there would still be enough for feed for stock but not enough water for the famous flower carpets.

'What do you think?' I asked Martin, meaning, did he like the look of the land? His childhood was spent exploring the jungles of Papua New Guinea: landslides, long-lost fighter planes, luxuriance and orchids. Could he like this arid country?

'I like it,' said Martin. 'I like the space. I like that this is how it has always looked.'

Finally, we reached Cue, the little town which is bordered by Austin Downs on three sides. Cue has a single main street. As it enters Cue, the Great Northern Highway adopts the name Austin Street, resuming its usual title a few kilometres out of town.

As we drove down Austin Street, I was overcome by a sense of familiarity. First came the long line of shopfronts, with their deep backs extending into the half-glimpsed street behind. Pavements nearly empty of people, a tiny dog flopped in the shade of a long-vacated shop's entryway. Then the old stone offices, glowing gold in the sun. I felt I had long known the way the corrugated-iron-clad buildings promised welcome and comfort inside, despite narrow doors and windows. And I took this familiarity as a good omen, that I would be happy here. I realised later that I had seen Austin Street drawn and painted and described a hundred times: it is the stereotypical Australian outback town, condensed to just one kilometre of bitumen.

I knew that we had driven through Austin Downs on our way into Cue, but I could gather little from the Great Northern Highway. I did not know how to read the land: was it in good heart or not? And the road verge never tells the truth because it enjoys the run-off from the road and is often less heavily grazed. But what I really wanted to see was the Austin Downs homestead.

Gran had warned me not to expect too much. Pastoral land is leased, not owned, and thus houses are also leased and not owned. Improvements to houses add little to the value of the property, she said, and so they are lowest on the long list of priorities.

I knew already that there were three houses but this, I saw as we came past the taller trees, was a little town. What were all these buildings? All had green roofs, some clad in corrugated iron, others in white weatherboard. Huge stone garden beds slowed our entry. Swept clean of leaves and twigs, they said 'outback' and 'desert' more loudly than the surrounding bush. Lawns were green, carefully edged and fenced around the tired, grand homestead and the two neat little cottages. All the houses were so close together! At the farm we were separated by kilometres. How could we live in this uncomfortable proximity!

Within the unimaginable flat sweep of the station, the homestead felt foreign to me — dry and cold and unfriendly. The sky was blue and I felt like a beetle in a petri dish underneath a shallow bowl lid through which a bright light shone down; there was no escape. It was not at all like the farm, with its soft soil, grassy pastures and gentle hills. There the sky appears over and between the hills, and it is a softer sky. The homestead offered no feeling of shelter; no house felt like mine. Houses are viewed not as they are, but with the filters of emotion and imagination and expectation clapped firmly over the eyes. I felt unwelcome; my expectations had been too high. I did not like the Austin Downs homestead.

I looked apprehensively at Mandy, who can no more live in an ugly house and unsympathetic surroundings than I can live without books. Her face was so determinedly unreadable, I was sure she was feeling as I did. Mum's expression was so eloquent of 'make the best' and 'could be worse' that it did not need her to remind me that 'the important thing is the quality of soil and water at the irrigation lease and the condition of the pastures.' I could tell she had felt no instant bond either.

We did not spend long at the homestead. Soon we were in utes and travelling through miles of bush to go to the irrigation site. The scrub was heavy — testament to the seven-year run of good summer seasons — and I noted with relief and pleasure a kind of tree to which I felt instantly drawn. These trees were the native poplars. Most have one trunk only and short delicate branches, and their gently green leaves adorn the little branches like scribbly curlicues. They looked frivolous and airy and totally uninterested in the earth. They seemed to be thinking only of the heavens. Here and there the poplars lay dead. With their leaves gone, I could see how this extraordinarily prayerful effect was achieved. They have many little branches, growing in opposing pairs up their thin trunks. Each pair of branches is crooked ever upwards, lifted to the sky, like a priest with arms upraised for the blessing.

We stopped. The low blue scrub was very thick. It was hard to believe that this had been irrigated land just ten years before, for I could see no sign of cultivation. Before us was a windmill, a trough, and three of the very fattest cattle I had seen in my life. Even though Austin Downs is a sheep station, in these good years cattle fattened quickly and were a quick and easy source of profit. The cattle swung away, breaking into a jubilant crashing gallop. A little way further on was an enormous pump. We waded through the scrub towards it.

Mum and Dad tell me that this pump was irretrievably broken down by the time we saw it. They insist that my memory of seeing it fuelled and cranked is not a real one. They say it must have been generated by the stories Mum's brothers had told of how this bore could be pumped for days on end without a drop in the water level. Nonetheless, I have a memory of water exploding from a pipe 30 centimetres across. I remember watching the water flowing on and on without diminishing, an abundance in abrupt contrast to the arid landscape. It turned the rich brick-orange soil to purple red. And I thought of the lack of water under the green paddocks of the farm and remembered why we had come. It is hard to believe that it is not a real memory.

But my memory of collecting soil samples at least is real. It was easy to collect those samples, for the soil layer was at least a metre deep. Easy to mound, easy to dig, easy for roots to tunnel. Samples were collected into neat little bags.

'Beautiful dirt!' cried Dad joyously. 'Tell me, what did you girls think of the houses?'

'They're different to farmhouses, aren't they?' replied Mandy, cleverly sounding as if she was answering the question without actually doing so.

'Well, it's much hotter here,' said Dad and then, intensely, 'I'm wondering about peaches at the irrigation. Bill Moses is growing them on a station at Mt Magnet and has been doing it for years, and he's doing well with them. What do you girls think?'

Back at the hotel, over the washing and feeding of the children, Mum, Mandy and I talked. The men talked too: tree crops, fencing and sheep. We women talked of houses. For the three of us all did feel the same way about the homestead. We examined these feelings in the light of the extraordinary potential of the soil and water; the potential for us to be a happy family again. We decided that there would be ways to make the homestead feel like home, ways to preserve personal space even though the houses were so close, ways to keep the children safe with the sheds so nearby.

That night, over dinner, the decision was made. Should the water and soil tests prove positive, we would make an offer for Austin Downs. It was as definite as we could be right now.

By the next dawn we were halfway home. Once again we stopped at Wubin for breakfast. To me the breakfast room seemed full of ghosts: the ghosts of the people we had been just two days before, the ghosts of the people we might have become if we had decided against Austin Downs. And then we were back to the farm, even greener against our memory of the station country. Back to the home we had decided to leave.

How easy I have made this sound! It was not. The soil and water had to be extensively tested. Approval from the Department of Land Administration for what we wished to do had to be gained. An offer on Austin Downs had to be formulated and accepted. While we waited for approval for the water and soil, we looked at other properties. Our farm had to be prepared for sale and sold, sooner rather than later. Despite our decision we had entered a period of terrible uncertainty.

There was a pet phrase of one of my teachers which came to haunt me in this time: 'To be held in the sacredness of not knowing'. How could this wretched limbo be in any way sacred?

I found it hard to think properly and clearly about the future. I found it hard to act at all, to do anything, in the face of not knowing what was to come. Instead I was gripped tightly in an emotion that seemed closer to sensation — my face was rigid with it; my muscles tried to lock tight in a body awash with oxytocin; I felt as if I was being pulled down to the earth. I wanted nothing more than to curl up with my children in a burrow. Fear is one of the most physical emotions there is, and this time it paralysed me even in my sleep. I had felt fear before and I had found ways to use it, but not this time.

My best and clearest moments were when the children were awake, when the present moment demanded my attention. And this was when I remembered another of this teacher's favourite phrases, 'The sacred in the mundane'. Unlike the first phrase, which tormented me because I could not make it true, this phrase and my children were my salvation — the nappy that had to be changed; the need to coax the baby into cooperation with smiles and singing; encouraging Tim to join me as an entertainer and help him enjoy his new role as a knightly and proud big brother and cousin, to link him to the other children with love and liking and respect. In every mothering task there is the sacred: the chance to show each child that he is loved, that life is to be trusted. Finding the sacred in the mundane is all about seeing that all the work we do is our life's work, finding meaning in the most everyday of tasks as we do them. It is how you polish the passing moment. But without the children to pull me out of my head and away from trying to find certainty where there could be none, I never would have lived in the passing moment at all, let alone found it shining.

How I wished I could have found the sacred in the housework and cooking! The housework seemed to be my cue for morbid fretting over the future. How ridiculous it seemed to be thinking of these signpost decisions while chopping carrots or hanging out washing. I would watch the carrot fall in the diagonal round which I used for stews, but I would not be thinking of stew but of what we would do if the station deal fell through. For now it seemed that we would not be able to buy Austin Downs after all.

There had recently been a change of government. Our application to put in an orchard on the special irrigation lease, which would have been quickly and easily approved just a month before, was now passed from department to department, desk to desk. Only approval contingent on other approvals was given. Eventually it returned to the original official in the Department of Land Administration from whom promises of a speedy resolution came often, but a speedy resolution came not.

Soon it became clear that this official would rather make no decision in case it was the wrong decision in the eyes of the new minister. Austin Downs forms part of five separate and disputed Native Title claims: did they apply to the special irrigation lease? Although this land had been in nearly continuous cultivation for years prior to 1995 (which would extinguish title in most cases), perhaps this case would be different?

This approval process had already taken two months, and we had reluctantly decided that we could not afford to wait for approval, for there was much to be done. In hindsight, this decision to act as if the approval that we needed had been granted was the riskiest of all. But we only imagined that we would be waiting days to hear. As the weeks stretched by it was harder and harder to find the confidence to do all we had to do: to pack, to clean, to paint, to sell, to grieve the farm, to resign from our jobs. Most of all I found it hard just to live my life, to leave the future and past, to stay in today.

~~~

The little boy is busy by the car. Good. The baby is in the bouncinette sleeping. Good! Now for a frenzy of activity coupled with constant listening for the baby's regular breaths, for the quiet noises of the little boy playing. I must make the most of this time.

I begin the washing-up, looking out at the view that would have once been my mother's because this sink, this house, had once been hers. Beyond was the gravel road and beyond it ran the creek where once I'd found tadpoles as a child, beyond *that* the Old Stone House and the mulberry tree. My hands are slowing in the sink. There were no tadpoles in that creek now, I recollected, for its catchment is cropped land, and chemicals have run in with the rain.

The wood floors of the Old Stone House were not quite safe when I was a little girl, and we would explore the empty rooms by walking the room perimeters, one hand touching the many-textured walls. In these rooms our grandfather's family had lived. The calm, flat floors, the glassless windows through which the dogrose climbed, the empty green-painted cement verandahs: a house without people, but going on happily without. As a child I had felt that the house had seemed not empty (although it was not occupied), but just preoccupied, thinking and quiet. Perhaps it was thinking about being built from stone and still being earth beneath, being lived in and being left, not greedy for more of any experience, but still thinking on each.

Two years ago the Old Stone House had lost its roof, and the wooden floor had quickly rotted away. The walls, the cement verandahs, the lovely wide steps that now led to nowhere were all that remained. In the same gale the mulberry tree had been uprooted, and we had mourned it, but this year it had shot new green leaves: there would be mulberries in November still. This would be the last year I would eat them. Where would I be next year? Around my slow-moving hands the water in the sink had grown cold, the washing-up was not finished, and the bouncinette was vainly trying to bounce the stirring baby back to sleep.

I had been lost in the murk of memory and speculation, but the sight of Sam's eyes, snapping blue and bold from the bouncinette, was like a dash of clear living water. The light around me lost its sepia tint. I was returned to the present. Did Sam need a feed? And what was Tim doing by the car? What should I make for tea?

I was always swiftly punished for falling into yesterday or falling into tomorrow. And not only by the tarnishing of today: bad consequences in the everyday world almost always followed. Sam and I went to see what Tim was doing by the car. Tim had removed the fuel cap from the car. He had found a bag of shell grit, tiny crushed sea shells which are given to the chooks: the extra calcium makes their own egg shells harder. Very carefully he was placing handfuls of grit into our fuel tank.

There were lamentations, there were reproaches and, until we sold that car, fascinated stares whenever we parked. At weddings, in car parks, at petrol stations. For from our just-parked car came the curiously loud noise of a thousand tiny particles of shell scraping back and forth as the fuel washed back and forth inside the tank.

My family had lived on the farm forty years, and there were forty years to be sorted out: for sale, to keep, for the tip. It seemed wrong to sell a single book, for every book is charged with the emotions felt on first reading. The once-loved soft toys: what to do with them? The old scales in the shearing shed, used to weigh wool bales once a year and the rest of the time functioning as a time machine for us children: into which pile should they go?

Mandy, Mum and I worked together, the little boys playing as we sorted and cleaned. The baby cousins were curiously alike: unusually tall and wide-shouldered, each handsome little face dominated by a pair of remarkable eyes. Placed together in a sandpit they looked like a pair of baby owls, heads swivelling as they watched Tim. He was their hero right now; they wanted nothing so much as to be able to talk like him, to run and dance with that same grace, to be big boys too. The three of us tried not to speculate on the decision by the Department of Land Administration as we worked.

And these were somehow good times too: my emotions felt 'clean' as we worked together. This feeling of being a team took me back to my childhood, where I'd learned (but forgotten) that when the job is shared, it goes all the faster; where the trouble is shared, it weighs less heavily; when the goal is the same, the work gains meaning and the relationship is strengthened. We had been pulling separately with our different ideas of how the farm would work best; now our goal was simply to start again as well as we could.

And it was in this shared work I learned something else. Mandy and Mum are busy people; thought quickly translates to action with them both. For me thought was thought, and while I would spend time embellishing it with evidence and nice words, I might not act at all. In their company I discovered how to loosen the grip of this awful fear of action. Carried along by their impetus to get the job done, I found that action is the only cure. Not just action in response to the immediate needs of my children — this offered respite but no cure — but action that showed a result in the material world. So even if we did not yet know which crop we could grow in the orchard or even if we wouldn't be allowed to use the irrigation lease at Austin Downs (which would mean we would have to start looking again for the right place), carrying on, taking action, was even more important than if we had been certain, for it was the only cure against that mind-killer fear.

A further two months passed and we still had no answer from the Department of Land Administration! Dad went and spent two days sitting by the desk of the official in question. At the prospect of a third day, the official crumbled, and we had our answer. Yes, the special irrigation lease on Austin Downs could still be used to produce irrigated crops.

With the approval, the sale could go through. And with the station out of their hands, the previous lease-holders wished to leave Austin Downs straightaway. It seemed that within minutes, Mandy and Kynan and Lachlan and six hundred of our best ewes were packed into trucks to make the long drive to the station, there to stay. How did Kyn feel, leaving the farm for the station? This was his land even more than it was mine. Working the earth, planting and harvesting, planning the crops for the new year, these are all more intimate engagements than just walking over the land.

As I watched him loading the ewes, I tried to guess what he was thinking. I looked at the upright set of his head, his eyes fixed not on the ground but on the truck where the ewes were settling. It seemed to me that he was simply determined to begin the adventure and not look back.

The farm had yet to sell and we had not yet set up for the clearing sale. We divided into two teams: I worked with Mum, Dad with Martin. All the machinery had to be cleaned, all the sheds to be emptied, all the farm to be tidied — the fences fixed, the gates painted white — while the everyday work of the farm continued as well. We worked from five in the morning through to eight at night, and through weekends.

Mandy rang from the station often; it was if she was calling from the future.

'I spent the first day crying over my house,' she said, 'but by the end of that day I had fallen in love with it. I know how I can make it beautiful. The homestead really is much nicer than we thought. And, oh Jo, you should see how green it is here! On the mill runs you go around a corner and you find beautiful, green feed. Austin Downs is so big you don't always know when there's been a storm, and then you find the feed, and it's just a wonderful surprise. Kynan nearly knows his way round now without the compass.

'And I have a tale to tell,' Mandy added. 'The day before yesterday we were driving to the far west corner of the station. We saw a new rock. We thought, 'Let's go to the top and see the view.' It was only a little out of our way: or that's how it seemed. In fact the way was windy and difficult, but finally we were there. We stopped the car, and the hackles went up on the back of my neck. Lachlan began to cry. Kyn looked uncomfortable, and then he admitted that his hackles were up too. So we left.

'Yesterday Kyn was talking about the experience in Cue and, I just can't believe this, he discovered that it was a male initiation site. Still active. No one is meant to go there.'

This was a nip of otherness I had not expected. We let the uncomfortable tingle of telling and listening to such a tale fade as we went on to share stories of the children.

It was the first time they had been parted, and they could not understand why. One-year-old Lachlan sobbed, 'My 'tousins!' in his sleep. Three-year-old Tim refused to talk of Lachlan or look at Lachlan's empty house, his deep-set eyes showing the first big wound of his life. Sam looked for his Great-gran (who had gone to stay with each of her daughters in turn until her house was ready at the station) because until now he had seen her every day. Martin and I had wanted an extended family for our children, but never had it occurred to me how deeply the absence of extended family members would be felt.

It had been a long time since I'd been able to work alongside Mum. These last three years she had become busier and busier with work, while I had become busy with babies. And it did not matter to me whether the work was occupational therapy, or housework, or stockwork, or packing up the farm — I loved working with Mum. Side by side we sorted and piled through bolts and bearings, buffed windows, swept shed and silo floors. As we worked, we talked. We sorted our emotions and laid them in neat piles — regret at leaving, excitement at the life to come, fear that we had taken on too much. We talked of the fine line we would need to walk — to be cautious but not over-cautious, to take risks but only the ones necessary for success. Together we readied the farm for sale and together we polished our attitudes and swept out old emotions, so we would be ready for the new life.

Often a neighbour, Kaye, came to help us too. How kind she was! For we had become curiosities in the district: not since the days Mum and Dad had removed us from the lcoal school had we been of such interest. No one could understand why we were selling, even less why we were moving so far away. To begin with Kaye did not understand either and would sometimes say, 'Must you?' But one day she announced that she had us all worked out and she knew why we were going. 'I can see it's the right thing for you all', she said. And as a surprise for Mum she potted many tiny cuttings for her to take into her new life. Nestled in their black pots, watered and weeded daily by Kaye, the multitude of cuttings waited by Mum's back door for the journey to the station. I felt heartened every time I saw them, for as the days grew longer and warmer it was hard to remember what we were working toward. It seemed we lived within the snake that bites its own tail, and the work of carving up the farm into separate boxes would just go on forever. The days grew hotter and dustier and brighter. I worked, I slept, I did not think at all.

Many of our hours had been directed toward one end: the clearing sale. Everything was laid out in 'lots' in a long snaking trail that doubled back and forth across the paddock behind my house. There were lots of all sizes: from tiny nut and bolt sets through to the very biggest machinery.

At four o'clock on the morning of the sale I went outside. I climbed the tank stand between my backyard and the paddock and stared out over the lots set out in the paddock. It would be a hot day, I thought. It was a good thing the roads were to be dampened. What would this day bring? It already had the feeling of anti-climax that some landmark events waft ahead of them: a bit like waiting for a last supper where you can already smell that they've burnt the roast.

And how strange it felt to be the ones having a clearing sale! When a farm is to be sold, a clearing sale is always held. They offer locals the chance to purchase second-hand goods at auction, but they are also social occasions. Farming and town families, everyone comes, sometimes from many districts away. Food and drink is sold. Some people follow the auctioneer from lot to lot; others stand and yarn. Sometimes they were openly sad occasions, when the farmer had been forced to sell.

From childhood I remembered those sales, and the faces of the kids whose clearing sale it was — outraged at the liberties being taken with their place and their things, burning to say 'get off' to the strange children climbing over hay bales and standing on machinery, but held silent by the knowledge that although it still felt like theirs, it would not be after today. So they stood looking on with frozen stares, standing by their parents who had to smile welcome and say, 'That's life,' and 'We can always start again,' over and over, to every face.

Today would be different because we had chosen to sell. I remembered gratefully that Elders were managing the sale. The week before, Elders agents had come to number and record the lots. Dad and Mum and Martin and I would stand aside while they directed the day. There would still be work for us today, but it would be at the behest of the Elders agents.

Today they would arrive at five o'clock, spruce in their red and white-striped shirts and cream moleskins. We would need to have coffee and tea and biscuits ready for them. It was time for me to climb down the ladder and descend into the day of the clearing sale.

By nine o'clock a line of cars stretched past my house, along the road, around the far corner and out of sight. There was a good turn-up for our clearing sale. The paddock behind my house had been transformed further by the importation of hundreds of people. There were those who moved in a clump with the auctioneer, as if he were a magnet and they iron filings. I caught words here and there of his urgent shout, but most words were scrambled and cracked by the driving beat with which he tried to force the price up and up. A group of those who were less attracted followed discreetly behind. Between the two groups a casual but regular exchange occurred.

There were families, easily identified by the balloons that bobbed about them. There were balloons tied to prams, tugging upwards on little wrists, bobbing like extra, bright-coloured heads as the families promenaded up and down the rows. Older children ran in little gangs, chasing along fences, dodging between people stopped in conversation.

I walked anonymous among them, disguised by the balloons bobbing from Sam's pram and Tim's wrist. Sometimes I would be stopped by an acquaintance and introduced. Eyes would suddenly brighten with curiosity.

'Is it really true that you are going to live on a station?' they would ask.

'Yes,' I said. But that wasn't what they really wanted to know, for it had become common knowledge.

'Why?'

And I would tell them about the water under the ground and the beautiful soil. But they already knew that too.

'How do you feel about that? I mean, it's not really a good place for a woman, is it?'

I said that I didn't know; I had never lived there. We were going to give it a go, and if it didn't work, it didn't work.

And then they would say, 'Well, I think you're very brave. I think that life would be alright for a man, but not a woman. I don't know how you can want to leave this nice farm. I know that I couldn't bear to leave mine! I would just say "no" if my husband wanted to sell.'

And I realised that it wasn't that they wanted to know about my reaction at all. They just wanted to give me their opinion on what we were doing. Not directly, but with unwanted sympathy. At first I wasn't disturbed, but by the tenth conversation that went the same way, I was beginning to feel angry and I had no way to let that show.

I began to understand the frozen stares of children at clearing sales a little better. They too must have felt hammered with curiosity and unwanted sympathy. I wished now I had never even glanced their way, for my intrusive glance must have been another hammer blow.

I had decided to retreat when Mum found me.

'Come and get the little ewes in with me,' she said. 'Once the wethers have been sold and loaded they're next for auction.'

We left Tim with Martin and Dad and, taking Sam, went to find the Rattler. The Rattler was the only ute left because all the other farm utes, cleaned and serviced, were being sold today. The Rattler had recently become difficult to start so, said Mum, we would keep it running.

'I must not stall the car,' I said to Sam on my knee, as we slowly circled in behind the ewes. I was driving and Mum was on foot, working the dogs.

It was all going well, and as I drove up one of the hills for which Hill paddock was named, I reflected on how much I enjoyed this. Working with Mum, Sam on my knee, Tim safe with his father and grandfather. It was nice that the clearing sale was here and that after today I would not have to set out another lot for sale. As I rounded the top of the hill, changing back down to first, I stalled the ute.

I turned the key hopefully. From the engine came a hum and a rattle, but it did not start up.

I let the Rattler run down the hill a little, and tried again.

Ahead of me the little ewes milled, found the gate, and pushed through, followed eagerly by the dogs. I could see Mum too. She was standing with her hands on her hips, watching me.

I tried again. No go. I noticed that the fenceline was rather close, it cut the hillside in two, mimicking the contour bank along which it ran. Mum had left the ewes to the dogs and was walking up the hill towards me. I decided with some cowardice that the next attempt could be hers.

Mum rolled the Rattler to within 30 metres of the fence, but it still did not start.

'There's only one thing to do,' she said. 'We're going to have to push. If we get some speed up, that'll get the motor turning over. I'll push and you drive straight towards the fence and swing away once the engine starts. That'll give us the longest straight downhill run.'

'Let's walk the sheep back,' I said. I didn't like Mum's plan.

'We don't have time,' said Mum. 'Are you hopping in?'

'We can call on the two-way,' I said, casting a horrified look at one of Martin's best fences. It bristled with upright steel-star pickets and barbed wire.

'No we can't. If the Rattler won't start, the two-way won't work,' said Mum. But I could see that even if the two-way had been working she would not have let me call for assistance. She was determined that we should fix the situation ourselves.

I wished again that I had not stalled the car.

'How about Sam and I push and you drive,' I suggested, trying to match Mum's calm tones, trying to hide my chicken-heartedness. Mum's lips twitched slightly. She was not fooled but she could also see there was no way I was going to drive straight at that fence.

'If that's what you would prefer,' she answered, and I knew she was laughing at me.

'Yes, it is,' I said, and hurried around to the back of the Rattler before the plan could be changed. I was determined to push much harder than she ever could so that there was no way I would end up being the driver. I put Sam down a safe distance away and told him to sit and watch. There would be no difficulty about that, because he too seemed to think I was being funny right now.

Then I placed my hands just above the dirty number plate and began pushing. I could hear the hums and half-hearted rattles from the engine as Mum turned the key. How much longer to the fence? I was running now, but my heart was going much faster than it needed, my shoulders braced for the crunch as we hit the fence line. Three metres from the fence the Rattler's engine fired. Mum swerved violently as I let go.

'See!' said Mum. 'I don't know what you were worried about.' We collected Sam, and gently pushed the ewes along, laughing like crazy women all the way back to the sale.

Later that afternoon the conversation began again, but I did not mind because my head was straight once more.

'It must really be a big sacrifice, I think. You are very brave. I couldn't do it.'

'Are you sure?' I asked. 'I think you never know what's going to happen, and what you will need to do, and how you're going to change. My Auntie Sue always reminds me that all through my childhood I said to her that I never wanted to marry a farmer and live on a farm. And here I am. I never thought I'd end up on a station either! Of course I feel nervous sometimes but I know I need a challenge to push me on. And I think we never really know where life will take us. Haven't you ever been surprised by your life,' I continued, thinking of the pushing of the Rattler hard toward the fence, 'and what you've found yourself doing, and enjoyed the challenge anyway?'

There was no more unwanted sympathy after that. Instead there were stories of unexpected life paths and achievement against the odds. So the day of the clearing sale had offered a resolution of a kind. Because of my adventure with Mum and the stories I was told, I finished the day feeling a little more courageous, a little readier to trust life to take me where I needed to go.

10

SAYING GOODBYE

'The birds that come to it through the air
At broken windows flew out and in,
Their murmur more like the sigh we sigh
From too much dwelling on what has been.'
ROBERT FROST, 'THE NEED OF BEING VERSED IN
COUNTRY THINGS', *COLLECTED POEMS*

S aying goodbye to our farm was not just something that the farmers of the family had to do. Steph and Megs had visited the farm to say farewell. So too had Cathi, who was now married with her own little son. Cathi found it hard to believe that the farm of her childhood would no longer belong to Auntie Barb and Uncle Tom. She had been brightly cheerful all day so as to not upset us — but was found crying by Mandy as she took photographs of gates and sheds in the late afternoon.

Steph and Brad had just returned from Brad's overseas post-doctoral posting to live in Perth. Part of the reason they had returned was so that they would see more of their families. It was just months after their return that we had decided to move to Austin Downs and sell the farm.

'I'm telling people it's just a coincidence!' Steph said, trying to joke, trying to prevent us knowing how hard our decision was for her.

Megan was now working for the Department of Foreign Affairs and Trade. On hearing that the farm was to be sold she wrote to me:

I find it hard to think of the farm belonging to anyone else. Even though I never wanted to stay, I somehow thought that you would all be there forever.

Even now I've moved to Canberra, I sometimes feel like I've just had a very long term away at school, the holidays will be coming up any day now and I'll be going home. When I think about life, I see times of good rains versus dry. When I'm miserable, I still just want to go home and go out walking through the bush.

But you can't stay just to nurse along my memories!

Megan had made a big decision of her own. She was going to Bougainville to work for four months. Here was my chance to support her decision, as she had supported mine to sell the farm. How I failed! From Martin's family I knew just how dangerous Bougainville was. Even as I remembered how supportive she'd been of the decision to sell the farm, even knowing how important it is to feel challenged and live a life of adventure, with all this in mind I still failed.

'Do you have to go?' I wailed.

'I want to go,' she said. 'I really want to do this.'

'What does Adrian say?' For after years of declaring that her soul mate had decided not to incarnate with her this time round, Megan had found Adrian. It was easy to understand now why he had been so hard to find! Adrian was a physicist who moonlighted as a lead singer in a rap band under the stage name Mr Harsh Reality.

'He understands,' she said.

As we embarked on the final stage of packing up the farm, Megan took a Hercules jet to Papua New Guinea.

Finally it was time for Martin, Tim, Sam and I to move to Austin Downs. I do not remember the drive at all, just Mandy's warm voice in the night as we arrived.

'Lachlan, come and see who this is!'

An amazed silence, then an overjoyed, dear little cry, as welcome as a candle in a dark and unfamiliar place.

'It my tousins! It my *tousins*!'

Still Mum and Dad were living between farm and station. A new house was being built for them at the homestead. The country on which the Austin Downs homestead is built is called opaline country. This does not mean that there are opals here. It refers to the metres-deep layer of silcrete that is barely covered by the red topsoil. It is white, concrete-like rock. It cannot be dug, only blasted. There was no way that Gran's transportable unit could be attached to any of the existing houses, so a new house had to be built for Mum and Dad.

Between two transportables — one containing a bathroom, bedrooms and an office, another containing kitchen, dining and laundry — they hung a huge one-room space. It was wood-floored and wood-ceilinged, designed to fit all the growing family around one table.

To Megan, now in Bougainville, I wrote:

We are here!

Yesterday Martin took the boys and me on a mill run to the southern-most part of the station … a 160-kilometre round trip. A 'mill run' is where you visit the windmills, clear out the troughs, check the windmill is working and look at the stock. With sixty-two windmills on the station, this is a never-ending job. There are six runs to different parts of the station, and I haven't yet been on all of them.

Finding the mill itself is the initial challenge. We set out equipped with compass, map and GPS unit (also lots of water and food). Finally you locate the mill, as strange as a steel sunflower towering above the scrub. You've then got to work out which mill it is! On our first run we cleaned one set of troughs twice, only realising that we'd been there before from the goat skull found again by Sam. He is teething, and the skull was just his idea of a good teething toy.

The introduction of the word 'skull' will give you the wrong idea. At the moment everything here is as lush as the Swan Valley in late spring. There are no bees, so the pollination of flowers and grasses is done by birds and butterflies.

There are so many butterflies that in the evening blades of grass sway under their combined weight. As many as twenty butterflies grip onto a blade, wings prayerfully closed for the night. Caterpillars are everywhere too, so big and juicy and full of purpose I feel I have to dodge them as they steam across the bare ground, around the sheds, on their way to a lawn.

With each different mill run is a new kind of terrain. They will all have proper names, but I don't know them all yet. But here is what I call them:

The Badlands, where sparse vegetation straggles out amongst piles of purple–brown rocks.

The Veldt: high lush grasslands (the proper name for these is Wanderrie Pastures) where a leopard or two should be lying along a high tree branch … but, alas, the only predator we saw was the perentie, the big lizard with a conquistador face and a gait so awkward it looks from behind like a turtle attempting to right itself.

The Fruit Tree Vistas, where all the trees are regularly shaped and regularly sized — a bush orchard without the fruit. Or perhaps it's there after all, but invisible to my eyes?

The Open Plains, which were over-grazed by cattle many years ago. There are no trees left, only hundreds of acres of poverty bush.

The Big Rock country: granite monoliths rising suddenly from the flat scrub as you approach. How they draw you in!

And there rock art 'hangs' in long galleries, beneath impossibly suspended outcrops.

Then there are the Washes, where regular flooding has left the ground smooth, a veneer of topsoil over white calcrete rock. The vegetation along these Washes is the smallest of shrubs. They have a thick, coral-like outline: my idea of 'amphibious plants'.

The creek lines are unmistakeable, marked by richly green gum trees. The creek bed sand is red. Up close it is composed not just of tiny red granite rocks, but also tiny rocks of sharp quartz, sparkly mica, white calcrete and purple iron. We stopped for lunch at Moses, a mill near a very wide creek bed. Sam and Tim threw themselves into this glinting multi-coloured sand, mouths open, faces down, pushing their fingers and toes through like slow swimmers.

It's so hard to get our heads around the scale of this place: the paddocks here are each as big as the entire farm! As we drove from mill to mill Tim kept saying, ever more hopefully, 'When we find the sheep, we'll push them into the yards, and Grandad will come over the hill and help us.'

I know how he feels.

The farm took until the beginning of winter to sell and just before the contract was signed, I went back for a final goodbye. The sheds were empty of the machinery around which I'd played as a child. But around the grain silos last year's spilled grain pushed up the earth in clods, just as it always had. And I lifted the clods to free the grain shoots and breathed in the steamy grainy earthy smell, just as I had done every year. But this was not the memory that touched me most. More poignant was the memory of sharing with Tim the new shoots hiding beneath the lifting clods.

Everywhere on the farm it was the same — my memories of the boys' baby and childhood felt sharper and more important than my own. I realised then how much harder leaving the farm must have been for my parents, and that most of my important memories were going to happen up here, on the station, with my sons and my nephew and children yet unborn.

The farm was sold. The journeys back and forth were done. Our energy belonged now to the station alone, and to our new life.

At Austin Downs Mum and Dad's house was finished, and Gran's flat neatly attached. From the first shared dinner in Mum and Dad's big room, Martin and I walked back to our house, each of us carrying a sleeping little boy. Above us the stars were bright, brighter here than they had ever been at the farm. How far we were away from everything now! And with that thought came an emotion for which I had no name, though it was not new. It was an emotion that somehow answered the question I'd asked myself for months now: what was sacred about not knowing? I'd hated not knowing. And I saw suddenly that sacred could simply mean 'what is true'. To be held in the sacredness of not knowing — this asked me simply to recognise that none of us ever know what is to come. Unless we are to be miserable, we must trust life regardless.

I had last felt this way sitting in a dinghy in the waters of the Torres Strait on the way to Yam Island. We had been navigating by island, but the last of them lay behind us now and we were out in open sea. The world's turning had taken us out of the reach of the sun's light. Now we were navigating by the stars alone.

11

THE FIRST MUSTER

'To look at landscapes loved by the newly dead is to move into the dark and out again.'

JUDITH WRIGHT, 'LANDSCAPES', *COLLECTED POEMS*

'You'd be better with men on horses and a good dog each,' said Des. He was referring to the combination of gyrocopter and men on motorbikes who were gathered for our first muster. In one of Des's many lives he'd been a stockman. Even now he dressed as a stockman, wearing R M Williams from boots to shirt, though he was in fact a regional manager for the Aboriginal Medical Service. Together Des and I were working on a cultural awareness package for the Health Department while Mandy looked after my boys for the day.

'I'd just sit on my horse, just walking along. Then the horse'd flick his ears. And through the scrub come the sheep with the dog behind them.'

But in spite of disapproving of the gyrocopter, Des could not resist watching it land and take off. A gyropcopter looks like one of Leonardo Da Vinci's flying machines, like a sycamore seed with a wheeled canoe beneath.

My fascination was tempered with some horror.

'Looks like it'd tip sideways in a good wind,' remarked Des, on first seeing a gyrocopter take off.

And it did, just days after this comment. Dad, who along with Martin and Kynan had been learning to fly a gyrocopter, had pranged badly on his first solo take-off. And then he had another prang a week later on landing. On both occasions he had walked away, but he had wrecked first a propeller and then the flimsy-framed gyrocopter itself.

These incidents had pushed Mandy and me from our position of reluctant support of the plan to use gyrocopters for mill runs and musters into fierce antagonism. Kyn and Martin were not to get into a gyrocopter again. If Dad wanted to, well, that was between him and Mum.

'But do you really want to miss out on watching your grandsons grow up?' Mandy asked sweetly.

We had prevailed and a professional was hired to fly the gyrocopter.

There were four grandsons now. Declan, Steph and Brad's son, had been born just six months ago. Since his birth Steph's hypoglycaemic symptoms, absent during pregnancy, had returned. But now she was having seizures where once she'd just 'gone off the air'; the sense of warning that had once preceded these attacks and allowed her to stave them off with food had disappeared. Extensive medical tests revealed a cyst on her pancreas. An operation to remove this tiny, but potentially fatal, cyst had been hurriedly scheduled and performed in a Perth hospital.

'Steph's operation yesterday went on longer than they expected,' I told Des. 'Is it okay if I ring Mum during the day and ask how she is going?'

'Sure, sure,' said Des.

Des and I had agreed early that we'd never seen a typical cultural awareness program — one where the history of colonisation was described — work. Yes, it *was* what had happened; yes, it *had* started the problems that exist today; but, no, we'd never seen any improvement in relationships between non-indigenous and indigenous people afterwards.

Des and I wanted to do something that had a better chance of working. We both felt that making people feel guilty just made them angry. It didn't motivate them to change. As Des repeatedly said, 'The question is: how do we go forward?'

In the end we turned to cognitive-behavioural theory, which describes the way your thinking influences your behaviour and mood. Identify the contents of your thoughts and you have a great deal more control. We also turned to Des's detailed knowledge about every step of the clinical process, using the way he phrased each question and the way he monitored the complex dance of body language between himself and his client and his client's family.

We were designing workshops with staff separated into their cultural groups. Each group would be asked the same questions: What is culture? What cultures do you belong to? What are your culture's rules? What are your cultural attitudes towards health and law? How does a typical family operate in your culture? And then we planned to ask them: What cultures do you draw upon when working? So we had scenarios in which they could describe the cultural rules that they would apply. We were trying to make staff members aware of themselves and how their culture influenced their assumptions at work. And how those assumptions created the actions they chose to take.

To begin with, we had wanted to talk about what Aboriginal people and those of European descent had in common. Instead we discovered how easy it was for us to misunderstand each other. The dominant culture in Australia — my culture — is not expressive or physically affectionate outside of our special people: our sense of personal space is large. In Aboriginal culture touch is very important. In my culture privacy is often linked to anonymity and a 'professional distance' by the interviewing staff member is reassuring. But for Aboriginal people privacy is ensured by a feeling of personal connection and they interpret 'professional distance' as 'cold'.

There are so many differences. Des was enthralled when I told him that one man has made millions of dollars out of explaining body language to people in my culture. Aboriginal people read body language as if it were flashing neon signs. They even use a whole-body sign language in their daily life. Des tried to teach some of it to me, but I couldn't even follow the quick movements of his hands, and that, he assured me, was the easiest part to see.

I left the two-way on as we worked. I was not used to this life where the men left at dawn on bikes to be away until late afternoon, and the women were left behind to care for children and cook, and to do the leftover jobs. I was used to us all working together. Keeping half an ear on the muster was my way of compensating.

The muster was not going well. The sheep were not where we expected them to be. Nor were they visible from the air. Where were they? Had they been stolen? Killed by foxes and dogs? On neighbouring properties? I longed to hear that thousands of sheep had been found. For on a sheep station the muster is the year's highlight, and our aim was a 'clean muster', with every sheep on the property brought in safely. Apart from the money made from selling feral goats, the wool cheque is IT. It is all the money the station earns in a year.

For us this muster was particularly critical, being our first and most vulnerable year and having little other money coming in and a lot being spent on the irrigation. Indeed, for these first three years our plan was to use the money from the wool enterprise to fund the horticultural enterprise until the horticultural enterprise could fund itself, which should be about three to five years into production. At first we had felt confident that we could manage the pastoral side of our new life. Sheep are sheep, aren't they? And how difficult could it be to just keep the windmills pumping? To keep the fences well maintained? These were all areas of long-established expertise. All we needed to learn was how to read the rangelands well enough so we could judge how much feed was left, surely?

But even before the first muster and shearing, we had begun to suspect that station and agricultural sheep were as unlike as the town mouse and his cousin in the country. My idea of wild sheep were the 'killers' on the farm. But for all their disdain for fences, the killers would still mob up eventually. It seemed that station sheep did not mob up. They were unused to moving together, and 'broke' and stalled repeatedly. Were we trying to do the impossible? Among those sheep mustered were 'double-wools' and 'triple-wools': sheep that had dodged the clippers over several shearings. I realised now that even the killers, the wildest of the farm sheep, were domestic animals. For all their delinquent air, they were but gilded town youths. And the station sheep resembled most the Man from Ironbark, with their determination never to be shorn ever again.

So the pastoral side of the operation was proving far more difficult than we'd anticipated. And the hoped-for winter rain had not come. We'd watched the wetland below Mandy and Kynan's big house slowly dry. All the long, wet summer we had fended off the mosquitoes and delighted in the waterbirds — pelicans and ibis, ducks and moorhens.

One day we saw a bird the size of a half-grown emu. The sight of its long, thick swan neck, big, stern butcherbird beak, eyes curlew-round and eagle-sharp, and waterbird legs, thicker than those of an ibis but hanging down in flight just the same way, set us to searching through Mum and Dad's collection of bird books. And there it was: the nomadic Australian Bush Turkey or Bustard.

The Bustard is so large that it can be tracked by satellite, and scientists do just that. This species gives a good indication of the condition of its habitat, from the rangelands to the tropical north. The numbers of Bustard sharply increase and contract in response to the good and bad years. There had been seven years of good rainfall on Austin Downs, so perhaps I should not have been so surprised and pleased to see the Bustard, but I read its appearance as a sign that the land was in good heart beneath the gloss of green.

There were a few final days of heat and the birds and water evaporated together. The paddock revealed was yellow with water-saturated grass, then green, and then it was the colour of dry land. As the land type varies, so does the colour it becomes in the dry. The opaline country is cream and peach and the leaves on the small shrubs the colour of dried herbs. The grass tufts became root clumps, just visible above the ground.

The Washes had been the last areas to dry. Away from the Washes, it had crisped and browned weeks ago. An air of waiting had crept over the land and settled, as though every tree had an eye cocked for the soft winter season clouds. They had not come.

So the mills still had to be checked every two days, just as in summer. This was expensive in time and fuel, and we had felt that setting up the orchard was all the challenge we'd needed at that point.

Although the pearly-blue scrub had retaken the once cropped irrigation site, there were still old sheds, hay rakes, seeders, and even an old chook shed waiting for us. They haunted the heavy scrub like a little ghost town, everything still in working order. We enclosed them, along with 20 hectares of the best soil, in a high fence to keep out the roos and emus, the sheep and the goats. Then we put up two enormous wire and steel gates. Then in came the bulldozer.

I was at the homestead on the day the bush was cleared to make way for the orchard, but I knew it was happening. We had never 'cleared land' before. On the farm we rarely even burnt dead trees, and Mum had taught us the way an ecosystem can develop around a log. My school and university holidays were spent planting trees to replace those that been cleared originally from the farm. So as I washed dishes, cleaned floors, and read stories through the whole of that long day, I prickled with guilt.

At my next visit to the orchard, the site was simply bare red soil, fenced and waiting, watched over by earth-moving equipment: diggers, graders, tractors.

We shaped the soil into three 100-metre long mounds. Each mound was a metre high: they looked like underground caterpillars. We put in the watering system, then trellises, and then two hundred peach trees. Every day we visited to water and weed, and watch. The irrigation was Mandy's and my responsibility now, for the men were fully engaged with the muster, and Mum with Steph, who was still in hospital in Perth.

I tried to imagine what it was like, riding through kilometres of the hypnotically same-and-different scrub, being directed from the air towards far-distant sheep. The muster was conducted by men travelling perhaps 2 to 3 kilometres apart from each other, in a long line across a paddock. They communicated regularly by two-way with the pilot. I wished I could see the station by motorbike to learn what each paddock was like. In my mind the station looked much like Tim's maps of that time: lines connecting circles. And that was how Austin Downs was mapped in my brain. The roads to the mills and the mills themselves; the paddocks were uncharted terrain.

We had employed three men to help on this first muster, local Aboriginal men who knew the land far better than we did, men who had grown up riding motorbikes through just this kind of thick scrub.

'Found deceased person,' said the pilot's voice on the two-way.

I had not been really listening as I was writing while Des talked, but I heard this. They must have found an old prospector, I thought. There were often prospectors on Austin Downs. Some followed the rules, leaving gates as they found them, not camping where the stock watered, not bringing dogs. But there were others who left every gate open, some who shut every gate they found, and others who cut fences when they could not find a gate. Des did not respond to my statement that it must be an old prospector who'd died far from home. Experienced stockman that he was, he had reached a different conclusion to mine entirely.

I rang the police at the request of the pilot. I relayed information back and forth between the pilot and the police. There had been some upset in town, I heard; they would be a little late arriving.

As I relayed the details I found myself puzzling over what I was hearing. Why was Dad staying with the body? It had been there for a while, after all. Why was Martin staying with Quentin? Where were Basil and Kynan? What was the upset in town? Still it did not occur to me what had happened.

Des had gone to sit on the verandah of my house. He sat and watched the road, as though waiting for someone to arrive.

The phone rang. It was Mandy and she was crying. 'Oh Jo,' she began, and then she told me who had died. It was one of the men we had employed. I shall not give his name for it is disrespectful to name the dead in Aboriginal culture, but call him the man-who-was-dead. How hateful, how invading is the cold you feel in your stomach when you hear this kind of news. A young man, a loved man, with no life any more.

I went out to tell Des. His face lifted with painful anxiety but no surprise; he had long guessed the truth and he was related to all the men on the muster. He had just been waiting to hear who had been killed: someone from my family or someone from his.

Des nodded just once as I said his name. The man-who-was-dead was a great loss; from our brief contact, I knew that. It had been awkward at first, employing three men we did not know to help us muster over unknown terrain. We were the employers but we knew less than they did. Perhaps because of my work with Des, we were all conscious of how easy it was to misunderstand each other. And that feeling of consciousness naturally translated into a loss of easy manners, into stilted conversations. Could this uneasy manner be interpreted as racism? Such a thought only leads to a feeling of super-consciousness! Martin was in the middle, both indigenous man and pastoralist. The first week of preparing for muster started very uncomfortably. It had been the man-who-was-dead who had delivered us from that discomfort. He had an extraordinary sense of humour, and it was this that had broken down the barriers. Soon, at day's end, Dad would recount the stories he'd been told, adding supporting comments such as, 'He's got a tremendous sense of humour, that chap.' It was this, along with the superb skills each man brought to the job, that showed us we had not made a mistake after all.

This weekend just gone, the men had moved into the shearers' quarters, to make it easy to get up in the morning for muster. The rest of the family had come out to be with the men.

By six o'clock a fourteen-year-old boy had knocked on my door looking for 'a rake for Aunty Noelene'. By seven o'clock five kids had come to the house to play with Tim and Sam. They were big kids, but in Aboriginal families big kids include little kids in their games. By ten o'clock they'd taken Tim, Sam and me to see the newborn chicks they were caring for and I discovered that the shearers' quarters had been entirely swept out, the kitchen cleaned, and the surrounding area raked up.

We all swam together in the Austin Downs pool, Lachlan and Mandy too. The women, all sisters and daughters, talked about growing up on Austin Downs. These sisters did not have a tribal or traditional connection to this land, but they have worked it for far longer than any owner. Their father worked here and, I think, their grandfather before that; perhaps one hundred years of family connection to this land. I wondered if the connection they felt to this land was anything like the one I still felt to the farm: out of my hands, but still part of me.

They were overjoyed at being back. One sister would note to another tiny details. 'It's nearly twelve o'clock, I bet,' they said to each other. 'What's the time you kids?'

'Ten to twelve,' said a teenager, checking his watch. The sisters were guessing the time by looking at the shadow cast by the shearers' quarter's roof, which was how they'd told the time there as kids.

It was from them we discovered that Mandy, too, has a family connection to Austin Downs. 'Meehan?' they said, after asking for her maiden name as Aboriginal people always do, looking amazed. 'You related to old Jack Meehan. He had this place for years!'

Straightaway Mandy had called her dad, and the story unfolded. Mandy's dad did remember a Great-uncle Jack who owned a station. 'He always carried a set of pistols,' said Mandy's dad. 'I don't remember a great deal more than that.'

Back went Mandy to the sisters. She asked for what they knew of Jack Meehan. And among the details that emerged (he held free movie nights, he was good to Aboriginal people), was the fact that he always carried a set of pistols! It was the same man.

The house that Mandy is living in now was once his house. Most of the work done to establish Austin Downs had been done in his time. After his death, his son had held the lease for a while before selling and, some owners later, we had bought Austin Downs.

'He still walks round at night,' said one sister. 'We felt him. An old man spirit come to see what we were doing, say hello.'

It had been a lovely weekend.

Outside the house the dogs barked, and soon I too heard the motorbike approaching the homestead. On went the kettle, and then I went outside to sit with Des. Tim and Sam were asleep at Mandy's house. How to tell the women what had happened?

It was Dad on the motorbike and rather than return to his empty house, for Mum was with Steph, he came to talk to Des and me.

Never had I seen Dad so upset. Slowly I built a picture of the day. The man-who-was-dead had hit an emu on the way out to the paddock that was to be mustered that day. The emu was killed outright. In Aboriginal culture birds are very significant, and this incident could not be regarded as anything other than a serious warning. But by the time everyone reached the man he was walking around easily and had lifted the bike off the ground.

He refused to go into the nursing post, leaving before Dad could reach him in the ute to take him into the nurse. Over the two-way he informed everyone that he was going to work.

All the early morning he was communicating regularly on the two-way, telling the pilot where he was, staying in his place in line. Then the pilot put down briefly for five minutes to refuel. In that small time frame, the man-who-was-dead disappeared from his position between Martin and Quentin. When the pilot returned to the air after refuelling, he could not raise him. Everyone was immediately concerned. An urgent search began. It took a lot longer to find him than they expected because he had broken from his position in the line.

Kynan and Basil found his trail and began following it, but it was Dad, directed by the pilot who had spotted the motorbike, who found him first. Dad discovered quickly that he was dead just as Basil and Kynan arrived. Dad broke the news, 'He's dead, Basil.' Basil said, 'I told him to go to the clinic!' and broke down. Dad put his arm around him and said, 'Go, if you want to. I'll sort out everything. Leave it to me.' Basil got back on his bike and rode away into the scrub very quickly. Dad stayed with the man-who-was-dead. He put his coat over him.

'The wind caught under the coat at one point,' Dad said, 'and I caught the movement out of the corner of my eye and hoped so hard that I'd made a mistake …'

Meanwhile Martin had driven Quentin home and found Basil there. He had gone straight back to Cue to tell the family what had happened. Martin called Dad on the two-way to say Basil was okay, because Dad had started to worry that Basil too had had an accident. Martin went into the house with Quentin and stayed with the family for a while. Des and I just sat and listened. Eventually Des stood up.

'He has a little daughter, you know. And a new young wife. She lost her dad last year. They were just starting to talk about a baby,' said Des. 'I have to go and see her, go see all the family in Cue. Now, the others won't be back to muster for you after this, not this year. You need to get thinking about how you'll get those sheep in.'

Tragedy and everyday living marched together, natural rivals and ill-matched companions.

It took some hours for the other implications of the tragedy to billow large in our minds. For behind the terrible loss of a good and loved man was the potential for us to lose the station. Like most musterers in the station country, the man-who-was-dead did not wear a helmet. Helmets on muster are a contentious issue. Most musterers feel they are more hazardous than protective as they prevent peripheral, upward and downward vision. This is dangerous in heavy scrub full of kangaroos and emus. So while we had them available as part of the equipment of muster, we did not make them compulsory.

Dad called the Pastoralists and Graziers' Association, who reported the incident to Worksafe. It was Worksafe we worried about because they had prosecuted before with intent to make an example. Such an action was likely to result in us losing and having to leave the station.

'So,' said Kyn to Mandy and me, 'this could be the end of our big adventure.'

We called Mum to tell her what had happened. How was Steph? we asked.

'Terrible,' replied Mum. 'Her lungs are infected. One has collapsed and the doctor in charge last night didn't read the warnings on her file and gave her penicillin, which she is still very allergic to. She's in a lot of pain from the operation and now from her allergic reaction too. I can't leave her, but I wish I could be with you all as well.'

Martin came home after taking Quentin into Cue. He told us that Kyn and Dad needed to return with him now to see the family today. The men all left together, and Mandy and me began cooking food to take in later.

It was then that our manager, Helen, arrived. She had heard what had happened from Des. She had come, she said, to debrief us. She was a pilot herself and she was familiar with the rigours of mustering station properties. She was a nurse too. She carefully outlined what was to come.

Worksafe, she said, was not likely to prosecute because the official ruling remained that helmets may in some instances be hazardous.

The men returned home. Going to see the family had been the right thing to do, Dad said. Every man there had shaken their hands. A couple of people said, 'That was the way he would have wanted to go,' and the other musterers told Dad they would come back to muster after the funeral. Dad said he was very flattered that they would even consider it.

Helen stayed on to debrief the men. She told us that the funeral would be weeks away, but the autopsy would probably be on Wednesday, and we would hear results by Thursday. She explained that soon we would hear from the Sudden Death Squad, the police department that deal with accidents like these. It was all so surreal: Sudden Death Squad, autopsy, funeral. He was riding, talking, laughing just hours ago, I thought.

Very early the following morning, I wrote to Megan, safely returned to Canberra:

In all this there have been the children. Tim does not want to talk about what has happened. Like Martin he is subterranean with his emotions, and there was plenty happening in the regions where light cannot penetrate today. Lachie just cried, and Sam was inconsolable if I went out of his sight.

Mandy and I had to take Sam with us on our visit to the family but left the other two with their dads. We walked in carrying the food. The men and children were lined up around the walls and fences of the garden, sitting, standing, with sad faces. In the centre of the lawn was a group of women, tightly surrounding his wife and his mum.

A table was pulled a little out towards us as we walked in, and we put down the food. We kept walking and were somehow drawn and pushed until we were kneeling opposite them. 'It's the bosses' wives from Austin Downs,' they said. His wife's head was sunk down, but she looked up and nodded as we said how sorry we were. She was absolutely silent. His mum was leaning back, her eyes deeply sunken but brimming with tears; her mouth open. She is a very old lady. All I could think, and Mandy too (she said later) was how I would feel to be her age and to have unexpectedly lost my son. We kneeled at her feet, holding her hands and cried. Around us were little murmurings of what a good man he had been. 'Always kind, that boy.' We said how much we had liked him. How sorry we were.

It's now the next morning, and twenty-four hours ago the man-who-is-dead was leaving on muster. Today we are joined by the men from Coodardy and Annean stations, who rang to offer their help, so we can finish the paddock, and maybe not get too behind with the muster.

Martin has gone out to say good morning and thank you to these men. I'm thinking I should make breakfast for the boys. Clean up the house a little.

I've just been out to say good morning too. Dad has asked me to see that the radios we borrowed from Nallan station are returned.

So this is life, going on, with one less person in it.

12

Planting an Orchard

'From little things, big things grow.'
Anon (traditional)

That first muster was eventually finished with just Martin, Dad and Kyn on bikes, and the gyrocopter. For several nights they camped away at the far end of the station. Then came shearing in late November. At the time I wrote briefly:

> The shearers are here. On the first night they had a blue amongst themselves and three of them left. Of those who still remain on Austin Downs, three now have chickenpox.

We had expected to muster 13,500 sheep, and we had found just 10,000: we were a long way short of the clean muster we'd hoped for. We felt sick at heart, all of us: at the death and at the financial consequences of so many missing sheep. As we waited for the judgement from Worksafe we asked ourselves, 'Had we somehow been negligent?'

Worksafe was very quick with its investigation and judgement. There had been no negligence. We had acted to address safety concerns before the accident. And wearing motorbike helmets is indeed a hazard rather than a protection when mustering in the rangelands. We began trialling bike helmets on muster at Worksafe's request.

At Austin Downs, a cross was placed on the road where the man-who-was-dead had hit the emu. People came with flowers; there were quick words in celebration of his life and in sorrow at his loss. He had been one of the bright particular stars in his family: their lives had been richer, warmer and lighter when he was there. I remember Basil, who had brought no flowers with him, walking into the dry bush and finding white and yellow flowers where I had seen none at all and with one easy twist, pulling them from the bush and gently placing them on the cross.

The day of the funeral came. There were hundreds of mourners, grief blurring the hot dry air.

After the funeral Basil and Quentin came back to work for us, but only for a while: they did not like our revamped safety policy. We understood how they felt, for the new rules did make managing the working day awkward. Still we had to meet Worksafe's requirements, and underneath this legal reality ran fear — the thought of this all happening again was unendurable.

It was the children who kept the circling fears at a distance during this time. Thoughts of losing the station, of another accident on a bike, would slowly dissipate as I watched the children playing their current favourite game. In the mornings one ray of sun shone through the narrow lounge room windows and into this Tim and Sam would spit. They loved watching their spit sparkle and fall. Sam, at one-and-a-half, gushed volcanoes upwards; four-year-old Tim was wiser and gushed his sideways.

But while the young families had each other, Dad did not have Mum: she was still caring for Steph and Declan. Every night Dad dreamed of finding a young man dead in the scrub of Austin Downs. He would turn him over. Sometimes the face was the face of the man-who-was-dead. But often it would be Kyn's face he saw.

In mid-December Mum came home, bringing Steph and Declan with her, for Steph still required a great deal of care, and Brad had to return to work. How glad Mum was to be back; how glad Dad was to have her home. How ridiculous that at thirty-three, with two children of my own, that I too should feel the world rocked less wildly now that Mum was home. Perhaps it was that since the accident, I had felt death sitting on my shoulder. It had been there all along, of course, but for the first time in my life I felt tugged down and unbalanced by its weight. Somehow Mum's safe return and Steph's safe recovery had me standing straighter. Every safe return is a gift: it was something I had not known properly before now. If death sits on one shoulder, joy has the other.

It was in January, the start of my second year on the station, that I realised Austin Downs had become home. The pattern of the days was familiar now. I knew where the sun rose and set through the year. If I had been away, crossing the boundary grid on the Great Northern Highway back onto the Austin Downs lease never failed to thrill me. It was both home and the big adventure: my own comfortable bed and the challenge I had only just begun.

Each day was both same and different to every other as weekends and weekdays were worked alike. One Sunday morning in July (midwinter) there was a phone call from Big Bell mine: could Martin go and fix a leaking pipe at a windmill? The little boys and I decided to go too. The leaking pipe was out along the Big Bell mine road. I often forget that hundreds of men and women fly in and out of Big Bell village to sleep, eat and work twelve-hour rotations on the mine. Their lives and mine rarely intersected, even though we lived so close together. Sometimes, hanging out the washing on hot summer evenings, I saw the lights of the mine in the distance like another cluster of stars in the sky and I listened for the dull rumble of the trucks in their ceaseless back-and-forth journeys. I wondered what it felt like to work on the mine and to have your working life and your family life so separate.

Almost every windmill on Austin Downs has a name: Tragedy, Jack's, Wattagee, Cavanagh's, Bitter Well, Dusty, Governess. We are slowly learning the history of each. Sometimes it's obvious. At Tragedy there was a tragedy, at Bitter Well the water does taste bitter. I would love to know who named Governess. It's just near the homestead. Perhaps it was the site of the governess's seduction one stormy steamy summer.

Boundary, naturally enough, is on the border between Austin Downs and Coodardy station. I'd not been here before. Around the mill is lots of the attractive grey Wanderrie grass that looks like it would be excellent fodder. It is but only after it's rained. There is little feed here and we see no sheep or goats. The dusty entryway is marked with the snaky lines of kangaroo tails. In a drought, the mills are as important to native animals as they are to stock.

As soon as we get out of the ute we are assailed by the noises from Big Bell up close. Tim and Sam seem not to notice the noise. They think that the dogs may have scented a fox; they want to paddle in the water washing over the ground; they see a windmill laid down. 'Why is the windmill down?' asks Tim. I tell him that this mill runs on mine water now, so there's no need for a windmill. It was part of the compensation agreement that the previous owners of Austin Downs made with Big Bell. The water and the free round-the-clock power to the homestead are part of the same deal. I wonder what will happen when the mine closes: who will pay for the windmills to be reinstalled, them or us? I wonder when the mine will close. I wonder when Sam will fall in the mud …

Martin has found the leak. A valve isn't working. I hand him tools as he unscrews it to take back to the workshop to repair.

Walking back to the ute, I see a tree in a puddle of leaked water, a tree which looks both dead and alive. A green stain alternates with dead grey patches and the occasional new green leaf is bursting from a black twig. A week ago this tree would have looked completely dead, and I know now that when the leak is repaired, it will look dead once more. But I also know that it won't really be dead but waiting, like us. Waiting for the rain. Even though it was winter, our second winter here, there had been no winter rainfall. In fact, there had been no rain since our first summer at Austin Downs, a year-and-a-half ago.

Tim ducks through the wire fence on his way to the ute. Running behind him, shouting for Tim to wait, Sam trips over a root of the dead-and-alive tree, and falls, finally, into the mud.

The ute is drafty and rattly, and there is not much room. One boy is on my lap; one is tucked between Martin and me. They fall asleep. I look at my sleeping boys. It seems that only on these long journeys in the ute do I have time to look at them properly. As they sleep in the bright daylight, I notice their black eyelashes and the paleness of their eyebrows, and how much bigger and browner their hands have become. At home they wake up, they are hungry. It is, after all, lunchtime. After lunch we drive to the orchard. The three lines of irrigated trees, high on their mounds, flash green through the high fence and the surrounding dry scrub. The peaches are dressed in their summer green, and it is on this summer's growth that next year's peaches will grow. There are two rows of peaches and another row of our experimental tree crop: the zizyphys, also known as the Chinese jujube or Chinese Date.

Even before we'd left the farm we'd been interested in growing this tree. We'd first heard of it at an Agriculture Extension evening. The jujube was described as early-bearing, salt-tolerant and prolific. Also shown that night was a chart showing dollars per kilo linked to product availability: once a market was established, the more common the product, the lower the price. We decided we needed to find a brand new product as well as something with a well-established market. The jujube was added to a long list of possible products.

The jujube is still new in Australian orchards. It has been grown for a hundred years in America and far longer than that in

China. Mum and Dad had investigated it further in South Australia. Their first sight of a jujube tree did not hearten them. The growers had been trying to propagate from seed: the resulting trees looked very sickly. But Mum and Dad remained interested as the Jujube has a strong Asian market, and we could provide fresh fruit to Asia in the off-season. From the West-Australian Nut and Tree Crop Association they located some West Australian growers, and eventually purchased about ninety grafted trees from local expert, Jim Dawson. Mum chose four varieties from the many that were available (the jujube has as many varieties as the apple!), and into the ground they went.

How exotic the quickly growing jujube tree looked under the blue Australian sky, even against the equally exotic peach tree. Tapering moth-silver trunks spouted a profusion of curly, fern-like, fruiting fronds and tiny, flat, yellow–green flowers. The flowering trees have a sweet powdery smell, like the perfume of the desserts you can buy on the streets of Bangkok. The fruit itself grows to the size of a small plum, and is as sweet and crisp as the best apple. It is not juicy but somehow stiff with moisture and as closely textured as a boiled sweet. Indeed, the Chinese make the jujube fruit into a candy, and it is from here that we know the name 'jujube'. The long shelf-life of the fruit also made it attractive to us, as the jujube keeps fresh for two months and when dried (a little like a date) it keeps for years.

Would they grow for us? Would they flourish in the soil and water and heat of our orchard? With relief we saw that they loved it here! Even on the very hottest days their leaves shone as gum leaves do after rain. There was fruit on nearly all the zizyphus trees, even though they had been planted just months before.

The success of the jujube was a comfort to us because, even after all the research that had led us to choose Tropic Snow cultivar peaches, we were still uncertain of their success. Indeed, so radical had this choice been that we could not find an agricultural consultant willing to take us on. With public liability laws the way they were, advising a client in a risky undertaking could make a consultant vulnerable to a lawsuit should the venture fail. Even though we explained to various consultants the careful research and problem-solving behind each irrigation decision, no one was keen to work with us.

For our peach trees we had mounded and shaped the soil so that salt would not buildup near the vulnerable root zone. We chose an irrigation system that delivered water to the roots but didn't touch the leaves. Our design wasted no water: we wanted our enterprise to be sustainable. Planting design, pruning pattern, everything had been carefully researched. But even though not one of these techniques was new, they hadn't been used before in the arid rangelands. So while agriculture consultants were happy to take money for writing a business plan for us, their recommendations were for us to do things quite other than what we had chosen to do. We were on our own.

Now it looked as though the consultants had been right. Six months after we put the trees in the ground the University of Queensland released a very negative study on the Tropic Snow and slightly saline water. In summary it said that the Tropic Snow cultivar would grow well in saline water, but this vegetative growth would be at the cost of fruit-bearing. Basically, our trees would not fruit. This ran counter to our own research, but we had to take it seriously. Did we need to pull the peaches out of the ground immediately and start again?

It was hard to believe the water was a serious problem because our trees had 'set fruit' not long after they had been planted. And this in itself had been a tremendous relief. But there are no European bees in the pastoral country so how would our peach flowers be pollinated? Without pollination no fruit could grow. Would we need to introduce bees? 'Look, don't worry!' said a Cue local, who'd once lived on the irrigation lease and grown a tremendous garden there. 'The ants will do it for you. We had some wonderful fruit trees. You can grow anything on that soil, you know.'

She'd been right. The tiny black ants had swarmed over the flowering peaches, and soon there were tiny, downy peaches swelling on every branch. Dad methodically removed every little peach he could find that first year. It's the correct thing to do: young trees need to put all their energy into getting taller and stronger, not into growing fruit. But Mum, who suffers from rampant curiosity, hid a few, nestling them up into their leaves as Dad walked by. She just had to know what the peaches were going to taste like.

The birds found them before we could pick them, of course, and the ants after that. But there was enough left for Mum to insist that we all had a taste, or more correctly, a suck.

'No thanks, Barbara,' said Martin politely, who likes his produce perfect.

'There's plenty left,' urged Mum, smiling and holding towards Martin a stone to which a few unappetising fragments of creamy flesh and pale skin clung. The other side of the peach showed the dry scour of a bird's beak. Unspoken was her disapproval of Martin's habit of throwing away fruit and vegetables that had begun to go bad. Even if most of an apple is bad, Mum doesn't give the good portion to the chooks. It is sliced out and saved for stews.

'You've all told me that it's terrific and I believe you,' said Martin, in his most courteous voice, though his eyes had begun to shift from face to amused face, in a vain attempt to find support.

'I want everyone to have a taste,' Mum rejoined, mischievous but implacable. 'You helped grow it, you get to taste it.'

Reluctantly, carefully avoiding the bird scours and dirt, Martin tried the peach. A faint look of surprise disturbed his usually impassive expression, and he shut his eyes for a moment. He nodded and smiled, and seeing that we all expected something more, went on to say that we were right. The taste of the peach made up not just for its poor presentation but for the hours of work he'd put in.

I began to look for a neutral expert on the Tropic Snow who could advise us on growing them using saline water. Someone outside Australia, someone who worked with growers and not just in the laboratory. I went on the Net and contacted growers and nurseries all over the world. Within two days I had the email address of the scientist at the University of Florida who had bred the Tropic Snow cultivar.

> Dear Dr Sherman,
> We have planted two hundred of your Tropic Snow variety in Cue in Western Australia. It's basically desert country, climatically identical to Seville, or possibly California. The water is 1000 parts per million (ppm) of total salts, and the soil type is red loam and drains well.
>
> We planted eighteen-month-old trees in August 2001 (on mounds for better draining) and they appear very happy indeed, even setting fruit in October 2001! We removed most fruit from the trees but kept a couple to taste — richly sherbety with a strongly sweet aftertaste — smashing!
>
> Our concern is some recent research out of Queensland: that low-chill peach varieties will not fruit well when irrigated with salty water.

Dr Sherman wrote back immediately:

> I know where Cue is. I suspect you can grow the peaches in the salty area if you don't let the water get on the leaves (irrigate with under-tree emitters) as the roots will take more salt (about 1000 ppm in total) than leaves will. You are in a dry area, but you will probably need a yearly rainfall to flush the salts downward to keep them from building up too high

in the root zone. I suspect you will get that most years in winter. You may find that the salt actually enhances the flavour of the peaches!'

Just what our own research suggested! We decided to leave the trees in the ground. But the truth was that we would not really know who was right until after our first harvest, in November — just a few months away. We hoped that first precocious fruit set was a sign of good crops to come!

We reached the orchard. The gate was already unlocked because the rest of the family was already here and working. Tim and Sam climbed out of the ute and proudly held a gate open each.

The orchard was changing once more. Beyond the three rows of trees more caterpillar mounds were growing. Dad was in the grader, Kyn the tractor. Together they were heaping and shaping the red earth. In long ditches the new irrigation system was laid out — giant white plastic plumbing. It waited to be joined and then it would be buried.

Mandy, Mum and Lachlan were bent with glue and fittings over the thinner segments of pipe — the pathway from the big pipes to the smaller pipes that took the water to the trees. Martin started the pump and took Tim to help, as it was Tim's turn to hold the funnel as Martin fuelled the engine.

A crisp high chug joined the boom and shuffle of the earth-movers. The little engine began pulling the water from the bore. With the little boys I began checking the sprinklers: some were blocked with ants and, bizarrely, feathers. How the children loved this job! To clean an ant-clogged sprinkler you require a hand to still the sprinkler for a minute. The trapped water would loosen the dead, clinging ants, then it would throw correctly. The boys laughed as the water tickled their palms and staggered, giggling, away from the pursuing water droplets to roll down the steep banks of the mound.

Kynan switched off the tractor and together he and Martin began installing the trellis poles. Two matching holes had to be dug, then the long poles placed and angled exactly. It helped, they said, that they were just millimetres apart in height, as it made judging angles and handling the heavy wood much easier.

One experimental crop and another of uncertain outcome, and yet we had to go on building the orchard as fast as we could so it was large enough to overcome the disadvantage of distance from the market. A small amount of produce was not enough to pay for the cost of transport. The goal was a good quantity of high-quality produce: only this would give us a good profit.

So we were engaged in a race against time, although it was being fought not over minutes or hours or days, but over weeks and months and years. The orchard had to be making a profit as soon as possible: we had to have as many trees in the ground as we could afford, growing high-value fruit as soon as possible. This meant long days of long hours digging and shaping the dirt, constructing the irrigation system of pipes and taps, and adding the huge trellis poles. Would we have it all ready in time for this year's planting?

Although mostly we worried that we were not going fast enough, occasionally we worried that we were going too fast. Would it be better to develop the orchard more slowly, so that our knowledge was some years ahead of our development schedule?

We had not yet harvested a crop, but we were planting more Jujubes and Tropic Snow peaches. Were the mounds high enough? Were the trees spaced correctly for optimum growth? The three hundred trees already growing had to be watered and weeded and pruned. How much water and how often? What kind of mulch worked best in this climate? These were the things that nobody could tell us.

Every day, through both research and practical experience, we learned a little more. We planned to change the sprinklers for long plastic tubes with tiny holes distributed along their length and hide them underneath hay mulch. We'd been told that this system would not require daily checking, and we were always looking for ways to save time.

The growth of the orchard was not our only concern. The pastoral enterprise was just as important, and we were in the process of changing the way we managed the sheep.

At meetings we talked of these enterprises and of our off-station work commitments, but more and more our minds were occupied with another threat: the dry winter had been followed by a dry summer. If this following winter was also dry, then there would be no feed left. If there was no rain by the first of May, we would have to begin to de-stock.

All this was in my mind as I watched the water flinging and falling from the sprinklers, seeping into the purple dirt from which the trees grew. Would we have the orchard ready for the new trees? But above all, would it rain? For without rain there would be no feed, and without feed no sheep, without sheep no wool. Without the wool cheque, how would we fund the development of the orchard? The trees were watered. We turned off the pump, locked the gates, drove home.

On the way home I looked out of the ute window. There was a set of low hills, though perhaps they were not hills at all but mounds left by mining from a century ago. Against the gold sky the trees that crowned each hill's soft curves made them lace-edged, and I was reminded of the curving filigreed edge of Mum's best tablecloth. Just as pretty, just as lifeless: the land no longer seemed to be breathing.

'It seems as if it has been dry forever,' I remarked to Martin, for there was no trace now of the wild lushness I remembered from our first summer at Austin Downs.

Martin didn't answer, but I saw his quick sailor's glance at the cloudless evening sky.

13

Of Sheep and Soil and Ghosts

'No red-hot branding iron
On a calf's soft hide
Ever left such a mark
As the sun
On a man's mind
In the drought.'

TOM JACKSON

It was May, and there had been no rain for months. The longing for rain began gently, like the feeling you have when you want to hear a song again, or the longing to finish a half-read book. That gentle pain of yearning grew sharper as dry day followed dry day. And on the days when you could smell the rain in the clouds as they passed overhead, your throat hurt with longing. Dry winter, dry summer, and now another dry winter seemed likely.

We were mustering once again, but not to shear. The sheep were being loaded onto trucks and taken off-station. How we'd hoped that we would not have to do this! But the rain had not come and we had to in the end.

The sheep we'd missed in that first muster for shearing had all been found in three 'straggler' musters later. I had never heard before of straggler musters. On a farm there is just shearing. It might take you a day to round up all the sheep and bring them into the shearing-shed yards. A few sheep might be missed: a late lambing ewe would be left in peace. But stations routinely have straggler musters.

We did not use the gyrocopter again as it seemed that our sheep were invisible from the air over much of Austin Downs. We had begun to suspect this, but for our neighbours aerial muster worked very well, and it was other pastoralists who were our teachers right now: we just had to ask the right questions of the right pastoralist. We weren't sure why aerial mustering didn't work for us until Mum, Martin and I met a pastoralist who casually remarked on the similarities between his property and Austin Downs.

'How do you muster, do you use a plane?' came the question from all of us simultaneously.

The pastoralist grinned a little at our urgency. 'No. The bush is just too thick, and the wool is the same colour as the bush anyway. We've tried a few times, but pilots can never see our sheep from the air. We just use bikes and trap.'

So our three straggler musters were conducted by Martin, Kyn and Dad on motorbikes. They also trapped sheep when they came into water. Over the three musters they found five thousand unshorn sheep, which well and truly made up the numbers we'd hoped for.

After shearing, we had begun to phase in a new way of managing the sheep on Austin Downs. Again, we looked to see how our neighbours did things. When we purchased Austin Downs, the sheep were spread over a large part of the lease. In the huge paddocks they travelled not in flocks, but in small groups of no more than ten.

But more and more pastoralists were moving their sheep from paddock to paddock and allowing each paddock time to recover before grazing it once more. The sheep were kept together in a few big mobs.

'Fifty years ago there were thirty thousand sheep on this place,' said Dad, as we began planning our new grazing strategy. Often people with a historical connection to Austin Downs dropped in to see us. Just as we asked questions of every pastoralist we met, so we asked questions of these visitors. From all of them we tried to gain a picture of how Austin Downs had been managed when they knew it, and how well that management had worked. This was Dad's latest gleaning.

'They were kept in big mobs. The shepherd moved them on from paddock to paddock when the feed was gone, turning the waters off as they left each paddock.'

It would have been nice if we could have afforded shepherds! But fences would do, we thought, and we would move the sheep regularly.

The emphasis on resting the land was partly drawn from the work of Allan Savory. Savory spoke at the first Pastoralist and Grazier's Association conference Mum, Dad, Mandy and Kyn attended, but we had heard of him well before then. Allan Savory was a visionary and educator who believed that holistic decision-making about the land could help build a better world. Savory taught that every decision should be considered in the light of environmental and community goals, as well as personal and financial goals. In 2003 Savory was awarded the Banksia International Award for his significant contribution to conservation and land management around the world.

At the conference, Savory began by asking the audience if all those present who believed that current agricultural practices were unsustainable would raise their hands. With resignation Kyn watched Dad's hand go up. He agreed with Dad in part, of course, but …

And then came the next question from Savory: would all those present who believed that pure organic farming practice was just as unsustainable now raise their hands? Kyn's jaw dropped slightly, and then his hand shot into the air.

'Both groups are right,' declared Savory. And he proceeded to show how both views could be synthesised into a single decision-making process.

Of all the risks we had taken in coming to Austin Downs, the risk that Kyn and Dad could not resolve their dispute about the use of chemicals was one of the greatest. Yet we had believed there was sufficient common ground between them for us to find a way through. For both Dad and Kyn 'sustainability' is the greatest goal. Sustainability is Savory's goal too, and he described a decision-making process that put long-term sustainability first. Instantly Dad and Kyn realised that this decision-making process would work for them both, and as simply as that, the problem of chemicals versus no-chemicals was solved. The solution is one I think Dad and Kynan would have reached on their own in time. There was enough common ground and goodwill for them to have worked it out, but now they didn't have to. Savory's process was a gift to our family — he saved us so much time … and perhaps grief.

With my family now riveted to his every word, Allan Savory began to talk about the management of grazing animals in arid lands. What he said proved very interesting.

As a young man he worked in southern Africa, much of the time within the kind of arid landscape that my Dad had known as a boy — the landscapes to which Dad often compares these rangelands. Savory spent years trying to understand the causes of land degradation in dry environments. 'Land degradation' simply means the loss of soil and plants on the land. I have seen the 'scalds' that result from this process. Scalds are bare stony patches of land on which nothing can grow. It is as if the land has been burned beyond recovery, down beyond the skin layers of topsoil, down to bone, down to rock.

Savory believes, as do many ecologists, that this process began simply with bare soil between plants. Bare soil is soil from which no plant grows and, just as important, soil that is not covered with a litter of dead branches and leaves. When it rains, less water soaks into bare soil because there is no litter to slow the water down and so give it a chance to sink in. The water runs away, carrying more soil with it. Now the top layer of soil is thinner, and less able to support plant life. It stays bare. More water runs off. More soil is lost. This is how a scald develops.

In the wettest years, the heavy rain that should establish a thick crop of annuals and reinvigorate the perennials does no such thing. Instead the rain becomes a flood, travelling through miles of bush, stripping plant litter from the ground, leaving its legacy — patches of bare soil that become scalds in their turn. Even gentle rain brings no succour. Water evaporates quickly from bare soil, with no trees and plants to shade the soil and absorb the rain. It may as well not have rained at all: the land is water-starved, drought-stricken, not for lack of rain but for the inability to absorb the rain that falls.

Once upon a time these patches of bare soil were repaired by animal activity. Slow-working termites returning wood to soil. The termites are still there, still working; so are the kangaroos and emus.

Their heavy sharp feet scratch up the dirt and crush and spread plant litter. Their eager eating of the plants also means that plants are 'pruned'. Just as peaches must be pruned for the sun to reach the wood before they will set fruit, so rangeland plants that evolved with the kangaroos and wallabies have growing points which the sun must reach for them to continue to grow. When a kangaroo is eating the leaves from a plant, it is serving the plant's purposes too: the growing points of the plant now can receive direct sunlight.

In the stomachs of all these grazing animals live bacteria that break down plant material and return some nutrients to the dry earth.

What has been lost are the small creatures that are almost faded into myth; I have only ever seen them at the nocturnal house at the zoo. The bandicoots and small wallabies. Stick-nest rats and bettongs. Bilbies! Millions of them, digging and foraging in the soil kept it aerated and soft, ready to absorb all the rain that fell. Even in the dry seasons, those little animals survived because they did not drink, nor did they require green feed.

Once, the soil on Austin Downs must have been rich in organic matter. But we had never seen soils with less organic matter than these! The 'beautiful dirt' at the irrigation ran through our fingers like beach sand. And we realised that without the earthworks by the little marsupials (and work it was, for research shows that a single bettong churns up 6 tonnes of dirt a year searching for fungi), the micro-flora and fauna in the soil had died for lack of organic matter.

Savory believes that introduced animals, if managed properly, could take up the role once carried out by the native herbivores. It was a matter of giving the plants enough rest between grazing periods.

The nibbling mouths of sheep, their sharp hooves, their bacteria-filled guts: all of these could benefit the ecology of Austin Downs if managed properly. The sheep had to be kept together in large mobs so that ungrazed paddocks could be properly rested, and the waters had to be turned off in those unused paddocks to keep the goats out too.

How we hoped we could get this right — we would pay our debt to the land and strengthen the grazing enterprise simultaneously. But there were always risks. There were many gaps in the research. The original ecology of the rangelands is not well understood. We could not know for sure whether or not this would work.

And we knew such a plan could get us into trouble if our stock movement planning was not based on an accurate estimation of the feed available. Or if we did not monitor that feed while it was being eaten. Or if we had any sort of a hold-up in mustering and moving!

If we had too many sheep in one paddock and it ran out of water or food, the consequences would be disastrous. We also knew that we might be able to exclude the sheep from the rested paddocks, but the kangaroos and goats would remain.

But we only had to look at a neighbouring station to see how well such a system could work. Mike and his wife moved their sheep around in big mobs and had been successful for many years, through droughts and out the other side.

'The guts of the matter is that if you look after your country, it'll look after you,' said Mike, adding as an afterthought that those stations that stay in the one family a long time are always managed well. 'They know if a station isn't looked after, the family will go broke. You're starting from a strong position: Austin Downs has always been well cared for.'

So we pressed ahead. We put our sheep into two big mobs. Instead of using shepherds, we reinforced the fences on the paddocks into which the sheep were put, and checked them often.

Immediately we discovered that the sheep did not want to live in flocks. They did all they could to avoid other sheep. It was change management where the key players were determined to resist! Only the six hundred ewes we had brought with us from the farm behaved as we wished. They had lived in mobs before, after all.

Moving the sheep into the next paddock to be grazed meant not just one muster, but many little musters to find those sheep that had fled the proximity of the mob. All the time we were learning how to read the land, as we had to be able to calculate how much feed remained. We read books, attended workshops, talked to scientists, talked to neighbours — all the time watching the feed slowly disappear. All the time hoping for the replenishing rain.

But the rain did not come, and the food was nearly all gone. We knew that if there was no rain by early May, we would have to move them off-station. The sheep would starve to death if they stayed on Austin Downs.

Now the fact that we had all the sheep in only a couple of

paddocks had another advantage. With all the sheep in just two big mobs, they were far easier to muster. But even with this advantage, we needed help because at the orchard it was time to plant trees. We employed a mustering team to help us muster, draft and drench the sheep ready to load onto the trucks that would take them to their new home in the south of the State. The mustering team stayed in the shearers' quarters. In the spare cottage, which we now called Frog Cottage, was Jim Dawson, with more jujubes for us to plant.

At night I lay in bed and listened to the country music played loud from the shearers' quarters. It is this music that gains most in texture and richness from these surroundings. Only since finding a radio left on in a ute parked outside the silent sheds had I understood this. It was piercingly cold and dry, and somehow this simple music coming from the old radio in the rattly ute and ringing against the iron wall of quarters and sheds warmed the air, warmed the soul.

As I lay and listened, I felt a romantic thrill. This was how it must have felt fifty years ago: the homestead area fully staffed, perhaps with the fencing, windmill and stockmen teams simultaneously quartered at the homestead area after weeks away on some far part of the station. The nights now were far noiser: more voices, more dogs, more activity. I wondered if it would have all sounded much the same fifty years ago.

There would have been fewer vehicles then of course. The station was managed by men on horses and motorbikes. Go back another fifty years, and it was men on mustering horses, and horses and drays and pushbikes.

On our family walks (children, parents, grandparents, dogs, pet lambs) we sometimes went to one of the old dumps near the homestead. There are several of these, where the discarded household and workshop items from different eras lie half-buried. At one dump is a collection of old vehicles.

Drays of different eras were parked next to each other for eternity: some with wheels made entirely of wood; some had wheels of wood ringed with iron, and some wheels of iron and wood with rubber tires. A lady's carriage and two 1930s Chevrolet trucks rest a little further on.

Beyond are humpies, made from wood and corrugated iron. Only twenty-five years ago many of the Aboriginal people who worked on Austin Downs lived here. Some of those families live in Cue still. On one visit to this camp with Mum she pointed out an old tin can half-hidden in a bush.

'Look,' said Mum.

'Yes, an old tin can,' I said.

'No,' she said, 'it's a toy.' Wire had been threaded through it so that it could be trundled along.

And of course, go back one hundred and twenty years and there was no Austin Downs. The reminders of that time are everywhere. In a wash below the homesteads is a tool-making site where discarded flints of granite, quartz and calcrete ornament the bare sandy soil.

Before daybreak I could hear men's voices around the sheds. Then the sound of motorbikes being wheeled out, the irregular repeated staccato of kicks, and the revving of reluctant engines that kept them firing in the cold, cold air. Then there would be a soaring vroom as they swept out of the homestead.

Never would I listen to that sound without cold invading my stomach. Never would I forget last year's tragedy. Throughout the day I prayed for safe returns and tried to keep busy while listening on the two-way.

It was easier on the days when I went out to work at the orchard or worked as an occupational therapist. And I had also begun a radio series that told of our lives week-to-week. I had to collect background sound and I was determined to record the sound of the first truckload of sheep leaving.

To do this I travelled out 30 kilometres from the homestead to watch the men loading the sheep onto the truck. It's always important to ensure that stock are loaded correctly — not too densely packed (or some might be squashed and die), and not too loosely packed (for this allows the sheep to be tossed around and perhaps injured). Once they are in the truck they are in a stranger's hands, but we follow their journey in our thoughts.

I crouched by the yards holding the microphone out, Sam beside me. Dad glanced over, waved a hand and pointed me out to Kyn, Martin and the visiting musterers. And where before the air had been as rich in men's voices, dogs barking and sheep bleating as it was in the smell of sheep and dust, there came a quiet. As the men fell silent one by one, the dogs began to look anxiously for cues, and suddenly the sheep could only be heard as the light thud of hooves on hard ground.

I stood up and explained that I wanted the sound that I'd heard as I came in. I wanted the dogs to woof. I wanted men's voices against the sound of the flock.

With an air of constraint they began pushing up the sheep. Rather than use words, as I'd heard them doing before, they all said 'shoosh' and 'shoo'. The dogs seemed to be muffling their woofs: the shrill air-shaking yaps I wanted had stopped.

I could — at least — faithfully record the transition of sheep hooves from the dirt, up the wooden race, onto the metal floor of the truck.

Now I wanted to record the deep bass of the truck starting and pulling away, and I waited by the cab of the truck. The truckie marched up and down, checking wheels and the gates within the crate. He saw me and his eyes fell uncomfortably to the microphone. He climbed into the cab of the truck. He looked at me, swigged from his drink, glanced back down at me, opened his lunchbox and started on a sandwich. Another long glug from the drink. Another glance at me, waiting outside the cab. More sandwich. I was starting to feel impatient. Then his face hardened with sudden decision and he got out of the cab.

He marched into the bush. About 5 metres into the scrub he turned back, and I suddenly realised that he was checking to see if I could still see (or hear) him. His expression was hunted; in his hand was a roll of toilet paper.

Feeling guilty, I retreated to the back of the truck. The truckie returned to the cab. I decided he'd prefer it if I recorded from a distance. The engine sounded and the sheep called in surprise as they felt the truck slowly ease forward.

I switched off the recorder. Took Sam from Martin. Kyn stood watching the truck as it pulled away, and I heard him say quietly: 'See ya fellas. Enjoy the clean green feed.'

How I'd have loved to have that on tape! It was a melancholy thing, watching the sheep leave on the truck. Each of them a fine big animal, bred to grow good wool in this semi-arid country. But it was the right thing to do because we couldn't have waited any longer for rain to come. In a few short months our sheep would have starved to death. But before that had happened, they would have done the kind of damage that the land would never have recovered from. They would have continued to feed but the only plants left, the perennials, would have had no chance to grow back, and they would have died.

We were working long days, and it was always on these very long, very busy days that we forgot to feed and lock up the dogs. In the early evening the dogs did not much care. Wanna, the Miss Congeniality of the pack, made up some wonderful games to play in the twilight. She would find goat bones or maggoty sheep wool and drag them along for the other dogs to snatch out of her mouth. She would set up races which she never won but after all, the fun is in the racing. She would tease the smallest dog of all (little Austin, who was named for Austin Downs, but was smaller than a cat) very gently with her tail. But by late evening the dogs were tired of games. They would stand outside the houses and howl.

I couldn't blame them. Austin Downs late at night is very different to Austin Downs at daytime. I never wanted to be the person who fed the dogs long after dark. But I had to take my turn when it came.

Out in the dark, on my way to the dog food, I would try not to listen to the decades-old conversations around the sheds. For there were human voices within the sounds made by the galvanised iron in the wind. I tried to forget the stories of an old man spirit who was reputed to wander Austin Downs at night. I tried to forget the hostility emanating from the generator shed that I felt was directed at me, at all of us, in our first few months on the station. It had faded now into acceptance and sometimes liking. I tried to forget the book that said that ghosts seek each other's company, that there is never just one ghost. I tried to remember the world of logic and sunshine, and the job at hand: feeding the dogs.

But out there in the dark, the world had changed. The air sang with the sonic bleats of the bats, reverberating against the iron sheds and tanks. Beyond and deeper was the rumble of the Big Bell mine. But I knew what made those sounds. It was the other sounds that worried me: the clatters in the shed, the footsteps which were not quite in time with mine, the changes in air temperature around the sheds.

Suddenly I could recall, word for word, a story that during the daytime I could only half recollect. The day before the man-who-was-dead hit the emu, he was seen walking outside the shearers' quarters. Seen by his nephews at a time when he was actually in Cue, getting provisions for the next day's muster. Then I remembered a walk last year where my dog Wilbur ran up to greet someone just near the place where the accident occurred and — even more chillingly — the way Sam, just past babyhood, had also waved to this person. And how, though I looked and looked, I hadn't been able to see anyone at all in the early evening twilight when I turned and looked where they did.

Half running I would tie Wanna up near the chooks and call Maisie and Noni to their cages. Finally, I would rush back to my verandah and feed Wilbur.

When I opened my door to warmth, light and the voices of the little boys, the cold dark night would retreat, leaving behind only a cobwebby feeling of fear that quickly faded to a slight unease. Martin told me that the farmer agisting our wethers had called. The sheep had arrived safely, the truckie had made good time and the sheep already had their noses down in their feed. And with this good news, the last cobwebby terrors of Austin Downs after dark disappeared.

But not all our sheep could be agisted, and some were sold. The money we earned from selling the sheep went into special bonds that were to be used only for restocking the property when it had rained once more. As I watched more and more sheep loaded onto trucks and carted away, I reminded myself that we hadn't come here just to grow wool. We'd come to build an orchard.

When the trees Jim had brought with him had been planted, we would have twelve rows of trees. And they would all be fine, I told myself, even if it never rained again. Irrigated and supported on trellises, weeded and pruned: a tiny patch of hopeful green in the big brown station.

Drought

Winter was nearly over and it had not rained. At dawn, at dusk, we looked to the sky. We watched colours, cloud shapes and height, hoping all the time for the low black clouds, the red mornings, the swirlings of steamy white clouds that herald the advance of a low-pressure system — anything that might mean rain.

No longer were the experts calling this a 'prolonged dry spell'. It was a drought. And to me this drought had a mythic, Murphy's Law feel. For we had been conservative in our figures in budgeting the profit from the wool enterprise: we had budgeted for years of low average rainfall. But we had not budgeted for drought. And at no other time would drought years have affected us so much. Now we were all occupied with thoughts of how to fund the orchard in the absence of a wool cheque.

In the end we decided that we could only slow the program a little. The jobs which we had planned to contract out, we would now have to do on our own. Rather than buy equipment, the men would build anything else we required. More trees would be the last big purchase until the drought had broken. Every expenditure would be considered and reconsidered. We would build tools and develop new methods so that the jobs that usually took four or five men to finish could be done by us alone. We would work harder and longer and we would somehow get everything done.

We decided too that we would look for more off-station work. Soon Martin found more Information Technology work at the Big Bell mine and at local shires. Mum, Mandy and I worked longer hours for the local health service.

We were behind with our program at the orchard. The drought had required us to spend time that had been budgeted for the orchard on mustering sheep and goats. Now we were losing the race with time — the race to build an orchard big enough to be a reliable income stream. It was more important than ever in this drought. The rain we needed now was not just light falls — the kind of rain that keeps plants alive and growing. We needed a lot of rain — 15 millimetres at the very least — enough rain for germination. Light rain would not make much difference now because there were no plants left to keep alive apart from the larger shrubs and trees. Only enough rain for germination and regular follow-up rain would be of any help now. I tried not to waste energy in hoping for rain because we were a long way behind schedule. I needed to put my energy into doing what I could to help.

There were over two thousand trees remaining to be planted and more trellising, more mounding, more irrigation system to be installed. I didn't have the skills or the strength for those jobs, but I could weed and prune the trees already in the ground. And I could plant more trees.

By late August we had put hundreds of jujubes in the ground: suddenly, we were one of the biggest growers of jujubes in Australia. Another eight rows of peach trees were in the ground and growing well. We'd not been confident of these trees at first. There were all eighteen months old but of varying sizes and unevenly pruned, their roots crushed and nipped. They were hard to plant: each hole had to be dug to a different shape, and we had pruned each tree back to just stem as we wanted that single-trunk growing pattern for all our trees. Would these unhealthy-looking trees survive this massacre of branch and root?

In late August more new trees arrived. They were a different variety of peach tree — UF Gold — growing easy-to-pick gold-fleshed fruit. They were little trees, their trunks pencil thin, with a few large leaves, like elegant and spindly flagpoles overburdened with flags. How easy they were to plant! Barely any pruning was required. In three days Mum, Dad and me had them in the ground.

There is no room in my mind for anything else when I am planting a peach tree. Roots and tree must be pruned first. Then the tree is placed in the hole. It must be angled so that it will lie against the trellis. The graft site must be 4 inches (10 cm) at least above the soil. The roots must be placed under the dripper. The branches that remain must not point into the middle of the row. If I think of something else even for a second, I find that I've made a mistake. The tree has to be dug out and replanted.

Sam and Tim would help me push in the dirt around the tree; they liked to stamp the dirt down too. More than anything they wanted to work the secateurs. They wanted to prune. They wanted to snip. I would guide the secateurs into the right place, and they would place their hands over my fingers and compress the handles.

At nearly five, Tim could be sent with secateurs to prune the water shoots — those unwanted stems that grow vigorously from beneath the graft site. His hands would get sore but he wanted to help. When the children were tired of working alongside us, we would say, 'The best way to help us now is to play nicely together until the job is done and we can all go home.'

How well they did this! They roamed the bush within the high fence. (Much of the irrigation site was still bush.) They found old cars, antique seeders, inexplicably shaped pieces of metal: rocketships, battleships, complicated weapons for fighting an unseen foe. Sometimes it was dark when we drove home. Without the cooperation of the little boys, Mandy and I could never have worked the long hours we did — the long hours we had to work — to get the trees into the ground. The children were part of the team, part of the business, and they shared our feeling of accomplishment at the end of a day.

Mum, Mandy and I took on some of the mill runs. Two women would always go together in case of difficulties. When Mandy and I had our first run together, I insisted that I would navigate. Mandy is by far the better driver, and I felt that to do my share I needed to navigate.

'If you keep the boys entertained and clean the troughs, I'm happy to drive and navigate,' said Mandy.

'No, let me navigate,' I insisted. 'I've got to practise.'

Mandy looked at me doubtfully, but I was filled with the zeal that comes from the desire for self-improvement.

I had been reading about butterflies and was fascinated to find that butterflies are a symbol of the psyche. The four wings of a butterfly symbolise the four functions of the psyche: thinking, feeling, sensation, intuition. And, like a butterfly's wings, most people have two functions that are better developed and two less developed. It is in one of these less well-developed functions that problems for a person tend to cluster. According to many Jungian psychologists, who believe personality develops at certain stages in a lifetime, it is an important task in the years between thirty and fifty to fix this problem area.

For me (now thirty-three years old) the problem area was sensation: I struggled to cope with the physical world. I still had problems with navigation, gardening, housework, paperwork and driving. Life on Austin Downs required all of these skills! I began to wonder if somehow I had chosen to come here to do this piece of growing.

At the outset I'd tried to improve these skills by reading books on them, only to realise how futile that was. If the problem was in the physical realm, it was in that realm that I had to practise! Slowly I was learning to garden by working at the orchard. But all the other areas were proving difficult. This day offered the chance to practise my navigation skills, and I was not going to pass up the opportunity.

Five hours later we were lost. The little boys were crying wearily from the heat and the hours of uncomfortable sitting, and there were eight mills remaining to be checked before we headed for home … wherever that was.

'Please let me look at the map,' Mandy pleaded.

I reluctantly handed it over.

'I think you've been reading it backwards,' declared Mandy, after we'd examined it together. 'How about improving your bush-driving skills while I navigate? All you have to remember is it's better to go over the top of a bush than go off the road.'

When we finally arrived home, the men were leaving the homestead to find us. Mandy said loyally: 'We got lost.'

'You let Jo navigate, didn't you?' said Kynan incredulously, one eyebrow raised.

Martin smiled — sympathetically at Mandy and in relief at the three little boys. 'Did you get them all done?' he inquired in a very non-judgemental way.

'I'm not sure,' said Mandy. 'It got confusing. I think we might have missed the last couple.'

'Thanks, though,' said Kyn hastily.

'Yes,' added Martin. 'Thanks very much.'

Their attitudes were suddenly so grateful and understanding that I could almost see a little explanatory sign floating in the air between the two men. It read: 'No matter what mistakes they've made, no matter what's delayed the girls, we are going to be very nice.' They were clearly determined to say nothing that would discourage us from doing more mill runs …

We did keep doing the occasional mill run, but from then on, Mandy navigated while I drove. (I kept my hand in by trying to keep a sense of where north was, relative to our position.) Mandy navigated partly because she was a better navigator but also because she was pregnant for the second time and too big to fit behind the steering wheel.

Soon, the jobs we had left to do fitted into the time we had left to do them. We could lift our heads, look out, and remember once more that there was a world beyond orchard and stock, that there were other dimensions to life on Austin Downs.

The Austin Downs lease contains a significant tourist attraction: Walga Rock. It is a wonderful place. A great granite monolith, it has stood since the time of the dinosaurs, and it has been used by Aboriginal clans for thousands of years. It is easy to believe as you walk up to it that Aboriginal families were coming here when Gilgamesh was written, in the long centuries before the towers of Babel were built.

Its very height draws you inexorably in and under. The Rock promises shelter, but there is danger too, for on the granite sit huge boulders, ready to roll. You walk closer, keeping one eye on the boulders that look as if they are restrained only by a pebble. And around you the vegetation grows wilder and higher, for Walga Rock is so large it has a micro-climate. Even in drought years, there are still flowers at the Rock.

When you are close, you find the long gallery; it lies beneath an impossible hanging outcrop, and there is rock art there from a time beyond human memory. It's just so old. It is like being under the stars or reading poetry. Your mind bumps bewildered against the big questions, the sacred questions: time, distance, the meaning of human life, what is forever?

Walga Rock is no longer considered an 'active' sacred site by government departments, yet activity there remains. From an Aboriginal co-worker I heard this story:

A group of school children from Perth had been staying at the Rock. It was full moon. One night a boy had taken a photograph as the moon lay huge and low behind the rock, against the flat horizon. Back in Perth the photograph was developed.

And not only did the photograph show the Rock and the moon beyond, it showed something else, something that bewildered the boy. For there had been no people in the photo he took. But from the picture gazed an old Aboriginal man, a traditional man, a lawman.

Walga Rock should have simply been a joy — a wonderful place to take our visitors — but with the public liability laws it was fast becoming a threat to our business. Walga Rock is steep, and people climb it as they do Uluru (although that goes against the wishes of its traditional owners). An accident at the Rock could lead to a claim against our business.

It was hard to refuse people permission to camp or visit Walga Rock. In many cases we were refusing permission to people who had visited this place for many years and their relationship with Austin Downs well and truly pre-dated our own. We were sure they were thinking, 'As if we would sue them if we had an accident. We've got our own cover and we would never do that to a little family business. What's the matter with these people?'

But we knew that insurance companies do not pay anything to anyone until all other avenues for compensation have been pursued. From our lawyers we learned the story behind the famous incident where a man sued a town council after a beach accident. The injured man had not wanted to sue the council. But then his insurance company had refused to pay his personal accident cover, informing him that he had to pursue the town council first. Reluctantly, he took the council to court, because only when he had lost would his personal insurer pay him out.

If a climber fell from the Rock, it would be our business they had to sue first. And our business would not survive paying such a claim.

At the same time we felt people should be able to go to Walga Rock. And we felt it should be cared for properly. Used toilet paper and things even more unmentionable blew around the Rock. Most visitors buried such items but not deep enough; the foxes dug it all up again.

Visitors burnt dead trees in campfires, not realising that this forever denied them the chance of rebirth. A dead tree provides a resting place for birds, and while a bird rests it may excrete a seed and that seed, protected from the sun by the litter of termite-digested old wood, will grow again. Over time a number of bushes and grasses will grow up, protected by the shade of the old tree. Eventually a cooperative community of plants can grow. All plants can benefit from combined shade; all plants gain from the plant litter that mulches the ground. Beneath such a stand, animals can rest, adding nutrients from their dung, trampling the plant litter ever finer.

If the tree was burnt a new tree could not grow. Only a bare patch would remain, and it would grow slowly over the years.

Each visitor seemed to want a pristine campsite: one free of old campfires. And so more and more bush was being turned into camping ground. It was interstate and Perth-based tour operators who were deriving an income from this too: nothing was being returned to the local Aboriginal people, to the businesses in Cue.

What could we do?

We discovered our dismay at the state of the Rock was more than equalled by the dismay of the shire president and local Aboriginal families. The shire appointed Jeff Barnard to unite pastoralists, traditional owners and Aboriginal people in the area and other concerned locals in caring for Walga Rock. Jeff was a local Aboriginal boy. He grew up in Cue and had been to university. Now he was back, determined to see the Rock properly cared for.

The task set him was one of reconciliation — notoriously difficult. But Jeff took time to get to know everyone. He won our cooperation with one simple courtesy: he asked permission every time he wished to come onto Austin Downs. One of the most common misconceptions about pastoral leases is that anyone can visit anytime, that they are as open to the public as unallocated crown land.

Dad once found a couple camped in a paddock with lambing ewes. He asked them to leave, describing how easy it is to disturb the mothering bond in Merinos. He outlined our response to the public liability laws in his explanation to them.

'Not all pastoralists refuse to allow camping,' he told them, 'but you should always ask.'

The woman seemed outraged.

'You've got no right to tell us to leave,' she said. 'We don't have a dog. We're not camped at a watering hole or a trough. And I've got a pamphlet that proves we can camp on pastoral leases. We don't need your permission. It's not like a farm!'

'Pull it out and read it to me,' challenged Dad. 'If that's what it really says, then you can stay.'

Out came the booklet. She began to read aloud, then stopped in puzzlement when she came to the line that should have clinched the argument for her.

'That's not what I thought it said!' she exclaimed, staring at the words 'a pastoral lease is private property' in bewilderment. She and her husband apologised, packed and left. Perhaps, in all the discussion of Aboriginal access to pastoral leases, people began to feel that this right of access must apply to everyone. And of course it does not: how could a property be run efficiently with stray campers all over?

After weeks of talking backward and forward, Jeff organised a planning meeting. Round the table sat Dad and Martin, traditional owners, local Aboriginal people, shire councillors, and the local tourist association. The meeting ended in agreement. All parties supported an indigenous tourism start-up — the employment of three Aboriginal people to carry out conservation jobs and to manage tourist access.

For our part, we set in motion the excision of Walga Rock from the Austin Down lease. To see it cared for, to see it treated with reverence by visitors and to have it no longer pose a public liability risk for us: those were the outcomes we hoped for.

And more and more visitors were coming. Like so many little towns in the Year of the Outback, Cue was having a festival. It was not going to be a festival with a raw outback feel. It was going to celebrate Cue's history — a forgotten history, but one of glamour and excitement.

Only three hundred people live in Cue now, but a hundred years ago the population in and around Cue exceeded that of Perth. It was the most sophisticated metropolis in Western Australia. The Cue newspapers advertised 'pure, crystal ice always on hand' and 'the choicest selection of tea gowns, ties, sashes, pure silk shirts, silk taffetas, kid gloves, fancy and black parasols'.

So large was Cue that many West Australians have family who lived and worked here once. Bradley's step-grandfather was sent to Cue 'off the boat' from Holland. He made a living servicing the mine camps — selling cabbages, doing haircuts. His stepson, Bill, (Brad's dad) kept an emu as a pet. All the kids did, Bill says. Painting the Austin Downs shearer's quarters was one of Bill's first jobs. Now art students were coming to stay in those same quarters for the Cue Festival. They were coming to make sculptures from scrap — installations to complement the air and the earth — in the paddocks around the great installation of the homestead.

In the old stories it seemed that the men of Cue had all been gentlemen once, that they had fled Europe for murder and, despite their blotted escutcheons, brought culture to Cue. There had been men of title, famous musicians who gave concerts for free; their mines are still here on Austin Downs. Some of those mines became satellite towns — Daydawn, Big Bell, Great Fingall — all with their own dress shops, bakeries and butchers. They are ghost towns now. Only Cue still shows the lustre of the gold money spent a century ago.

In 1902, Cue town council built a cathedral and a racecourse, discussed issues of drainage and prostitution and frequently posed for official photographs. It was a gentleman's town, with handsome buildings and pretty residences of stone and galvanised iron on the outside and pressed tin inside. Flowers, such as fleurs-de-lis and other fantastic shapes were embossed on the thin metal, like three-dimensional wallpaper.

For the celebrations, each of the stations near Cue was to host an event for 'Q-Fest'. We had offered a Bush Breakfast. Regrettably, family meetings were being taken over by the discussion of menus, how to make traditional coffee brews, and logos for cups and plates. And Mandy was not there to admonish us not to stray from the really important issues because in the thirty-eighth week of her pregnancy, she had gone to Perth to have her baby.

That's how it is up here. To give birth, a woman must travel to the city at least two weeks before her baby is due. And only when baby and mother are ready to travel do they return home.

'Fifty years ago there was a hospital or at least a doctor for every little country town, no matter how remote,' says my mother's mother, who for many years lived on a station in Yalgoo (only a few hundred kilometres from Austin Downs).

But there was no local childcare nurse fifty years ago. Station women relied on correspondence with Nurse Nicholson in Perth. My grandmother weighed my mother and sent a record of this to Nurse Nicholson. Any other concerns would be noted down too. And then she would wait for a letter in return.

It was on that same station in Yalgoo that my grandfather grew up. Ninety years ago, when he was born, the situation for women on stations was different again. There were fewer local hospitals. My great-grandmother had to travel to Perth by train to give birth, and her babies were a month old by the time she returned to the station.

So the way things are now is similar to how they were a hundred years ago! The little hospitals that were so painstakingly built in every country town and the local doctors whose lives were intertwined with their patients are gone. The quick, life-saving dash to a hospital and medical expertise is no longer possible.

Mandy had been away for nearly six weeks. Before leaving she had cleaned her house, planted trees, completed all her outstanding speech pathology work and written a scholarship application for Federal funding to help us market the jujubes. She and Lachlan then travelled to Perth. Kynan had travelled back and forth between his family and the station.

Now it was nearly time for them to come home, the whole family. And with them would be someone new — someone coming home for the first time.

It's hard to believe in a baby you have not met. I wondered how my great-grandfather had felt, farewelling a pregnant wife, worrying that neither baby nor wife would return, then waiting for a baby he knew only from a letter.

On the afternoon Mandy, Kyn, Lachlan and the new baby, Benjamin, were due home, we had all found jobs to do close to the homestead. As the big red four-wheel drive pulled up to their house, Dad and Martin left the workshop to offer help with the unloading of the car; Tim and Sam ran for the house, followed by Mum and me, who were calling vainly after them, but it was my gran who was somehow the first person there, making better time even than the little boys. We found her holding the new baby, both of them radiating contentment.

Mandy and Kyn and Lachlan had the tired glow of a family falling in love with a newborn. And I saw the same look in my dad's eyes, when it was his turn to hold his new grandson.

Not until I was holding Benjamin did the excitement of having a new person to love sweep over me. He looked very like his dad and, at the same time, just like Mandy's dad — symmetrical features and a handsome little head, with his dad's long, heavy eyebrows already marked out.

Tim and Sam plainly felt the same excitement. Sam, who had spent much time gazing at the photographs of Ben emailed to us two weeks before, told Ben quietly that he loved him and tried to poke his fingers into Ben's tightly shut eyes.

The whole family had somehow squeezed into Mandy's lounge room. We knew we should just have welcomed them home and gone back to our own houses. We should have left Mandy and Kyn to unpack, but none of us could walk away from the serenity radiated by Ben.

So we moved in and out, making cups of tea, taking turns to hold Ben, shepherding the little boys out to play with balls on the lawn, bringing them back when they asked to look at Ben again. They hung over him, singing his name out in a little chorus, touching his head gently, wanting (vainly) to hold him.

He's the first new life in our new lives here. We've christened Austin Downs with a baby, we said — the first Jackson baby on Austin Downs. Of course, that's just on one side of his family. Ben is the first Jackson baby here and at the same time, the latest in the long line of Meehan babies to come to Austin Downs.

It was for Benjamin I wrote:

In coming to Austin Downs we had so many dreams and aspirations for our children. We hope for a strong friendship that will last all your lives. As you get older it's clear that the relationship between cousins is closer than usual. In many ways you are like brothers who have different mums and dads. Sometimes I hear the big boys discussing this:

'He's my Uncle Martin and he's your dad,' says Lachlan emphatically.

'You don't sleep at my house,' Tim will say, sounding confused, 'but Sam does.'

They're still sorting it out. But they're very clear on how important you are, Ben. You're a cousin, a brother, and you belong to the gang already. Tim, Lach, Sam and Ben. It sounds good.

So welcome, Benjamin! You've only been home a day, but already we can't imagine life without you.

15

Festival Time

'Life is a festival only to the wise.'
RALPH WALDO EMERSON

Summer had come several months early to Austin Downs. By early September the frogs had returned. They appeared as it grew dark and adorned our toilet and bathroom walls. The same frog would choose the same spot as the night before. They glistened against the whitewashed walls, crouching placidly and waiting for their moth to come in. Their skins were faintly iridescent in the artificial light, palest gold through to beige through to soft green, like small, plump jewels.

The frogs ignored all but the most intrusive human movement; their eyes, unblinking, contentedly followed the moths. They lived in the drains and in the toilet cisterns. They croaked excitedly (and somewhat disconcertingly) when they thought the toilet was going to be flushed or when the sprinkler was going on the lawn, and also just before it rained. Even just a few drops from a storm cell racing overhead would bring forth joyous and frenzied sound.

I found it hard to deal with the frogs with hygienic firmness. This is not a problem for Mandy, who can always call to mind the horror of frog poo on a toothbrush! But I suffer terrible pangs of guilt as I empty out the frogs from under the cistern lid (when it's no longer possible to depress the button). I turn them out onto the bare earth behind the house. In the sunlight they lose their glistening, delicate, individual night colours to become a uniform, unhappy leaf-brown.

The one thousand spindly young peaches that had been so easy to plant had not done well. With the summer heat and wind coming a month earlier, some of these trees were now dead; they would have all survived last year's cooler October. The frizzled remains of these little trees were dotted about among their sisters, who had left the flagpole stage and seemed almost fuzzy with new growth. They made me feel far guiltier than I ever did over the frogs. I helped plant those trees, leaving them to face the wind and the heat when they were not ready. Summer had come too early for these little trees: if September had remained where it was supposed to, in spring, they would have lived. It felt like I had asked too much of a child, and they had not coped, and had been damaged by the experience. It was that sort of guilt. The older trees — the rough-looking and slightly damaged trees we had brutally pruned — had done well.

We decided that we would never plant trees later than July again. And we were thinking more and more about growing peaches from seed. These would be root-stock peaches, that is, the part of the tree that has roots in the ground. When the root-stock grew tall enough, we could graft on a variety of peach that grows nice fruit. It still seems strange to me that trees cannot be bred with good root growth *and* nice fruit, but this is apparently the case. You need two different varieties to grow one good tree! We hoped that trees grown here would have greater resilience to our climate.

The reappearance of the frogs was followed by hot water in the cold water taps and plumes of dust on the horizon: the willy-willys were back. The first time Sam saw a willy-willy, he called out, 'I want to play too!' and ran into the little wind that was so jauntily swirling the dry leaves and dust.

The wind seemed to grow stronger every day in October until the day of our Bush Breakfast for the Cue Festival, when a hundred people came to the shearing shed to eat and be entertained, and the wind became a storm — a front of wind hundreds of kilometres long with a sound like a bullroarer. The air was full of dirt and dead things.

To our astonishment, not one visitor complained of the wind. There was straw in their home-brewed coffee and grit in their lamb chops and mushrooms — and in their eyes as well — but this was how it really was out here, they said, and this is what they had to come to see.

The shearing shed was built around 1903, and it has technologies such as counter-weighted gates between the yards. A gate can be hoisted into the air and sit there indefinitely, balanced by stones on ropes either side. It's all dark wood and tin, with the dark, starry-sky ceiling of every shearing shed in Australia. The visitors were enthralled. I found one man raking the ceiling with his video cameras.

The yards around the shed are older still. The races are raised well above the ground and have a protective canopy of vines. (Races are long, fenced pathways which are only one-sheep wide so the sheep are forced to move in single file, making it easier for us to tag and drench each animal.) It is hard to believe that these yards were built over a century ago and not just because they only look fifty-years old. Their innovation in limiting bending and sun exposure for workers is remarkable.

The visitors loved it all. They loved their souvenir stencilled tin plates and mugs. (One hundred of each, painted then baked in Mum's oven by Steph and Brad, who had come to holiday with us but had found they were working instead.) They loved the souvenir Austin Downs ear tags. They ate enormously of the outback breakfast cooked by art students Ed, Amanda and Adam. They loved the entertainment, which included a surprise appearance by 'the Prime Minister of Australia, John Howard' in business suit and statesmanlike tie. And suddenly the day seemed to me closer to a dream than reality. It had been so long anticipated, getting ready for it so fatiguing, and here was John Howard played so nearly straight. (He was gracious as he lined up for his breakfast, ready to be pleased in any company.) We have no mobile phone access in Cue shire, and he presented Dad with the first mobile phone in the district. It turned out to be a tin can. John Howard apologised because it had no string attached. I felt quite unequal to meeting him and wandered away, Sam asleep in my arms, to discover people taking photographs of Tim as he sat eating a bun on a wool bale.

Mandy and Ben joined us, but before we could speak there was a tap on my arm. Could we spend a few moments with a journalist?

Together Mandy and I sat down, each holding a child, waiting for questions.

Instead the journalist looked at Ben sleeping in her arms, Sam sleeping in mine, and remarked, 'So you girls up here just have babies. Isn't that quaint!'

Mandy now tells me only my intervention saved this man from annhilation, and I did indeed begin to talk very fast. Later she confessed it was the word 'just' that annoyed her. 'There is no just about it!' she said indignantly.

I told him about Mandy's latest project, a toy library and family fun centre in Cue. It was a new concept, I said, a place for carers to bring their very young children, where the games and activities are ready to go. A place where children can learn all the skills they need to be ready for school.

Mandy read the latest child-development research, then she began talking to carers of children about what they thought would work in Cue. In small communities your work role and your home life cannot be separated. Mandy drew upon her therapist's knowledge as well as the networks set up in her life as a local mother.

Already in Cue there existed two facilities for little children. There was the old playgroup which had met in the town hall, but that had been for the white kids. There was the group that met at Aboriginal Progress Association's hall, but that was the place where the Aboriginal kids went. Both Aboriginal and white mums wanted somewhere new — a place for reconciliation as well as play.

'The kids go to school together, why shouldn't they get used to each other now?' asked one mum.

Within months of Mandy initiating the project, the Fun Centre had opened. For the children who attended the Fun Centre to play, scissors and paints and books were old friends; moving from one activity to another was practised so that finding and following the teacher's instructions in a room crowded with other stimuli wouldn't be new. The rules of school would be familiar even if they were not the same rules as home.

'They will go to school ready to learn,' said Mandy, and the journalist, now looking alarmed at this torrent of information, nodded to show he understood. The Fun Centre was in our thoughts just then, as we were about to run a stall to help support it.

The three-day Cue Festival was the best fundraising opportunity of the year. Little stalls were dotted all over Cue. We had set up a little café, selling percolated coffee and tea, and homemade muffins — spicy apple, chocolate chip, juicy pineapple. By early afternoon I could see that we were not going to sell all our fundraising muffins. There were people everywhere, but we had muffins to spare. This was because we had competition. The Lunar Circus Café was also selling coffee and cake. I had spent the morning resenting the Lunar Circus's café. I hadn't known there would be competition, and professional competition too! So it was with a feeling that I was admitting defeat (and a simmering resentment) that I went to ask if they would be interested in buying our muffins to sell in their café.

I walked into the big white tent, sawdust beneath my feet and up to the long silver Lunar Circus bus, which had been parked to form a wall. A long door had been pulled back to reveal a silver café kitchen, beyond it I could see bunk beds. Where was the manager? There were lots of busy people. Who was in charge?

Finally the oldest person in sight put down his broom: he had been sweeping sawdust from a white canvas floor. He didn't look like a manager. He was very thin, with straggly hair descending from either side of a neatly bald dome, a casual, composed air and an overlined face, as though someone had carved out exaggerated lines of expression around his mouth and eyes.

'Just let me change my shirt,' he said. As the shirt came off, I could see that this man didn't just manage. He was undoubtedly one of the acrobats who performed in the Lunar Circus.

He bargained for the muffins with no thought for my fundraising dreams:

'Either I sell them, or they'll be food for the crew. I can't pay more than a dollar each!' And he searched his own wallet for money.

Suddenly I lost my fundraiser's resentment in a feeling of small business solidarity. They were like us, like my family! The circus was a business, the café just an extra enterprise. Like us, they were looking for ways to make money all the time, to be able to keep doing the things they wanted to do.

On Saturday night I saw the manager perform. He was ringmaster, guitarist, clown, acrobat, character actor, artist. It was a wonderful show, and I hoped passionately that they had made a good profit on the muffins.

The art students staying in the Austin Downs shearers' quarters had been building big sculptures out at the ghost town of Big Bell, building them to burn at the festival's end. One of the art students, Rachel, could be seen every morning, rhythmically throwing, turning and then catching what looked like juggling clubs. They flashed as the sun caught them, and this too matched the rhythm. To finish she threw, knelt, then swiftly caught each club, and bowed her head.

We arrived at the Big Bell Sculpture Burn at twilight. Once Big Bell had been a prosperous mining settlement. Now nothing was left but the occasional cement slab — to show that here was once a house — and tumbles of bricks from long-since collapsed chimneys. Even though we stumbled over these remnants of old buildings, the usual melancholic air of long-lost human occupation was absent. Hundreds of people streamed from cars, children running, all drawn by a towering sculpture. It was apparently a dancing girl, but to me it looked like a sun god, a crown like the rays of sun on its head. Its fingers, also like rays, fanned out. Attached to the wires that held it upright were little dancing sprites.

The barbecues were lit long before the sculptures. I was cooking bacon for the Parents & Citizens' bacon and egg burgers; next to me was Jonathon from the Sirocco band, on fried eggs rather than his usual Chinese flute. Out beyond the blinding cloud of oily smoke, I could hear the other members of the Sirocco band: percussion, strings and voice.

It wasn't one of their gigs; they were playing their trademark world music for the joy of it. The sound was strong and sweet — a gift to the night. As I flipped bacon, I found myself wondering if it was their playing that had called the wind storm to the Bush Breakfast the day before, for that had been a real sirocco: I'd found a layer of dirt 2 centimetres deep in my back room.

Jonathon persisted with the eggs. The rest of the band had swept the line of waiting bacon-and-egg-burger patrons into a laughing, twisting dancing circle. Jonathon's eyes streamed in the acrid smoke. I had long retreated from the barbecue to take over the job of separating and chopping the bacon. Finally Jonathon, now quite blinded with smoke, unsteadily left the barbecues and weaved his way toward the rest of the band to add his fluting to the music that was now calling the fire to the sculptures, in tones both plaintive and ominous. The sound reached out to the quiet desert beyond.

As I waited with everyone else for the fire to come, I realised we had grown a community for one night, built from people giving in whatever way would help, local people and visitors alike.

Then the fire came — twin flames wheeling into the dark, dry air, one after the other. I recognised the rhythms and knew who was carrying both birth and death to the sculptures before I saw her. Rachel the art student knelt to touch the flame to the straw that lay at the foot of the sculptures, and the music stopped so we could listen to the sound of them burning. The sun god had been still and stiff and wooden; now he was alive. Fire brought animation to him — he expanded in the dark sky and glowed, and the dancing sprites sparkled and jerked on their wire — and then came death. In our hundreds we stood and watched as the sun god lost limbs and his crowned head and the sprites stilled.

The festival was over. The visitors were gone; the art students were gone; only the sculptures remained. There were shearers in the shearing quarters, and the shearing shed was was once more just a place to shear sheep. The sheep waiting for the clippers had scattered the sculptures in Shed Paddock, and the winds were gently reversing the students' work everywhere else: from scrap to sculpture and now back to scrap. We noted the decay sadly on our family walks.

There were only a few sheep to be shorn, all ewes and hardly any lambs. There was enough feed to keep this small remaining mob on Austin Downs for a little longer. But if there was no rain by the end of December, these sheep too would be agisted or sold.

Our first crop of peaches was almost ready to be picked. The trees were veiled in netting, and the peaches were nearly invisible unless you were standing close and looking carefully, but I could smell them from some distance away. Not ripe, not yet. It was the scent of the promise: that there would be peaches and they would be sweet and warm in the sun.

To see the peaches on the trees! We had conjured them from water and sun and earth, and this conjuring had been matched by care and time and careful thinking. Perhaps the water would have proved too salty without the mounding. Perhaps the salt would have proved a problem with a different water-delivery system. They were not a miracle, the peaches, I knew that, but in my awe and gratitude, they felt like one.

At first we had wondered if we should even pick this first crop of peaches. There would be no financial advantage in selling such a small crop. Eventually we had realised that this first crop would provide a wonderful learning opportunity, greatly outweighing the short-term cost, because we had never picked fruit before. Never marketed fruit before. Never stored or transported fruit before. Never done any of the many things you need to do to get fruit to market. So this would be a useful, practical exercise in what worked and what didn't.

First we had to organise some way of chilling the fruit and then of transporting it to Perth. (There is a coolroom at the homestead, next to the meat-hanging room, which is perhaps fifty years old, but it's now a haven for mice.)

We decided that the answer was a coolroom trailer. We could both chill and transport the peaches in it. We wanted one that would be big enough to do the job for the next two years, so it needed to have enough capacity for next year's harvest. Our budget was not going to stretch to purchasing such an item, even second-hand. We would have to make it, and the first step was to buy the materials required.

Mum and Dad left at three on a Friday morning for Perth, which is an eight-hour drive from Austin Downs. They had the job of finding cheap, second-hand coolroom panels, coolroom doors and a chilling unit. They were back two days later, and within four days Kynan and Dad had built a very beautiful coolroom trailer.

In this time Kynan had been trying to find a market for our peaches. This was much harder than we had hoped. Placing product at big supermarkets is notoriously difficult — often the producer has to pay the supermarket to put their product on the shelf. This wasn't something we were prepared to do. Our aim was to become one of the producers sought after by supermarkets — something that only happens after you've been in the market a few years.

But even the smaller fruit and veg shops were not interested. They already had enough peaches: yes, even of the white-fleshed, thin-skinned, free-stone variety that you're talking about, thanks.

It was hard not become despondent, but Kynan persevered, though he had to grit his teeth against the next round of rejections.

Finally he found a broker who was interested in selling the fruit for us, even in the tiny quantities we had available. The broker said that he knew our peaches would be sweeter and more intensely flavoured than most. He talked about the soil and the sun and the water and said he thought we had made an excellent choice of location for horticulture. He asked about the other things we were growing and expressed a strong interest in marketing those too.

I'm not sure words have ever been so sweet and, of course, they were all the sweeter for the lack of interest that had preceded them. We awaited the first ripe peach with nervous excitement: we had cooling and transportation ready; we had a market sorted, but we had yet to learn how to pick and sort and pack!

In summer the sheep change their watering patterns. In the cooler months they are out grazing in the middle of the day, but on the long hot days of early summer they camp by the water during the day and go out to feed in the early morning and evening.

And our pattern of work and sleep had likewise changed — we worked very early and very late, and went home to sleep (and water) during the hottest part of the day.

How hot was it? I wasn't exactly sure. The cold taps didn't ever run cold now. By eight o'clock in the morning there was a heat haze along the horizon. By nine o'clock the illusion that a little further on there is a puddle of water lying on the road began. The puddle dissolved and reappeared repeatedly, just ahead of wherever you were.

We had begun to hope for some early summer rain. The occasional storm cell appeared, racing overhead, and one day I saw one like a giant man-of-war jellyfish, crested with lighter clouds and richly grey and bulging underneath. It drifted over Austin Downs, rain shafts streaming from it like tendrils, but never quite reaching the ground.

It got hotter and hotter. One afternoon in late November the sky brewed up a late afternoon storm. Feathery, ice-bearing clouds mixed together with the rising heat from the land. Martin, the children and I were having a week on our own on the station. This particular afternoon Martin was working off-station, so the children and I were going to water the trees at the orchard and check for ripe peaches.

I love lightning but I'm scared of it too. And the storm was between me and the orchard. In an attempt to avoid attracting the storm's attention, I drove very slowly, trying to crawl and scuttle between the lightning like an insect dodging a foot, while trying to explain what lightning is to the boys, and also trying to battle a stream of paralysing thoughts: 'Does it really matter if the trees don't get watered? What happens if lightning hits a car?'

I had the window open so I could count the gap between the thunder and the lightning. I counted one, two, and then came the bang!

Then it began to hail. Tim and Sam had never seen hail. I stopped the car and the boys and I quickly and nervously gathered some lumps to suck on. The peaches! I thought, just days away from ripening. Would I find them damaged by hail?

Hail lay white at the gates of the orchard, and the ground beneath looked as though it had been pecked, in the same pattern that is left by the beaks of galahs when they peck up fallen grain. Had the peaches been damaged? We found that the hail had stopped at the gates, 50 metres short of the peach trees.

The storm thundered on just a little way distant from the orchard, moving backwards and forwards over the same terrain on a little circling pattern of wind. The boys and I turned on the pump and checked the sprinklers, all with a wary eye on the sky.

At seven-thirty Martin arrived at the orchard, come to fetch his family in the ute, as the road to the orchard was now impassable by car. He found the boys and I lying on our backs on the warm dirt, watching the lightning snaking from earth to cloud and listening to the thunder.

I wanted a new way to describe the bold roar of this thunder across the flat plain. Rattling, reverberating? No, clichéd, hackneyed, I thought, discarding one term after another. Then Sam whispered suddenly, 'It's like a lion, Mum!'

Martin lay down with us. As the lightning and its attendant lion moved away, to the far south-east horizon — perhaps it was over Yarraquin station now — the clouds above us cleared. The full moon shone down, a long note held to end a piece of music.

16

RAIN

'In the lonely, silent places
Men lift up their glad, wet faces
And their thanks ask no explaining —
It is raining — raining — raining!'

C J DENNIS, 'A SONG OF RAIN', *BACKBLOCK BALLADS* (1913)

Until now the peaches had been invisible under the white netting, green on green. But suddenly the peach trees looked like rows of dressed Christmas trees.

We had been pruning them to achieve just such a shape — a central leader and many little fruit-bearing twigs. Now they were hung with peaches, and the peaches had turned pistachio and lemon-coloured with crimson streaks. December was so close that the comparison with a Christmas tree was unavoidable.

Now we had to learn to judge when to pick a peach. This was not easy, and the next day we would discover that we had got it a little wrong again. And I suspect that having found that we had got it wrong, we would then overcorrect. If we found over-ripe peaches, we would know we had left peaches that needed picking the day before. This would lead to us picking greener peaches. Then the following day we would find that there were hardly any peaches left to pick — which told us we had picked them too green.

But it was still a very enjoyable job. We would leave the homestead at just before five o'clock to be at the orchard at daybreak. First light among green and growing things!

I would climb under the netting and walk up to the first tree in the row, box in hand. Each peach had to be examined separately and while towards the end of picking I could see at a glance if a peach needed to be picked, on those first mornings it could take as long as a minute to decide.

As a peach approaches ripeness, the light seems to penetrate deeper into the flesh; the background colour moves from a hard green to a softer, more gold-tinged shade. I would look for the beginnings of translucence or for colour change on the bottom of the peach, or I would watch where the ants went; they seemed the first to know when a peach was ripening. In the very early morning I would sniff the peach, but as the morning grew hotter the sniff test would work no longer. The warm air was not just infused with the smell but the taste of peach.

During peach-picking my sister Megan came to stay with us. She had exchanged her Canberra suits for the women's overalls Gran sewed for us. Gran was still sewing: workshirts for the men, all kinds of things for the little boys, and for us, these overalls. They were of pale seersucker or gingham, with a long zip up the front, a half-elasticized waist and a big sun collar. Gorgeously comfortable and extraordinarily unflattering!

With us Megs picked peaches and planted vegetables. Mum gave her a handful of pumpkin seeds to plant in the gaps where peaches had died and at the beginning and end of rows. Megs spent an hour wandering the orchard, planting here and there.

Megs and I decided that picking peaches was a bit like picking mushrooms. There was the same calling out to each other over a paddock, the same exulting over a really good one. And as we graded them into firsts and seconds, thirds and peaches-for-home-consumption, we found ourselves carrying out a ritual left over from the days of mushrooming — nominating the best, the smoothest-skinned, best-coloured, best-smelling, of all the peaches we had picked that day.

Megs was so competent so quickly with all of the jobs at the orchard — the pruning as well as the picking — it was hard to believe she fitted in equally well with the life she had chosen. (Indeed, both my sisters would suit my life better than I do; they are gifted fixers and makers — and excellent navigators!) Megs has chosen a different kind of adventure to mine of family and land, but still a life that will force her to grow. She is a shy person and working for the Department of Foreign Affairs and Trade means that she has a very public life; it is her job to represent Australia overseas.

So easily did she fit back into this life that it seemed sometimes that she could never have been away at all, that her other life of learning new languages and diplomatic policy did not even exist. But not so long ago, I had been longing for her to arrive and now she was here. I was beginning to remember that each day closer to her arrival was also a day closer to when she would leave again. But there is always the telephone and the Internet. My sisters and I can share each other's lives no matter how far apart we are. And perhaps it was the almost daily contact between us that helped Megs slot so neatly into this life — so like the life of her childhood — once more.

Eventually we had picked enough peaches to take them to the broker, at the Canning Vale Fruit and Vegetable Markets, which start at four in the morning. What would the market think of our peaches?

I have never been to a big fruit and vegetable market, and as our peaches were about to have judgement passed on them, an image, which I knew to be wrong, entered my mind and persisted. In a crowded town hall, full of agricultural produce, there is a plate on a table. And on that plate, plump and fragrant, sits the very best of our peaches. A panel of peach experts are paused before it, examining it, cutting it open and tasting.

And the verdict?

'The flavour of Austin Downs peaches is wonderful and they have reached the market in excellent condition but they are too small and too pale.'

(A common fault, apparently, in first crops with inexperienced growers.)

This was valuable feedback, and we decided that we needed to be more aggressive with our bud-thinning, so there would be far less fruit and the remaining peaches would grow bigger. And we needed to thin the leaves so that more light reached the fruit.

So did we make any money from our peaches? No. As anticipated, the costs of picking and marketing were greater than the money earned from the sale of the peaches. And of course they did not sell at all well, being too small and too pale. But with those faults corrected and more of our peach trees reaching fruiting age, we knew that the return from the peach trees would be better in 2003 and good by 2004.

We ended up giving away a lot of peaches! But this turned out to have its own reward too. Everywhere we heard, 'It doesn't look like much, but this is the best peach I've ever tasted.'

Trips to Perth were now enlivened by people who asked when the next crop would be ready, people who offered to sell our peaches for us in their town, people who just wanted to put in an order for their own tray. Now I enjoyed travelling to Perth far more because I could never hear too much praise of our peaches!

At the same time I worried that the market requirements for colour and size would come at the cost of flavour. The advice from the broker was that consumers buy with their eyes, not their tastebuds. This puts Tropic Snow peaches at a disadvantage in the market. The glorious gold colour of most peaches is not theirs. They are classified as a white-fleshed peach, though their flesh is not exactly white. It is a creamy greeny-lemony mix. They are known mostly to foodies and restaurateurs. To most people they look unripe, even when gilded in blush, for next to the crimson blush is a stripe of soft green.

How I wished I could stand next to every peach-buyer in every market. To each I would say: 'This is a Tropic Snow peach. Look! It has white flesh and smooth skin; it is a dessert peach. Each peach has the brief, agonising sweetness of the best apricot. Each mouthful tastes a little different to the next. You can taste where the sun has fallen most. Beneath the crimson the flavour and texture is that of treacle and custard. Beneath the lemon bursts first tartness and then sweetness which grows ever stronger. Closer to the stone is different again.

You can taste everything that has gone into this peach! Beneath the skin you taste the sun, in the middle you taste the saltwater from under the ground and the rain from the sky, close to the stone you taste the earth.'

But it was for 'eyes' that we had to grow our fruit. We did wonder if the smallness of the fruit had contributed to the intensity of its flavour. And so would flavour be diluted in a larger peach? Certainly, the very large peaches often have a 'pale' taste, despite their splendid looks. But we had to sell our peaches! We decided that we must take the advice of the experts, and hope that we were not going to compromise flavour by increasing size. There was no point to growing fruit that no one would buy.

It was nearly Christmas, and still we were picking. Now that we knew these fruit could not find a market, we decided to keep them for ourselves. Fruit and vegetables are expensive this far north, and usually I purchased only what I knew would be eaten in a week and what was in season.

Suddenly I had an abundance of fruit! For the first time since moving up to the station I needed to contrive many different ways to use up a single fruit. As I made peach chutney and peach and banana muffins, I realised I'd missed this. I made beef curry with peach (this didn't work so well). I dried, baked, stewed and froze peaches.

I think the most successful meal of all was the feast of fresh peach fritters Meg made for a family breakfast. She diced green peaches into tiny pieces and added them to a sweet batter made of spelt flour, rice syrup, honey, olive oil, eggs and milk. Each fritter was equal parts fruit and batter. The frying pan was sizzling hot; she gave each side just half a minute. The fruit was soft but still tart; the batter was crunchy and sweet.

Four days before Christmas came a phone call from a farmer who'd been our neighbour before we came to Austin Downs. 'I thought you should know,' Dave said, 'that your old farm was pretty much all burnt this afternoon. The houses were alright, but everything else went up.'

'All the trees we planted?'

'Yeah,' he said. 'They went too.'

I waited for the news of the fire at the farm to hurt, and it did, but it was curiously blunt. The next morning, though, there was a haze over Austin Downs. As it did not smell, Dad and I disagreed over whether it was a dust haze or smoke. It was ash-coloured and yellow-tinged so I thought it was smoke from the fires down south, and some of it smoke from the fire at the farm. You cannot really draw a line between your old life and your new. There are always connections forward and back, and this smoke from a fire 500 kilometres away seemed one of those connections to me.

As the day went on, the hazy horizon began to fill with steamy clouds, outlined in white. I tried not to hope for rain but hope I did, and I noticed how very sharp a pain was my hope. So often in these last months it had looked as if rain was inevitable, but either it had not rained or it had not rained enough for germination. The land was now so dry that only consecutive heavy rains would break the drought.

The sky slowly filled in, but with a different type of cloud to the usual ground-to-sky grey that meant rain. In the early evening the thunderstorms started. It was a night of many lions. There were storm cells in every direction semaphoring and sending long lightning tendrils out to each other across the steamy sky. And then it started to rain.

For half an hour, the brown land reflected the white sky everywhere I looked, as the rain fell so rapidly that it could not soak in and sink away. Martin and I tortured ourselves with guesses about how much rain was falling, belief bubbling more confidently in our chests.

'We're going to get a germination out of this,' we predicted. 'The very best Christmas present of all!'

In the end we had 27 millimetres. More than enough for germination, and for puddles too.

On Christmas Eve I was inside cooking when Dad stuck his head through the door. 'Come on,' he said. 'Come and look at the boys playing with boats in the puddles. The big boys,' he added with great satisfaction, as I walked outside. There were Martin and my brother-in-law, Bradley, building boats for Declan, Tim and Sam. They made them out of wood, old cartons and styrofoam, with twig masts and leaf sails. They were all playing in the puddles that had turned the raised garden beds into an archipelago.

Like every family, we have our own Christmas traditions. But that first Christmas at Austin Downs, with no one to keep Mum and me up to the mark, those traditions were neglected. Mandy and Kyn spent Christmas with Mandy's family, and at Austin Downs our Christmas celebrations were meagre. We had opened presents, and then we went out to work at the orchard. We had then hastily pulled together a shared meal at night and gone early to bed. Mum and Dad did not even have a Christmas tree. But this time Steph had come to spend the day with us. She informed Mum and me that we would do the thing properly: work was to be confined to the must-do jobs with a proper meal and games to follow the chores, and there was to be a Christmas tree at every house!

During the Cue Festival, Ed the art student had sculpted a tree from fence posts and branches and given it a foot instead of roots. As Ed stood explaining to a group of his peers and his supervisors the origins of his idea to make a tree, Noni, our dingo, came closer and closer. Ed talked about interconnections between the natural and man-made, of above the ground and below the ground and in the air. Noni came up and sniffed the tree. Finally, just as Ed was waiting for some feedback from the group, she lifted her leg and marked the tree. Retrieved from the shearers' quarters and washed down, this contructed tree became Mum and Dad's Christmas tree. Sparsely decorated with the most artificial and modern of Christmas baubles and lights, it looked wonderful.

Bradley wound scarlet flashing lights around two poles on the verandah too.

'Landing lights for Father Christmas,' he informed the little boys, 'otherwise he might get lost. Your presents might go missing.'

The next morning, walking across the still damp ground to Mum and Dad's house, it was obvious that Father Christmas had found us after all. There were sleigh tracks gouged into the earth, coming very close to the house.

'It looks like the sleigh very nearly ploughed into the verandah!' said Martin.

'Yeah, that's right,' replied Brad. 'I was woken up in the night by Father Christmas. He said the landing lights were too ...', Bradley coughed to conceal a very rude word, '... close to the house!'

The children had no difficulty accepting that Father Christmas had woken Uncle Bradley up. Steph's stories of Brad's adventures had never stopped; now she told them to the children too. So the night Uncle Bradley had been woken up by termites chewing several rooms away was a favourite, as was the story of the night Uncle Bradley had thrown a chair at a sheep that kept bleating.

We made all our traditional salads. I made the one invented by Martin for Christmas many years ago: avocado, peeled granny smith apples and firm bananas, sliced together in equal quantities and tossed gently with just a snifter of balsalmic vinegar. It was the first time that I, not Martin, had made his salad and afterwards I realised how clearly it showed a change I'd not even noticed in our lives — both of us had taken on more traditional gender roles.

Peaches dominated the Christmas Day meals. We had peach muffins and brewed coffee with present opening; peaches for dessert after a light lunch; green peaches in the rice salad, dried peaches in the Christmas pudding and fresh peaches in the fruit salad after Christmas dinner.

There was one box of cherries too. Bradley's parents grow cherries and every year send one box to us. This year I saw them differently. For the first time I saw the art that goes into growing fruit as perfect as these. They were just 'seconds', but each cherry looked as if it had come from an identical mould to every other cherry. They were as radiantly and deeply scarlet as the Christmas lights.

It is wrong to eat a cherry quickly, even though they are so small. First they should be held in the mouth to feel and taste the sweet, smooth skin. Then comes the bite through to the tiny stone and the intense brief pleasure of the juice and flesh. I felt humbled as I realised how amateurish our first crop of peaches had been

But the main event for us at Christmas was not the food, but what we did after dinner. We played games — the same games every year. This was a tradition developed many years ago in our extended family. No longer can we share Christmas with them for we are too far away now, but we can play the games still. Early in the evening we played the more challenging games, like racing charades or pictionary. Fictionary is a favorite too; we use *Mrs Byrne's Dictionary of Unusual and Obscure Words* and compete to create the most convincing definition. Later on in the evening come simpler games: wink murder and spoons.

The games have evolved to include the children now, and the words and phrases we write for charades and pictionary often refer to nursery rhymes or children's fiction or the daily routine of the station. In wink murder each child sits on an adult's knees and whispers observations of winks and looks; in spoons the children are employed by an adult to dive for a spoon.

It was a great Christmas. Mum and I resolved afterwards that for all the Christmases to come, we would remember to stop work and celebrate this special day with special people. And remember it on our own, so that the special people didn't have to remind us how very important they were!

By Boxing Day the brown land looked as if it had been washed over in green water colour. Tangles of grass that I would have sworn were long dead had begun to sprout, and the salt bush was putting up new shoots.

We began the New Year, our third year at Austin Downs, with a business meeting. We had to review our drought management plans as, despite the rain, it wasn't yet time to restock. This was a time of renewal, but also a time of great vulnerability for plants. Although the new growth was prompted by the rain, the real energy for new shoots came from the plant's roots. And there had to be a quick payback, that is, the energy had to be returned to the plant's roots or the plant would be overextended. Should such a plant be heavily grazed at this point, it would die. We had to wait for more rain to support this germination, and more rain again.

But our hopes were high. The cyclone season was due to start in the Far North of Western Australia, and cyclones in the north would mean rain here for us. We had been told that the El Niño effect was breaking down once more. We believed we had a better than fifty per cent chance of drought-breaking rain in the next few months.

We knew that much of Western Australia would share this good season. This meant that it would not just be us looking to restock. Many farmers and pastoralists would be looking to buy in more livestock. Naturally this meant the prices for sheep would rise. The thing to do, if we could, was to buy before everyone else did: to gamble that the rain would come. Or perhaps not to buy stock at all, but find another way to use the feed.

We sat down and worked out our cut-off dates. For example, if there's no rain by such and such a date, we will not buy Merinos. And our contingency plans: if it does rain and the price of merinos is too high, then here are the other options.

In our meetings we tried to make sure that every idea was considered and that one idea wasn't honoured above another because of the depth of knowledge possessed by the person whose idea it was. At this meeting it was Mandy, the not-so-long-ago city girl, who spotted an opportunity for marketing feral goats.

We were still deciding what to plant in the coming year. The experimental fig trees put in by Mum were doing very well. Figs often command good prices, so naturally we were keen to grow them. But there was a difficulty. Figs have the shortest of shelf-lives!

Living eight hours from Perth, we had to store our fruit until there was enough to make the expensive trip to Perth economically viable. The extremely short shelf-life of figs meant that no matter how well they grew here, no matter how high a price they commanded, the problems with storage and transportation were going to be too complex. But we were still working on it: developing budgets with different numbers of trees and checking out the latest research. We'd been fascinated to discover that figs travel best wrapped in fig leaves. New research and old knowledge often tell the same story!

When we bought Austin Downs, it had experienced a run of good seasons. The land was lush and wild with new growth, the washes that were now bare soil had been a paradise for water birds, the bush filled with the sweet rattle of breeding insects, and the many sheep had been fat and healthy. The Christmas rain had not brought any of those things back, but the soft green blooming on the soil had reminded me that they were possible.

But swift on the heels of our delight in the new green came the worry that it might not rain again, that these tiny plants would wither and die in the long hot dry days of January.

Out in the orchard we pruned back the peaches, now empty of fruit. We moved the netting onto the jujube trees, as now they were hung with tiny clumps of fruit. The peach trees had become just two rows of trunks and branches with a few leaves. They were heavily mulched, but in our cupboards and freezers their peaches dwelt still!

In early January there was a tropical low in the north. Not a cyclone, but still our best chance for rain in nearly two years. Would it mean rain for Austin Downs? Would it rain enough for one of us to have to race to Perth and buy Merinos?

The sky went grey. We could smell the rain in the clouds. But it did not rain, and did not rain. I tried to stop looking at the sky, tried to stop hoping. But looking down meant looking at December's germination, only a couple of centimetres out of the ground, and I imagined it frying pitifully in the sun. And then, late on the second afternoon, it started to rain gently. Then it continued, soft and constant, into the warm grey night. Martin and I lay awake, listening to the sound of rain on our roof.

When I woke, one thought was uppermost: the Christmas germination would keep going a while yet. My next thought was: had we had enough rain to restock?

I went outside and saw with astonishment that the children's paddling pool on my lawn, empty yesterday, was now full nearly to the brim.

There was a yellow dawn. No more rain then, I thought, but count your blessings, my girl! The new sun was butter-coloured and the light a soft primrose. In the paddock below my house, where sheep were being kept ready for yet another straggler shearing, I could see only water. A lake! Yesterday there was only bare, compacted soil there.

Where were the sheep? Had they drowned? I ran down the driveway, to be assailed by an extraordinary sound. A thousand frogs that had been silent for two years were calling to each other in the wash. A monumental chorus of deep, lusty ba-booms, frenzied clicks and seductive chirrups. The air seemed to beat against my eardrums, vibrating with the piercing rattle of insects: cicadas, grasshoppers and huge black beetles.

Of course, I should have recorded this sound for the radio program, but I did not realise that within two days it would be gone. It was all gone so quickly. It was the first time I'd seen insects and animals respond like this to rain. It seemed that once some quantity of rain prescribed millions of years ago had fallen, a switch was flicked. Life crawled and blossomed and hatched. There were the flying ants who held us hostage for just one night; our house lights drew them as they do moths. The flying ants were of all sizes: little ones who kept their wings on as though uncertain of a final destination, big ants who on landing purposefully shrugged off their wings, ready to hunker down and build their new nests in every corner of my house. I was too entranced to consider that it would be gone within hours.

When I returned from checking the sheep (they had moved to higher ground), I discovered the rest of the family in their pyjamas in the driveway. Mum and Dad said they had been to check the rain gauge early this morning. It was so early they'd needed torches.

We'd had 47 millimetres of rain! The usual procedure is to check, note down the figure and then empty the rain gauge. But Mum and Dad had not been able to bring themselves to tip out the precious evidence.

We were all giddy with relief and sleeplessness. Martin and I had not been the only people to lie awake waiting for the rain to stop. We had all listened in our beds, under our tin roofs. We surrendered to the sound the way sun worshippers surrender to the sun, trying not to become anxious as the rain lightened off but to simply treasure every second. We all knew just when the rain had stopped: at twenty past one. We'd all gone to sleep smiling.

In the days that followed, the plants grew quickly in the hot, wet soil. The road verges were now brilliant green where the smaller puddles had been. If hope has a colour, it must be green: this new growth lifted our spirits as we went back to hoping for rain once more.

17

EVERYDAY PLEASURES

'Good fences make good neighbours.'
ROBERT FROST, 'MENDING WALL',
COLLECTED POEMS

In the puddles left by the rain were shovel-headed shrimps. They appeared on the first day after the rain. At first I thought they were tadpoles. In the water they seemed to have the same gentle blunt head, the same paddling tail, the same wriggling motion. I was thrilled. As soon as I heard the frogs calling in the washes, I told the children about tadpoles. Just the thought of them made me happy — a leftover from my childhood.

For me, the wonder of the change from tadpole to frog is equal to that from caterpillar to butterfly, yet I have never seen the frog celebrated as a symbol of transformation. A butterfly gets the job every time.

Seeing this tadpole shape in the pond, I called Tim and Sam and together we pored over the puddle, waiting for another to appear. It waggled up from the shallow depths, and I scooped it up. Immediately I could see that something wasn't right with my first tadpole in three years. It was too pale, the tail was too short, the head looked hard. Then it flipped over in my hand.

The back part of its head lifted up: it was a kind of shell, jointed onto the tail. Underneath were gills mounted on a tiny plate of shell. As it flipped again, the tail flicked off some more water and I saw that the tail was not the innocent tail of a tadpole: it was forked in two. All of this hit me in seconds but I still could not quite accept that it was not a tadpole I held. Then I was seized with revulsion, even though this thing was so tiny and so harmless. I dropped it back into the puddle. I felt relieved to have it off my hand.

What was it? We went to find Mum, who usually knows about this sort of thing.

'It's a shovel-headed shrimp, I expect,' she told us. 'The other name for them is tadpole shrimp. They have a very short life-cycle.'

She explained it carefully to the boys, and now Tim can tell me exactly how it goes: 'They wait in eggs for a big rain. They hatch and mate. They leave the eggs in the soil. Then they die. And then when it rains, their eggs hatch.'

They seem to be able to mature and lay eggs in four days, if that's all the time they have. Four days. This seemed to add to their fascination, because I had become fascinated with them in a horrified kind of way and I could not walk past a puddle without picking one up. They seemed primeval and alien.

Some of the smaller puddles were drying on the fourth day. Trying to swim, contorting, flipping over and over in the sticky mud were millions of shovel-headed shrimps. Too many to save.

'They've already mated,' my mum comforted the boys. 'Next time it rains their babies will hatch.'

I wondered if was it worth it for the shrimps? Hatching, swimming, then dying slowly in the mud? What did they think? Did they think? What kind of consciousness would a shovel-headed shrimp have? Did they enjoy life at all? Some of them could be seen lying on their backs, their gills pulsing.

I began to get vicarious existential angst every time I walked past a puddle. It was with relief that I finally found my tadpoles in the dogs' drinking bucket below a rainwater tank. I made sure

I kept the water high, so they were not gulped down by thirsty dogs. Just the sight of their round soft heads and long gentle tails made me happy, but Tim and Sam were far more interested in the shovel-headed shrimps.

Soon the vivid wash of green over the enormous paddocks began to fade. February, supposedly the best month of the summer season, had brought no rain to Austin Downs.

I had been watching the plants race through their life cycle in January's 5-centimetre rains. I noticed in particular a little grass with just the one flower — a perfectly symmetrical four-petalled green flower which became a quartered seed pod, containing four little burrs. It took just three weeks.

I wondered if conditions had been right for any of the perennial bushes to germinate. For some of them conditions are right just once in thirty years! Some of those perennials go on to live for three hundred years, if they are cared for, that is. Looking at the land, we were still reluctant to bring back more sheep. Three thousand, moved often, kept bunched together, was enough.

The feed from the germinating annuals — 'green pick' is what it's called up here — was making a difference to our remaining Merinos. We were checking the sheep every two days now the puddles were gone, checking the solar-powered pumps were still working and the windmills as well. The solar-powered pumps were proving a success. They tracked the sun the way a flower does, following the sun from daybreak to dusk. We planned to buy more solar pumps when we could because although sometimes there is not wind enough for windmills, there is nearly always sun enough for solar power.

On these mill runs we have found some sheep that are not ours. It's not unusual here where 'strangers' (as visiting sheep are called) can come from stations several hundred kilometres away. Strangers are usually discovered at the annual muster for shearing and sorted into a separate pen in the yards, where they await collection.

The Austin Downs sheep wander too, and I love the trips out to other stations to retrieve them. I look at the land, of course, and the vegetation but what I really like to see is the other homesteads, their outhouses and their shearing sheds. Some places seem like cousins to the Austin Downs homestead, but in other places the problems of heat, dryness and more people than there is accommodation are solved very differently. Some stations have a single, grand homestead. Other stations have a main house with the other sleeping quarters very close, often placed around a shared garden courtyard.

We had discovered some stranger sheep on a mill run, but they were not Merinos like ours. They were Damaras, fat-tailed meat sheep. They are pretty animals with stipples and spots in tan and black and dark brown. Nonetheless, they are not a welcome sight for any wool producer.

African fat-tailed meat sheep were introduced to Western Australia about twenty years ago by the Department of Agriculture. They are the preferred sheep for live export to the Middle East. For wool producers there is one big drawback to having Damaras nearby: their coarse, coloured hair can contaminate white Merino wool.

The most likely way for contamination to occur is for the two breeds to mate, then the resulting cross-bred lamb, in rubbing against its Merino mother, will contaminate her wool with coarse fibres. Should the lamb later die before it's been spotted by us, we would have no idea that contamination has occurred. And the contaminating fibres are difficult to detect until the wool is made into cloth.

Just recently a firm bought $120,000 worth of wool (that's about 120 bales of wool). This wool would have come from a number of different producers and after the wool was made into fabric, it was found to be contaminated with non-wool fibres from meat sheep. The contaminating fibres had to be picked out of the cloth by hand (after it had been made) at a cost of $50,000. This money had to be refunded by the producers who'd grown the wool!

Merinos and Damaras can be run side-by-side: one of our neighbours has had Damaras for three years now, and not one has gone wandering. It is a mattter of the right fencing and good management. And this is where the dispute often begins. Some Damara breeders don't accept that the Damara requires special fencing. They are bigger animals than Merinos, with the same fence-testing propensity as cross-bred sheep (like the Poll Dorsets we had on the farm) or goats. A six-wire fence will only just hold them, whereas a five-wire fence is fine for Merinos.

Some Damara growers also don't accept that fencing their stock is their responsibility. It adds to the cost of their enterprise considerably. They doubt the likelihood that contamination will occur, they say, and they feel that Merino growers should fence to protect their own stock if they are worried.

At first we found it difficult to understand the Damara growers' perspective. In farming, every farmer's responsibility to fence in their own stock is accepted. But up here in the pastoral country, where fences are hundreds of kilometres long, paying for fencing is far harder. Of economic necessity there has been give and take between neighbours so in bordering paddocks there is always a mix of home and stranger sheep. It's very different from the accepted practice in farmlands.

The pastoralists' practice has worked well in the rangelands while neighbours have the same breed of sheep. But there cannot be the same give and take over shared boundaries when one neighbour's stock could spell ruin to the other's enterprise.

When we first spotted Damaras among our Merinos, we were tempted to shoot them, say nothing and hope that contamination of the wool or the flock hadn't occurred. But in the end we decided that wasn't a good long-term option.

If we did not report the Damaras and then contamination occurred, we would not only lose our registration — our wool clip and our business would become known as dishonest.

So we took the other path, the one of protest. We did not all agree on this path at the start. When the risk of a straying Damara was isolated to one or two found on the property a year, then all of us (except Dad) felt that going public with our concern was hardly a sensible economic choice. But a nearby station's introduction of six thousand Damaras swiftly changed our minds.

This station had just changed hands and immediately began moving from Merinos to Damaras without stock-proofing the fences. And although we only had a short boundary with them, the fences between us and them were one hundred years old and falling down. It took a lot of talking before an agreement to replace the boundary was reached. And before the fencing was completed, they had to muster much of Austin Downs to retrieve their Damaras.

We did not want their choice of enterprises to force us into changing our own. Switching to meat sheep would go against our philosophy: that only the minimum must be taken from the land. Of course, this is Dad's philosophy in particular. He does not look at the land in terms of just his lifetime, or mine, or even his grandchildren. When he says long-term, he often means hundreds of years. And while some people might say that the difference between selling 5 kilos of wool per sheep per year and selling the whole 45-kilogram sheep will have an infinitesimal impact on the land, in Dad's view of the long-term, that impact will count.

We still hope there is a future in white wool in the rangelands. Many of the Damara growers were once woolgrowers themselves, but they have lost faith in the future of the wool industry. This philosophical difference underpins the disagreement over fencing. In their heart of hearts the Damara growers believe their sheep are the right ones for the rangelands, and that the woolgrowers should make the same change.

But despite the philosophical differences and the day-to-day worry over contaminated wool, every pastoralist wants to stay on good terms with neighbours. For we are all on the same side really: all of us are trying to find ways to combine caring for loved land with making an income.

My hopes of more summer rain at Austin Downs had evaporated at the end of a dry February. But then March was a wet month. I could not keep my eyes from the skies, looking and looking to preserve snapshots to treasure when it turned dry again. I saw half of the sunset entirely blotted out by a black cloudburst one evening, and the gum leaves glittered like diamonds in the blue storm light. Feeding the nervous dogs, I watched the lightning shine off the old buildings near their cages. And one night a rain cloud turned rose and lilac by the setting sun and from it streamed shafts of pink rain. I called the men from the shed to see this.

'There's nothing in it,' Kynan observed, meaning that the rain was not reaching the ground, 'but, yeah, it's pretty.'

There had not been more than 30 millimetres all up, but the rain had gone a long way into the warm ground; everywhere I looked it was green. Still, with the month-long gap between rains, much of January's germination had died. What I could see was the annuals, germinating yet again into brief life.

About 2 kilometres from the homestead is a creek which crosses the road. After January's rain it flowed, and now it was running again. This creek line travels tens of kilometres through the scrub, all the way to Lake Austin, which has been nothing more than a huge saltpan these last two years.

I was very surprised to hear that, in wet years, fish can be caught in Lake Austin. How could any fish survive the drought years in this country? Apparently there is a waterhole, so deep it never runs dry, nearly 50 kilometres away on Karbar station. There are always fish there. After heavy rain, this waterhole overflows into creeks which run to other waterholes and eventually to Lake Austin. Now shoals of tiny little fish puckered the slowly running water as they waited for their turn to cross the road on their way to Lake Austin.

The creek is just a millimetre deep over the gravel and very puddly in some places. The little fish have to jump and some jump wrong. We find them stiff and silver in the sun. I wondered how there could be hundreds, just a week after the rain.

The vegetable garden at the orchard was suddenly repaying all Mum's efforts now it had rained. Mum had planted pumpkins, parsley, okra, zucchini, squash, tomatoes, basil, rockmelon, watermelon, beetroot, broccoli and carrots. She had planted at the end of rows, in between the fruit trees and on the bare mounds which awaited the new fruit trees. The pumpkin vines planted by Megs became mini-jungles, their leaves as huge as those in rainforests. There were vines rioting down the banks and herbs poking confidently from the hay mulch. These vegetables were for us to eat, but they also doubled as experimental crops. For we were looking for new crops all the time, new ways to make more dollars.

The hay mulch was downgraded agricultural hay. This is hay that has low nutrition value, so it's not suitable for stock. The hay has made an enormous difference to the soil. When we began work at the orchard, the loamy soil was remarkably empty of life. There was no humus, so there were no earthworms and none of the markers of microscopic life. Now there were earthworms — little white tendrils ran through the soil and the earth clumped together instead of running through our fingers.

For me the vegetable garden was full of little mysteries. Why was it that some of the tiny gold zucchinis rotted, and others did not? Some hours of observation and thinking rewarded me with the rather obvious conclusion that some zucchini flowers accidentally collected water droplets. When that happens, the zucchini rotted slowly away from the flower. I was very proud of myself for working this out! I began ripping open the female flowers on all the vines to let them drain.

With so many pumpkin vines, pollinating the pumpkins took some time. As I pollinated the voluptuous female flowers (with their giveaway blouse 'hey boys' va-voom shaping) with the male flowers, I felt very relieved that the flowers were mostly on the perimeter of the plant. Who knew what lived beneath these vines? There were suddenly hundreds of lizards at the orchard; they had bred up on the insects in the hay mulch.

The perenties are the king of all lizards up here, with their dignified, conquistador face and ungainly walk. The next largest are the bungarras. They are the lizards in all the outback stories that you hear. The ones where a man's dogs accidentally frightens the lizard up the man's body and onto the top of his head and there the lizard clutches on, defying the barking dog and the screaming man. We liked to see them and their winding tracks, as we'd been told that where there are bungarras there are no snakes.

Then there are the little dragons. They run on two legs like tiny dinosaurs, their little bodies seeming to sail upright, their heads remaining utterly, impossibly still.

Not all of the dragons were so quick at that time; some of them had unmistakeably swollen stomachs. I was reminded of the moths I found every morning, their abdomens so swollen with eggs they could no longer fly. It was like a little springtime.

'Look how much closer the horizon is now,' said Mum to me, as we weeded the garden together. 'You can't see as far because the bush is so much thicker!'

This was the first time I had cared for and cooked from a garden as extensive as this. How quickly such a garden shapes the way women use time! The pattern of planting, tending and harvesting, of cooking to store the food. I loved the feeling that stirred in me when I did the things that had been done by woman after woman for generations. Even, and this is a horrible confession, plucking the feathers and removing the innards of roosters. It was in carrying out that particular task when I was about fifteen that I first noticed the feeling of satisfaction and strength that comes from doing this 'women's work'.

Now, of course, I am doing them all the time. Rocking a child to sleep, cutting nails, reading stories, making up games. All of these are part of women's lives everywhere. When Steph visited at Christmas, she and I managed to get five little boys to go to sleep at the same time. We turned to each other with identical smiles of satisfaction because we had both been reminded of one of our favourite games as children. It was a game Grandad taught us. We would always get in trouble afterwards, as it put the hens off the lay, but no amount of bad consequences could ever stop us. It's well known that if you put a chook's head under her wing she will go to sleep. The game involved drawing a circle on the dirt and getting as many chooks as possible to sleep around the ring. We would run the hens down one by one and force their heads under their wings. Once they were all sleeping the idea was to keep them there as long as possible. We would stand there watching like hawks for the slightest awakening movement. If we saw an unsteady rolling or a quiver of a feather, we would quickly set to work, making crooning noises and retucking the puzzled head.

Eventually Mum would be spotted coming towards us, and we would hurriedly shake the hens awake and scuff out the ring mark.

I still remember my annoyance with the hens who continued to look dozy when Mum reached us. We would deny like mad that we had been playing the game, but Mum always knew, she told us later, by the drop in egg numbers. Now, of course, I am

Mum. Mum and Dad are Gran and Grandad. I count myself lucky that we share the same chooks: if we didn't, I'm sure my sons and nephews would have been taught the game by now, and I would have no eggs.

The orchard was growing more and more beautiful, the bush too, but the gardens around the homestead were not. There were empty beds everywhere. The water at the homestead is much saltier than at the orchard, which makes it hard to garden even in raised beds. A thin glitter of salt coats the soil in many places. Mandy's beloved roses died almost on arrival at Austin Downs. Now she uses rainwater and pots to grow any plants that fall out of the 'tough as nails' category.

I'd not been at all successful in my garden — even with pots and rainwater. I had many ideas but the garden seemed to resist somehow those I implemented, and I found myself discarding or forgetting the others. The truth was that I had not bonded with my garden!

In her book *The Rosemary Tree*, my favourite writer Elizabeth Goudge writes:

> He had very soon discovered that one can have very odd sensations while gardening. A close union with the earth seemed to involve one in union with a good deal more than the earth.

I'd not ever felt that in my garden at the homestead, but at the orchard (and Mum and Mandy have felt the same thing) I often felt an approving and interested presence.

Just across from my house is an old sleeping quarters — two bedrooms with a verandah. Even this tiny set of quarters has a raised garden bed made from moulded white stone, perhaps salvaged from one of the nearby ghost towns. I wonder who would have had responsibility for tending this garden. Was it the stockmen themselves? What would they have grown? My guess was vegetables, but then I was far more drawn to the growing of things that can be eaten. Mandy had to remind me often that flowers are food for the spirit! Although I had not yet succeeded with my garden, my determination to do better in the practical realm was finally showing results in the house and kitchen. And in this I was aided by the wealth of fresh produce from the orchard garden. Nothing can be more satisfying than finding your old recipes lifted into art by ingredients just out of the ground or off the vine or freshly cut!

With every meal I grew more confident, and that feeling of confidence soon extended to my house. It is one of those old station cottages. It had begun life as a thick-walled square, divided into four small, equal-sized rooms with verandahs all round. Once the bathroom, laundry and toilet had been located away from the house, but over time verandahs had been enclosed in thin weatherboard to make extra rooms, and the original rooms functioned as passageways as well as living space.

Martin takes up a full one-quarter of any of the original little rooms once he is sitting down, and so we added two more big rooms.

In the small rooms I discovered that furniture was best organised along only two walls in each room: take up a third wall and the room would be cluttered. I discovered that putting out my clothes every night for the day to come and doing the dishes every night made the following day run better.

I began to fill vases with flowers: the pink mulla-mullas, the violet statice, the red — and cream native hops that grows wild around the homestead. Soon I noticed how disconsolate and reproachful a vase of flowers looked set among papery clutter piles! I began to throw away the ever-accumulating clutter so the flowers could rule as they wished.

It seems hardly possible that these discoveries for me could rank in importance with discovering my life direction, and yet they did. And I had made them just in time. I had switched from sending Tim to Cue Primary School to teaching him myself with the support of the School of the Air.

Tim and I drove together to Meekatharra, which is 120 kilometres north of Cue, to enrol him in the School of the Air and also to check on one of my clients at the hospital.

On the long drive I told him stories about the other times he had come to work with me. He liked my stories but he particularly wanted to know about the School of the Air. He is fascinated with the name. But soon he had used up my stock of knowledge, and I directed his attention to the land outside the window.

The rain had worked magic. What a month ago had been a sad twisty tree, a few starved bushes and bare orange ground was now a grassland, enhanced by an ornately carved tree and flowering bushes. There were great, still slabs of water filling the depressions in the flat land. Lake Nallan — which is Cue's place for water sports — was filled nearly to the road's edge.

All this water! The miraculous easing of my spirits at the sight of it was akin to the relaxation I felt on the nights when the house was tidy and the boys sleeping and healthy. Winter was coming: surely there would be rains to follow this rain, and this germination at least would not die.

Past the gigantic, goblin workings of the Saint Barbara's mines we drove, and into Meekatharra. To the hospital first, to see my client, and onto the School of the Air. A dragon lizard had invaded the School of the Air headquarters, much to Tim's delight. I'd not seen one up close before either. It was pale and striped, with an unexpectedly big head, made bigger by frilled ear protrusions.

The School of the Air is a virtual school, really. Soon the radios for which these schools are famous would be replaced by satellite-linked computers. On the walls of the little building I saw noticeboards, brown with gold writing, naming the head boy and girl for every year, and children's work displayed everywhere. There are assemblies (but they happen on air) and merit awards. There is a principal, a receptionist and teachers, although the teachers are often away, visiting their students who may be hundreds of kilometres away.

We went home rich in workbooks and reading books, art materials and toys, radio and antennae. Late that night I unpacked it all and felt increasingly nervous. It was not the prospect of teaching Tim that scared me, but the many workbooks and worksheets. How was I to keep so many pieces of paper organised? I could not help remembering the large messy pile under the stairwell which had served as my locker at school. Surely I could do better this time.

18

TRIAL AND ERROR

'Do you suppose adventures ever have an end?'
JRR TOLKIEN, *THE LORD OF THE RINGS:*
THE FELLOWSHIP OF THE RING

The Big Bell gold mine was shutting down, or downsizing or maybe just resting for a while. We were not certain exactly what was happening. Even Kynan, who is always beforehand with the news of who is buying and who is selling, could not separate rumour from truth. The unmistakeable fact was that people were leaving. The town of Cue, which is, after all, a gold town, was shrinking once more.

These dramatic decreases in size are the lot of mining towns. Many vanish altogether when their mine closes. There was a town called Reedy's, located between Austin Downs and Meekatharra. It had a population of fifteen hundred, two boarding houses, a shopping centre, a hospital, schools and a picture theatre. I knew about it only from local history books because I'd seen no trace of Reedy's at all.

I don't think Cue will disappear, but Cue had lost some important families by the end of that autumn. People who do their bit are just as important to a community as its buildings, and there were a lot of goodbye parties and speeches and presents over a couple of months. One autumn night we all went to Nallan station to say goodbye to Chris and Janine Varly — one of those important families. Chris's job at the mine was finished, so the whole family was moving to another mining town.

As you drive into Nallan station, first you see a dear little cottage. Further in comes the grand main homestead, the front half of which is the old sandstone hospital and the back half the old Cue Shire Hall. Colonial verandahs have been added on, knitting the two old buildings into one. A large shadecloth room containing a swimming pool has also been added onto the house, creating a courtyard at the front of it. Some way beyond, out of sight, are the shearers' quarters.

Perhaps because the people at Nallan, Sandy and Michael Clinch, also run a tourism enterprise, or perhaps just because it was their style, there were party lights on the verandahs, collections of old iron tools grouped around the jacaranda trees, pretty mismatching mats on each large step leading into the house and, in a large wrought iron cage, was a pet rabbit.

The adults sat quietly on the lawn, in a ring of chairs around two big tables. In the darkness beyond the children played, finding a pool table in a bough shed, finding the rabbit on the outskirts of the lawn.

There were no speeches; everyone simply took a turn to say goodbye and thankyou to Janine. Her husband, Chris, had not been able to attend. A volunteer ambulance officer, he was out on a job on his last night in Cue, doing more than his bit once again.

There are people who come to a community but don't put down roots.

'I call them potplanters,' Michael said to me.

It would be easy to be a 'potplanter' if you worked in the mining industry, but Chris and Janine had chosen to put down roots. Even if it was going to be just for a little while, even if it would hurt more when they had to move on.

Michael went on to talk of the experience of leaving loved land, the pull of the old land and the need to bond with the new. Like us, the Clinches were new to Cue. Unlike us, they have always lived on stations. There are few other farmers or pastoralists I could discuss this with: the mobility of the modern worker is still alien to the majority of people who work in farming businesses.

It is hard to leave land that you have become attached to. I tend to put down roots where I live and already I was beginning to worry about what would happen if I had to leave the station. Indeed, I had already begun to feel torn. I had grown to love Austin Downs, but now Tim had begun primary school, boarding school did not seem so far away. And I did not want to live eight hours drive away from my children.

'What's home to you now?' I asked Michael, wondering if he would nominate Nallan station or the station he had left behind.

'Western Australia,' Michael said simply, revealing how far ahead of me he was in his thinking.

Just as easily as the knowledge that you must move on can stop you putting down roots, so can love of land stop you trusting life to take you where you need to go. Michael's way — to be neither a 'potplanter' nor too deep-rooted in only one place — was quite new to me. Straightaway I decided to try and emulate his approach because it is rare to stay in one place through a whole lifetime: you never do know what is to come.

At the orchard we had been trialling tomatoes and rockmelons as new crops. These are both low-earning crops, and although we had no intention of growing such crops when we first came to Austin Downs, the drought had changed our minds. We just needed cash: even the small profit earned from crops such as these would be helpful. We were looking for something that would thrive simply on water and occasional care and fit a niche in the market.

On the advice of food buyers, we had planted a row of rockmelons and a row of tomatoes, hoping to fill the niche markets of late autumn rockmelons and early winter tomatoes.

But some rockmelons rotted where they touched the straw, and our tomatoes vexingly ripened with all the other tomatoes in the State. So while both of these products found local markets, neither proved to be the easy annual crop we were looking for. Instead it was the Jap pumpkins, grown from just those few seeds planted by Megan, that we took to market in Perth.

From twenty vines, not merely neglected but stomped on and sworn at by the men, around whose feet the pumpkin tendrils anarchically curled as they trellised and pruned peaches, came 2 tonnes of pumpkin. Perfect pumpkins, many weighing over 6 kilos, attractively green and speckled and sweet-flavoured from all that summer sun. The fruit and vegetable broker was impressed with their size and their early timing.

The accidental pumpkins were early, but we knew we could make them earlier still. We prepared new ground to plant more Japs in August. In most places this is way too early to plant Japs, but here — where the water comes hot out of the earth and the winter days are warm — we thought we would get away with it. Next year's crop of pumpkins would be among the first to market.

We were relieved beyond telling to have grown something that was just right. Because it wasn't just that our first crop of peaches had not found a market, the feedback on our jujubes was even less promising.

We had spent quite some time regrafting our jujubes as many of them had reverted to tiny-leaved, tiny-fruited root-stock, and we had to to start again. It seemed the bark had grown over the inserted bud on many trees. Grafting is fiddly work. First a bud of the variety required must be harvested from a tree of the right cultivar. Then the bud must be picked clean of all wood. This was a task of excruciating delicacy, during which my fingers had seemed to swell with self-consciousness and become blunt and unfeeling and unable. But finally what you have left is a 2-millimetre long bud of soft green flesh.

The root-stock tree is then pruned a little, a cut is made in the trunk, and the cultivar bud is pushed in to nest against the growing wood that is revealed by the cut. The wound is gently bound, and all you can do then is hope that it will take.

Jujubes fruit twice a year. It was now time for their second fruiting, which proved far heavier than the first. With great expectations Kyn and Mandy took the jujubes to Perth for a market test. With Perth's high Asian population, we felt confident of finding a strong local market. We were wondering too about a 'lunchbox' market. Jujubes are small and sweet, with the highest vitamin C content of any fruit. But the feedback we received could hardly have been worse. The fruit-buyers who had not seen jujubes before were not impressed. One man said they were so underdeveloped that they were 'the equivalent of the crab-apple to the apple'. The Asian buyers said that our jujubes had been picked too early, were too dry and, finally, were the wrong varieties for the Asian market.

It's always hard to listen to such negative feedback, take it in, and work from there. And of course, because we were one of the first Australian business trying to grow jujubes in such quantities, we had been able to find no one prepared to share their knowledge. It seemed that our long hours of research and thinking, planting and caring had been in vain.

Were we going to have to begin again on the jujubes? Prune back to root-stock and graft on new varieties? Should we look for another new crop entirely?

In the end we could not bring ourselves to give up on the jujubes. We knew we needed that brand new product to run alongside the peaches and we could not forget the chart showing the link between product availability and price. Our variety of jujubes might be wrong for the Asian market, but perhaps they would suit Western palates. And surely we would be able to fix their dryness by the next harvest.

So we changed the watering regimen for the trees and experimented with a different style of pruning. And we drew comfort from the fact that Kynan's scholarship (which had been written by Mandy before Ben was born) would take him to China, where he could buy some trees of the right variety.

Then China too joined the list of countries that the Department of Foreign Affairs recommended against visiting. Indeed, none of the original countries on his list were good places to go in 2003 because of the fears surrounding either SARS or international terrorism. So Kyn and Mandy decided to go to to California instead, where jujubes have been grown commercially for over fifty years. They grew them there for nutriceuticals, health food, and juice. Perhaps these would be things we could do too.

It was time to plant the new peaches: not trees, but seed. We had decided that if the trees were grown at Austin Downs they were likely to be more resilient, and seeds are much cheaper than trees. We could still develop the orchard but spend less of our rapidly decreasing captial to do so. The meeting in which we developed the design for growing the peach seeds was a triumph of synergy. It took half an hour to put together a comprehensive plan for irrigation, planting design, and the degree of mounding that would be required.

We designed our own irrigation system for this: the thin pierced tubes, 'state of the art' though they were, had not worked. Finally, I was beginning to understand those growers who flood-irrigated their plants. I'd felt those practices were unsustainable because so much water was wasted that way. But as we lost trees to water starvation, I realised that flood-irrigation was the easiest way to be sure plants were getting enough water. That said, we believed this new irrigation mechanism would work better; indeed, as the plan was committed to paper we all felt sure every detail would work.

And it did. The 3000 peach seeds — like slivered almonds — were planted in two days into low seed beds. There were four at each point of a square, set around an irrigation point designed to ooze water four ways. When I looked down at the seedbed, I saw butterfly shapes strung along a black pipe — the water had gently washed the ground into four linked circles at each irrigation point. And at the tip of each 'wing' a peach tree was growing.

As they emerged from the ground, the baby peach trees looked like the tip of an artist's brush — curled-up feathers, dipped in crimson and jade, slowly unfurling as they grew. They had to be watered every day and the trees were at first so tiny it looked as if they were bathing in the warm water, rather than just drinking it. The peach nursery rapidly became everyone's favourite part of the orchard, although it didn't have a lot of competition. The adult peaches were dormant — simply a collection of branches and twigs, row upon row, with the occasional cluster of wrinkled leaves sitting atop a high twig like a tattered nightcap. The jujubes were dormant too. They had black thorns on grey stems and were as elegant as bonsai, even without their softening green fronds.

Beyond the irrigation fence and all over Austin Downs, the green was browning off once again. We had brought back some of our agisted sheep, but not all. As the puddles dried in the paddocks, we had to restart the mill runs. Among the brown paddocks was the occasional area of wetland. Water birds rose shrieking from the long rushes as we drove past; mosquitos noisily clouded the air.

And at the homestead there were butterflies: they were back at last! Our first butterflies in over two years. During our first summer they had seemed a manifestation of the butterflies in our stomachs, so anxious were we about the outcome of our move to Austin Downs. Now they were evidence that the drought was easing. It would not be over for sure until there were several consecutive heavy rains, but there was more feed than there had been. Rain was coming, but intermittently, as if rainfall were the responsibility of a slapdash gardener (like me), who remembers only to water when she sees a plant dying.

The butterflies hung languidly from the flowering trees, occasionally exchanging one tree for another, but in a casual and haphazard way. What a striking contrast to their businesslike attitude as caterpillars! The little boys caught them carefully to take them to nine-month-old Ben, so he could admire their white-speckled black bodies and orange wings. Then they would let them go so he could watch their slow rise back to the trees.

The past two years had begun to take a toll on the men's bodies. Heavy physical work means that the men are fitter, healthier and stronger just as athletes are, but it also puts them at greater risk. If one man went down, the other two men had to do his share of the heavy physical work. And that put them at risk of injury too. Being one man down is a risk factor for the other men, and so for the business. So as much as possible, the women did some of that extra work.

Dad and Martin had both been injured; now it was Kynan's turn. For the latest straggler muster we had arranged that Martin would be rouseabout and classer for the single shearer, but the shearer foiled our plans by arriving early. Martin had left for the irrigation and would not be back for some hours. So, for the first time since having children, I got to be the rouseabout, while Kynan classed the wool, a job that would not overtax his injured back.

It was very noisy in the shed. The generator is probably older than the shearing shed itself. It has the uninhibited regular thumping of the very old engine. The smaller engine driving the clippers sings over this bass with a dentist-drill whine, then there are the yelled comments of the men and the worried cries of the sheep.

Being shorn can't be the nicest of experiences. First the belly is done, separate to the rest of the fleece. The rouseabout must grab the belly wool from the floor without startling the sheep, then skirt it quickly (which on the belly means to take off the most stained wool, which goes into its own pile), and throw the belly wool into the belly basket. There is a place for everything in a shearing shed.

Then the shearer stretches back the sheep's neck to run the clippers up the midline of the sheep and over its throat. The long clipper strokes are called 'blows' and the one over the sheep's throat is the blow that requires the most skill of all. Then the head is done, and the shearer works back down one side of the sheep, pushing back the wool from the skin on the forelegs, shoulders and then down to the hind leg. The clippers saw in little blows until the shearer can take one long blow up the animal's curved spine to work on its other foreleg. The shearer leans right over the sheep with his weight partly taken through a knee on the sheep's stomach as he does this.

('Would you want a really big bloke shearing sheep?' I ask Kyn. 'The big blokes can be very quick,' he answers, 'but sometimes when sheep have had a big bloke with a knee on them, they get out into the yards and they just collapse. Punctured lungs.')

Now the fleece is unpeeled down the back, then the final hind leg is done.

It is the fleece from the hind legs that the rouseabout must first find and grasp in each hand. Then the rouseabout swarms their arms and body around the rest of the fleece, walks to the shearing table and casts the fleece out, still grasping the hind legs. This is called throwing the fleece.

I get a lot of satisfaction from a perfect pick-up and throw. A perfectly thrown fleece should lie underside up and spread out on the table of steel rods, ready for skirting and classing. I am not a tall person; for Martin and Kynan, both well over 190 centimetres tall, the fleece simply needs to be flicked and dropped. For me, 30 centimetres shorter, achieving a perfect throw requires both concentration and luck.

Once on the table the fleece must be skirted. This means that the fleece is cut so that the wool around the base of the legs and backside runs in a continuous line from which it is easy to strip the dags, the stains and the prickles. The wool from the head has its own pile too. The fleece must also be checked over for strips of pink skin. There is not too much skin. The shearer is doing well, I think. But then one sheep is cut badly. The whine of the shearing stand is shut off, Kynan runs to hold the sheep still, and the shearer pulls out needle and thread to sew the wound closed.

'Mop up, Jo, quick!' Kyn shouts, for bloody wool doesn't have a pile, it must be thrown outside; it's the only wool for which there is no market at all.

In seconds the wound is closed, the rest of the sheep is shorn, and the bloody wool cast out a nearby window. As the morning goes on, my throws get better and better. Then the job is done, and the generator engine is shut off and slowly cranks down. In the sudden silence my eardrums continue to pulse, as if the barrage of sound jolt them still.

The morning's school had been rescheduled to the afternoon. Tim and I sat down together. His work arrives in blue bags, organised into 'sets', each with a theme. We were studying turtles right now. I told him about his first birthday party, for which we had returned to the Islands. Martin's mum had cooked turtle meatloaf.

Each set came with many books — reading books, maths books, handwriting books — which were all cross-referenced back and forth. Each day started with physical education, moved onto writing time, then project work, then maths, then art. Once a day Tim would have an air lesson. It started with a rollcall. Children were carefully encouraged to speak in full sentences on air.

'Tim is here. Good morning Mrs Morling and everyone else, over.'

Then comes the lesson.

'Turn to page 15 in your Monday air lesson book. At the top of the page you will see a picture of a jungle. Tell me when you've found it.'

And the quick, simultaneous responses:

'Megan has it, over.'
'Tim has it, over.'
'Joshua has it, over.'
'PJ has it, over.'
'Katie has it, over.'
'Matthew has it, over.'

And so it goes on for half an hour.

Often the school cannot hear us. 'Sun spots,' says the weather bureau. And soon there will be no more lessons over the air in this State: the school satellite disk was waiting outside my house for its computer. The new year would bring the teacher's voice into the home far more effectively with no crackles. The children would even be able to collaborate on assignments!

For the turtle project we drew turtles, made turtles, did turtle maths, learned about turtles' lives. Tim decided to make a non-fiction book for his project, and on his grandad's suggestion researched turtle migration patterns. When we discovered that turtles got caught in fishing nets and drowned, Tim was horrified and upset. (The story of the birthday turtle meatloaf was no longer a favourite.) I could find nothing that would bring him solace. Eventually his Auntie Megan suggested he wrote to the Minister for the Environment to ask for 'Australia's position' on protecting turtle corridors. The letter took a long time to write but the arduous task of typing seemed to bring him comfort. And the letter in return more comfort, for Australia is doing its best for turtles.

My struggles to keep Tim's work orderly were noted by Mrs Morling. One day little folders arrived in the mail with instructions on how to use them to achieve the most efficient organisation. I was not surprised at this thoughtfulness; by then I had discovered the lengths the teachers would go to support the 'home tutors'. A casual mention of one of Tim's special interests would see a computer game on that very subject arrive the next week. A request for an extension would lead to the writing of a new workbook. Reporting a difficulty in teaching a particular subject would be rewarded with 'how-to' articles, phone calls and visits from support officer Sylvia Byers. She is a woman so remarkable that she should be 'sent out with General Despatch', as one mother said. General Despatch is the very first post you receive from the School of the Air: it contains the essential equipment for the schoolroom.

When Mrs Morling came to visit (the teachers visit twice a term to assess the children), Sylvia came too. I confessed to her my worries over my poor organisational skills, my anxiety that I was not providing my boys with an education the equal of metropolitan children. Sylvia listened as actively as a hunting fox: nothing less than a gunshot overhead could have broken her concentration.

'School of the Air children go on to do very well. They win more than their fair share of scholarships. It's an excellent curriculum. This is a first-class education that you are providing here.' Sylvia's words are always delivered with verve and authority. I was comforted straightaway and even more comforted later when I discovered she is a famous innovator in education, known Australia-wide.

'What is it that you ask of Tim?' she asked. I answered a little incoherently, because I ask so many things of him. Sylvia held up a finger and continued, I could tell this was something she said often.

'Do you ask him for perfection? No. So don't try for perfection yourself. You simply ask him to try his best, whatever his best is on that day. It's about getting it done. You do that — and that's all you can do — and Tim will be fine.'

How quickly Sylvia had pegged me as a perfectionist! It is not a helpful trait. Just lately I had come to see that it was perfectionism that led to my battles in the practical realm. When there was not time to make something 'perfect', I felt too discouraged to undertake it at all. Only when I began to aim at 'better' and 'good enough' (which I had a chance of achieving), would I feel confident enough to begin such a task as cleaning the kitchen.

Now I saw I had brought this same trait into the schoolroom and had been inflicting my perfectionism on Tim. (And Sylvia must have known this too!) How lucky I was that he was resilient enough to stay interested despite this discouraging approach. I realised that I needed to change my focus from 'how can he be taught to do this perfectly' to 'how do I provide Tim with what he needs to find learning satisfying and do whatever his best might be on that day'.

One way was to allow Tim to choose his own rewards for enthusiasm and persistence. At the end of the turtle set, Tim announced that as a reward he wanted a fire outside. Martin and the little boys built a fire. I half-cooked potatoes ready to wrap in tinfoil, and from somewhere Mandy found six sparklers.

The evenings were becoming chilly now. Cold enough to remind us of how very cold it would be when winter arrived in just a few weeks. The fire, which Martin had trapped in a grill, glowed as orange as the dirt around the homestead, the smoke mixing with the dust kicked up by the boys as they ran with their sparklers into the darkness.

'Twinkle, twinkle little star,' we sang to Ben, as he watched the sparklers fountain in the darkness, and the stars in the sky overhead. Then it was suddenly too cold; the children began to cough, and we went inside leaving the fire to burn out in the cold night under the stars.

Suddenly it was winter. Cold days, and colder nights, the coldest winter so far at Austin Downs. Now and again it rained. How quietly this desert country responds to winter rain! I had only seen before the busy puddles, joyously noisy paddocks and sudden green brought by summer rain. Winter rain is met with a hush. Puddles are still and the greening of the land slow. The cold wet air became thicker with distant human noises. The low engine sounds from the Big Bell mine were suddenly closer, but there was no sound from the birds and geckos, the frogs and beetles.

Soon it would be time for Kynan, Mandy, Lachlan and Benjamin to fly from our winter to the North American summer. Jujube growers had offered homes and farms and factories: would their success be something that could be copied in Australia? For this trip would not just benefit us, Kynan and Mandy's report was to be published Australia-wide. But, of course, we felt that their findings were of more concern to us than anyone else. Would our many rows of jujubes ever make a return?

A few weeks before their trip, Mandy decided that we were all becoming dull with work and that it was time for play. So one morning, carrying sausages and sauce and matches, we drove to Junga Pool on a nearby station. I was running low on enthusiasm — so low that Mandy had needed to take me and my children in her own car to stop me from weaselling out of the expedition.

Surely, I thought, there had not been enough rain for this pool to be particularly nice. In my mind were mosquitos and mud and scratchy, browning rushes and all the things I still needed to do in my house. The country we drove through to reach Junga Pool was in poor health — overgrazing, poor planning of roads and mining had led to great eroded scours, red and hard, bare of life. My heart sank a little more.

Then in the distance I saw a great line of trees. As we approached, I saw that Junga Pool was not a pool but a wide canal of blue water stretching well out of sight in both directions. Tall trees and rich banks of rushes and red granite rocks bordered both edges of the water.

Later, at an environmental planning sesssion involving half a dozen station families nearby, I was to discover this canal was the heart of the Junga system, and it was so full of water precisely because of the poor land surrounding it. When the scrub and top soil is thin, little rain soaks in. It becomes run-off instead and travels to the lowest point in the landscape. The run-off from the Junga system goes on to produce more damage. In the wettest years it floods through kilometres of bush to reach Austin Downs, stripping topsoil and seeds, which results in more bare patches, which again produces more run-off. Breaking this kind of cycle, wherever it occurs, is the shared goal of the local station owners.

But on this day I was not thinking of anything except how glad I was that Mandy had persuaded me to come here for a picnic. The family from Annean station were there already. The fire was down to coals and ready for cooking, the smoke wisping over the water. The picnic spot was near a little rocky promontory. The boys climbed up the rocks then down to the water's edge, where they sat, calling out to us at the sight of the fish flashing silver around the red rocks, of the ducks at takeoff, and even at the sight of the weed in the water.

After the sausages were cooked and eaten, we left the fathers to mind the fires and the babies, and we (Mandy, Melissa from Annean station and me) took our boys for a walk.

We walked north along the river, bending beneath low branches, picking up rock pieces crumbling from the granite rocks that line the water and throwing them in a vain attempt to reach the far bank. Our eyes skimming over the blue flat water had been deceived into thinking it was not far, but it was well beyond throwing distance. The canal was probably 150 metres across.

We found ourselves before a ledge extending into the water. The water was shallow above it then invitingly and suddenly deep. And the day was hot, as winter days can be in the desert. How cold would the water be? How would the reeds feel on bare soles? Would we always regret it if we did not take this chance to swim, with nothing but sky and space around us?

I said that I was going in and that Tim and Sam could each come in with me. I put a foot toward the water and felt the chill air just above it.

'You've promised the boys now,' Mandy reminded me.

So in I went — in we all went. The water was gaspingly cold, the reeds soft on the soles of my feet, and when I came out of the water, I felt free and eased and heartened, ready for the days to come.

19

PEACH-PICKING TIME

'My long two-pointed ladder's sticking through a tree
Toward heaven still,
And there's a barrel that I didn't fill
Beside it, and there may be two or three
Apples I didn't pick upon some bough.
But I am done with apple-picking now.'

ROBERT FROST, 'AFTER APPLE-PICKING',

SELECTED POEMS

It's peach-picking time once more, but how different to last year! We know what we are doing, and it seems that the peach trees do too. The peaches are bigger and smoother and brighter. They are hung at regular intervals on trunk and twigs. Those on the trunk hug into the wood like clams on a rock.

We are picking them riper this year. We have discovered that when a peach is ready, it pulls easily from the tree. At the moment of separation of peach from tree comes a most satisfying sound: a sweet, woody 'thunk'.

Our days are spent picking and sorting. Tim is on holiday from school, and the children climb on the sorting table and sort with us. Our peaches have found a good market: they are finally reaching the kitchens and tables of foodies, the very market we have so long wished to supply.

Indeed, the previous few months had brought much good news. First came Mandy and Kynan's letter from America. In their absence we had transplanted the jujubes: spacing them more widely to grow them hedge-style. As we worked, we wondered if this effort — if any of our efforts with this crop — were going to prove worthwhile. How wonderful it was to read their first long letter to us:

Dear everyone

We are currently in Dallas, Texas, and loving it. The boys are being angels. Texas is a much larger and more multicultural version of Perth, except there are bigger utes and houses. It is a very friendly town, and people smile more than in Los Angeles. This is not surprising as in LA there is concrete from ground to clouds, and it is smoggy and noisy. Texas is green, open and relatively quiet.

Yesterday was a highlight of our trip! We met Chris Jacobson, who has done a lot with the Jujube and wants to work with us! He has made anti-ageing moisturising creams and capsules, and both sell well. Once people have tried the product they come back — the hard part is getting people to try the product. Heavy marketing is required. Also more research into the chemical composition of the jujube is needed. The research into the moisturiser and melanomas is exciting. There are two active ingredients in the moisturiser that have been show to reduce cancer cells. More research is required. Here is a list of the products he has made:

Wine (not so good)

Tonic

Jujube leathers/jerky (yummy and could be good for
lunchboxes)

Tea (sells well)

Capsules

Moisturiser

Honey

Juice (a good seller when marketed)

Chocolate and carob bars. (These sold very well when marketed for a premium. Chris spent money on good packaging and it went well, but he won't do this anymore as he philosophically disagrees with mixing a health product with chocolate.)

The varieties he uses are Lang, Li, Sherwood and a medicinal variety that we will need to look into. It has small fruit and grows well. This may be our root-stock.

I joyfully read and reread this letter. It was quickly followed by Mandy and Kyn's return. They brought with them sample products. We eagerly drank the juice and the tea, applied the moisturiser (lovely), gave Gran the anti-ageing capsules to try. (She says they really seem to help.)

We were really just beginning with our jujubes. We had learned how to grow them. But being able to grow the fruit was not enough. It seemed that the value-added market promised more than the fruit itself, though we believed that we could still earn well from the fruit alone. But now we had to research the Australian value-added market. We needed to test the DNA of all our varieties and our root-stock and perhaps graft on more varieties. Choose our products. Learn how to make them. It was going to take more money and more time.

As Mandy and Kynan returned, the trees in the orchard woke. The peach trees flowered first. At first the jujubes sent forth leaves but soon they were blooming and bursting in the dry, warming air. Spring had come, but there had been no rain for many weeks. The only clouds were stripes of white against the hard blue; sometimes a high fog fuzzed the sky over.

The drought went on. It had been the worst dry, they said, in one hundred years. And in the light of this, the Federal government declared that the Southern Rangelands (the area into which we fell) was eligible for 'exceptional circumstances funding'. This funding would help. It would provide some income support and assist with interest rates on loans.

Despite the drought, there were flowers. Where the autumnal rain had been heaviest and where puddles had lain for many weeks, there were scatterings of flowers. I liked especially the masses of tiny pink flowers that overlaid the red dirt. Each plant was no more than 10 centimetres high, each flower only a few millimetres across. Where they grew, the land looked lilac, not red, from a distance.

I've been told that in a wet year the wildflowers grow as a big as a man's fist. Tiny as these pink flowers were, I could not help feeling they were a promise that someday the wildflower carpets would return. The forecasts for the coming summer season suggested that it would be a poor one. But one day I would be able to say to my children, 'Listen to the rain. The sound of rain is the sound of grass growing. And the sound of grass growing is the sound of coins clinking in the bank.'

But, then again, my boys aren't growing up on our old farm. At Austin Downs we do not need rain for our orchard; we don't need it to rain to hear those coins clinking.

All our research on transport and figs suggested that we would be able to find a way to get the figs to market on time. Our figs would ripen in early December and give us a good niche market. We will send them to Perth, accompanied by the bulk commodity of rockmelons or perhaps herbs. Even small sheaves of herbs sell well and ours, grown under a desert sun, are very aromatic. Thus the cost of fuel can be covered by the rockmelons or herbs, and the substantial profit from the figs will be the cream on top.

The figs were placed alongside the baby peach trees in the tree nursery. Just as with the peaches, we were all waiting for the first leaves to show. With figs, whole large leaves unfurl over days from the cutting stick, much like a butterfly hatching from a cocoon on a leafless twig. I was looking forward to showing this to Tim and Sam because they had worked hard to get the cuttings into the ground. They had counted out and carried the sticks to the adults, dipping them into striking gel and slipping them into the holes.

Next it was time to thin the peaches. Thinning is often described as a job you should give to your enemy. It is only your enemy who could be ruthless enough to rub out the many flowers that must go if the few remaining fruit are to reach a marketable size. Last year we had not thinned sufficiently. Our peaches had been too small — partly as a result of this and partly because it was a first crop. This year we were determined to thin as ruthlessly as an enemy might.

Yet on that first day of thinning, my hands hovered in an agony of indecision above every tiny peach inside its flower. I had memorised the rules. On every stem you should have only two or three peaches. Those fruit must have as much distance between them as possible. But what should I do when you have a branch where all flowers are clustered together at one end? I longed to bend the rules. I wanted to transplant peaches so that there could be, after all, three peaches strung at intervals along the branch. But under these circumstances only one peach could be allowed to grow. I found that I was screwing my face tight as I nipped the surplus flowers from the wood.

As the days went on I grew quicker. Repetition dulled my angst as I culled each flower, but I was glad when thinning was finished. Now we just had to keep pruning the trees so the sun reached the fruit. In one hundred days the Tropic Snow peaches would ripen. Our new variety of peaches, the UF Gold, would ripen ahead of them, because they go from flower to fruit in just seventy days.

Life on Austin Downs was beginning to fall into a pattern, which wavered a little as we continued to add and subtract elements of our business and our lives, but growing more distinct all the time. I knew that every September would see us mustering for shearing, pruning peaches, planting rockmelons and other annual crops, and mulching trees for the summer months. This September we also had to build the infrastructure for irrigating rockmelons and fix kilometres of fencing. But for next year that work would already be done.

So each month had a few main jobs that had to be done, in addition to the routine of checking mills, sheep and fences, and watering, pruning and weeding the orchard. But on top of the main jobs we will have to build the infrastructure for each enterprise. One day the infrastructure will all be in place, and we will spend our time just on the main tasks and the routine jobs. But that day is still some years away.

I have joined the attenuated community of the School of the Air. The Meekatharra branch stretches all the way to the Northern Territory border, and serves fifty-four children over 540,000 kilometres. I attended my first Cluster Camp, where families close to each other (relatively speaking) converge on one station for two days of learning and social activities. Tim, Sam and I went to Challa station, land that has belonged to the Dowden family since it became a pastoral station. This is a very unusual thing and a comforting thing, too: it says that drought can be survived and that families can stay on good terms despite hardship. But what particularly struck me was the tidiness of the homestead. The lawns were precisely clipped — they rose high above the swept dirt — and there was an archaeological sense of generations of lawns beneath, lawns played on by generations of Dowden children.

In the grounds were old and special treasures cared for by the children of each generation: a little windmill that pumped water, ancient living tree houses where wood and iron had long united.

The Dowdens were building a new shearing shed. Designed, says Debbie Dowden, by the collective wisdom of the family, the visiting shearing teams and the shearing shedbuilder, and her own strong preference for a shed that is good for holding twenty-first birthday parties. This is confidence in the future!

The Dowdens are not just sheep people. Debbie and her husband were both pilots and ran an aerial mustering business in addition to their main enterprise. There were two other families on camp. They, too, had extra enterprises. Anne and her husband from Kirkalocka station ran a tourism enterprise; Kirsten is a practising vet, and she and her husband also kept pigs.

Just as comforting as the fortitude of the Challa homestead was the sense that these people were like us. Their talk was of caring for the land, of experimenting and building enterprises, of revitalising these arid rangeland communities. All of it reminded me of the talk around the dinner tables at Austin Downs and resonated with my own beliefs. These families were all on their own journey, but it was a journey a lot like ours. I felt a kinship with these women that went beyond those first common factors of station life and the School of the Air.

I was particularly curious to meet the children. Some research indicated that children from stations were less socially advanced. It suggested that they had difficulties talking to their peers, were awkward in groups and more prone to misreading social cues. Not what I wanted for my children! But that visit put my mind at rest — there were six teachers present, but the children still preferred to be with each other.

They shared that confidence that was so often part of country children's characters. It was the confidence that came from competence, but there was another dimension to their behaviour too. And I quickly realised that it stemmed from having meaning in their daily lives, from knowing that their family was on an adventure of which they were an important part.

Behind the Challa homestead stood a long array of solar panels. Somehow they did not look alien, because station homesteads are all about acknowledging the power of the sun. The solar array stood like flat-faced sisters, and looked oddly crestfallen when the sun set.

Soon, I knew, there would be just such an array at Austin Downs. When the Big Bell mine went, so would the twenty-four-hour power to the homestead. Already, we were making room for the huge batteries in the old workmen's quarters near my house.

But for the long-term Dad had an alternative solution: he wanted to build a solar pond. They were not well known, but their advantage over solar cells was enormous. They worked day and night, so neither the very expensive batteries nor back-up generator power were required.

Solar ponds are used in other parts of the world but there were only a few in Australia. And it was easy to see why: a solar pond is hardly an 'off the shelf' item. It takes up a lot of land, so the land must be very low-cost. A very large supply of saltwater is required, and the sun must reach the water most days of the year. In the parts of Australia where this power is most required, these are not the prevailing environmental conditions. But at Austin Downs, land, saltwater and sun were in plentiful supply: it would be a perfect match!

Like all alternative power solutions, solar ponds are cheap to run: it's getting them set up that is so expensive! We were gently trying to interest government agencies in helping us: a pond on

Austin Downs could easily power Cue and nearby mines also, replacing the huge unsustainable diesel generators.

Sustainability was our goal in the pastoral enterprise too. Three years of reading books about this land, talking to pastoralists and scientists and, of course, reading the land itself, and we thought we knew how to set about ensuring that Austin Downs was a working station five hundred years from now. We believed that sheep and all other grazing animals should be allowed to eat only what was surplus to the requirements of the ecosystem for survival and regeneration. This was commonsense, of course! It was finding ways to achieve this on Austin Downs that required so much new thinking. But finally we had a plan! First we had to gain control over all the grazing animals: the sheep, the goats and the kangaroos. If the animals were not controlled, then the land could not be properly rested between periods of intense grazing.

Many people believe that animals can be kept out of resting paddocks simply by turning off the waters in those paddocks. But goats and kangaroos can travel many kilometres without water. There is some anecdotal evidence that a well-insulated sheep (perhaps with a double or triple fleece) can go days without water. Even in these drought years, when the many natural pools and rockholes on Austin Downs had dried up, we had found that turning off the water doesn't keep animals out of a paddock. We were going to have to put in fences, really good fences, to control not just sheep and goats, but the kangaroos.

On the great map of Austin Downs on Mum and Dad's spare table, Dad had drawn in where each new fence was to go, and where the old fences could remain. Each had been plotted so it would divide each ecosystem from the other. And each new paddock was sufficiently large that enough resting time would be possible. Once these new paddocks were fenced, each ecosystem would be able to have exactly the amount of rest and grazing that it required.

We didn't completely understand the requirements of each ecosystem. We needed to know how to monitor the status of each. How would we estimate how much feed was available? How would we know when plants had been eaten down so that their growing points were exposed, but not too exposed? No one had this precise information: it was knowledge that we would have to develop ourselves.

A program as extensive and expensive as this as would take us many years to put in place. But it was cutting-edge stuff, which qualified us for a 'natural resources innovation' grant. So Dad had submitted an application to help us fund the new and upgraded fences, some new water supplies that would modify the grazing patterns, and more training in 'reading the rangelands'. Receiving this grant would let us put our vision into effect much more quickly. But we knew what we wanted to do: we were making a beginning, and we would slowly keep on.

We decided to revisit the marketing of our peaches. The drought meant that the profit from the peaches was far more critical to our survival than it had been in those far-off days when we had planned the orchard. We rang Deborah Pitter, whose company, Business Today, specialises in marketing agricultural products. She could give us an hour, she said, and she refused to charge for her time. 'We don't do the small volumes you are producing at this stage. You are going to have to do it yourselves,' Deborah informed us. 'All I can do is tell you what I think you should do. Tell me how it goes. And when you are big enough for export markets, we can do business then.'

We followed her advice precisely. She gave us a list of growers' markets to call. She told us to emphasise the growing conditions of sun and more sun. Mandy made the calls and reported that every proprietor sounded interested, but that one man had been particularly interested.

'Promise me,' he said to her, 'that you will bring me some of those peaches. Tony at the Herdsman Fresh Essentials. Please don't forget us.'

Shearing was carefully timed to finish just before peach-picking began. Our hopes for the wool clip were not high. We had set for ourselves the goal of a 5-kilogram fleece for each sheep, but there seemed little chance that our sheep could grow a good fleece in these conditions. We continued our program of resting and grazing paddocks. But we could see that in one way at least the program was working because there were lambs — far more than we had hoped for, and they were all big and healthy.

And then came the very surprising results of shearing. The average weight of our fleeces was 4.8 kilos. One hundred and three bales of wool came from just under four thousand sheep. Even a dip in the wool market couldn't quite shake our pleasure because it was clear that our new management style was working: these were excellent results for a drought year.

The peaches were ripening fast. We picked four trays of our best Tropic Snow peaches and one tray of the new UF Gold. The ripe UF Gold glowed rose and apricot but this first crop was small, half the size of this year's Tropic Snows. We liked their taste, but to us it did not compare with the flavours of our Snow peaches. (All our concerns over losing flavour if we grew the peaches larger had proved groundless.) We had included the Golds just to show Tony that we aimed to grow a range of fruit.

Mum and Dad took these five good trays to Tony at the Herdsman Fresh Essential in Perth. Mum and Dad walked through to the back of the market in search of Tony, noting the troubling perfection of every piece of produce displayed. Were our peaches going to be good enough?

After the meeting Mum relayed the story to us over the mobile phone.

'When we showed Tony the trays he went straight to the box of little Golds.

'He picked one up and sank his teeth in. There was juice everywhere. "These are beautiful," he declared. And he called over two of the girls who worked there. "Taste these," he said, giving them one each. He told them where we lived, and how it takes a lot of sun to grow this kind of taste. He told them we were new growers.

'Of course, your father and I were just dying for Tony to taste a Tropic Snow. But he hardly looked at them, he just said casually, "Of course we'll take them. I'm very familiar with this variety, I know they are sweet and I know yours will be sweeter than most."

'He explained his buying policy to us. The fruit comes in ripe, goes out that day. His market is based on everything being ready to eat and tasting good. The people who go to the Herdsman buy their fruit and vegetables daily. They don't want to wait for a tray of peaches to ripen. They want to hand a peach to their children to eat as they walk from the shop.

'Eventually he gave us a bit of feedback on the Tropic Snows. He said we had to pick riper, that they needed to be a bit larger, but that we were beginning growers growing in the right place so he was going to look after us. He asked what else we were growing. We said, "Figs." He said he'd take them. We talked about the jujubes, and he said he'd give them a try. He said he would take our rockmelons and our Japs.'

'How much a tray?' I asked Mum.

'It never came up,' she confessed apologetically. 'It was just so exciting hearing that he would buy them that we forgot to ask! We were just so pleased!'

We found a carrier that would take our small loads of peaches (thirty trays a time) down to Perth every Thursday. And on

Sundays Mum and Dad would take down another load. On these trips they left our 'seconds' peaches at the roadhouses and hotels: where they were sold on. The cost of the fuel was nearly covered by the earnings from the seconds peaches.

But, regardless of fuel costs, we knew we must keep in touch with our market. Mum and Dad walked through the shop to check that our peaches were ripe and unblemished, that they were selling. They spoke to Tony, but never did they seem to get around to the subject of how much we would be paid per tray.

In the next year we would have around eighteen hundred trays of Tropic Snow and four hundred trays of UF Gold to sell. It was a lot more fruit and a lot more work. We would also have to graft a cultivar onto the root-stock peaches that were growing in the peach nursery and then replant them.

In two to three years time we will be producing too many peaches for the local market. It will be time to find an export market — that will be another layer of learning. So we still have a lot to do, and a lot to learn. The Austin Downs peach enterprise is just beginning.

How will we be able to do all this with just six pairs of hands? We don't think we will be able to in the long-term. Mum and Dad often remind us that they are rapidly approaching sixty. Those words actually mean, 'We need to slow down.' The need for extra help is growing more urgent all the time. The challenge will be finding a way of paying for the extra hands if the drought goes on.

Dad is talking of offering tours on Austin Downs. It would be another income stream for the business; work that won't require him to heft shovels or ride motorbikes for days on end, and work that would fit in with sheep-checking and mill runs.

In the New Year we will discuss all of this in earnest. But right now our days are taken up with peaches, moving sheep and weaning lambs. We begin work at five o'clock; we stop at six o'clock each night.

At night Martin and I are reading *The Hobbit* to Tim and Sam over dinner. Unlike their Auntie Stephanie, they showed no sign of screaming as the back of the cave split open. They don't seem to find it a particularly scary book; instead, they find it funny. Indeed, I think it was written to suit the humour of little boys. When the trolls insulted one another at Gandalf's connivance, Tim and Sam laughed so loudly they could not hear the next insult.

I tell the boys that we are on a journey a little like Bilbo's. I say they are part of a company of eleven adventurers. Grandad and Gran and Great-gran, Uncle Kyn, Auntie Mandy, Lachlan and Benjamin, Dad, Mum, Tim and Sam. Some days I say that the journey is halfway through; some days I say it is only just beginning. The truth is that I don't know for sure where we are on our adventure. But I do know that I could not have had better companions.

In the few spare moments between peaches and sheep, we were preparing for a party. For, after Christmas (our third here) Austin Downs will be *en fête*. Family and friends — lifelong and new — are coming to Austin Downs to stay and celebrate with us.

The lawns around the homestead are being clipped and watered. All the expertise we have developed at the orchard is being directed to the long-neglected gardens at the homestead. Hydrangeas, rosemary, lavender, petunias and bougainvillea have been ordered to dress every yard. Fences will be white once more.

The sculptures left by the art students will ornament the homestead instead of the paddocks. The best treasures from the dumps will come to live in the high raised garden beds. Tree trunks will be lit up from the ground, and the branches will flower with fairy lights. The houses and bower sheds will be made ready with extra beds. Unfinished rooms in each house will be finished.

We are discussing menus and recipes. We think crayfish and turkey and many kinds of salad. Florentines and cheesecake, bottled peaches and sweet fresh rockmelon. Mum's friend Pam is coming to help with the cooking, and finally, we are discussing what we will all wear to the party.

The dress code is 'elegant summer'. Steph is planning on wearing a soft floating dress of lavender and pink. She is making her dress herself. Gran is making my dress in darker jewel shades with a skirt on which flowers delicately interlace. Steph and Megan and Gran will make Megan's dress together. It will be flowing and long and ivory, for after all, this day will be Megan and Adrian's wedding day. We are determined to make it the very happiest of occasions. We want to enjoy Megan while we have her because she and Adrian have been posted to the Middle East for two years.

But the peaches are still on our minds right now.

On Mum and Dad's last visit to Perth, Mum noticed a palette of Tropic Snow peaches outside the Herdsman. Were they our peaches? Did this mean that our peaches were not selling well? Were we going to hear that Tony could take no more of our Tropic Snows? A day of anxiety followed until Mum could stand it no longer. She rang Tony to ask how our peaches were selling.

'You saw the palette outside, did you?' said Tony.

Mum admitted that she had.

'Don't worry,' said Tony. 'Your peaches are selling very well. And I notice you are getting better at picking them ripe all the time.'

'We are trying hard,' Mum replied, very gratified by this feedback and now confident enough to finally ask the question that had been haunting us.

'Can I ask how much you will be paying us per tray?'

'Around eighteen dollars a tray,' answered Tony. 'I want you to hang in there. Keep on growing.'

Mum thanked him fervently, said goodbye, and left for Mandy's house at a run. On her freshly mowed back lawn the boys were playing. Mandy and I were watching them, considering how best this part of her garden could be made ready for Megan's wedding.

'Guess how much! Guess how much!' Mum cried by way of greeting.

'How much what?' I asked, distracted by the sight of Ben swinging a golf club twice his length.

'A tray of peaches,' she said, and on the same breath cried, '… eighteen dollars!'

It was far more than we had expected. Our wildest dreams had been of the lower market standard of sixteen dollars a tray. It was wonderful news.

'I can't wait to tell your father,' exclaimed Mum, eyes shining.

Ben swung the golf club ever more wildly, narrowing missing Lachlan, Sam and Tim all in turn. Mandy said, 'How wonderful!' and removed the golf club. Benjamin roared in fury.

'That is wonderful news!' I added, and then to Benjamin, who can always be soothed by music (and because it was the first day of December) I sang: 'On the first day of Christmas, my true love sent to me: a partridge in a pear tree. On the second day …'

'No,' interrupted Mandy. Mandy never interrupts. I fell silent with shock.

'No, that's not right, Jo,' she said, in her very firmest and very happiest voice. 'At Austin Downs that partridge is sitting in a *peach* tree.'